DAILY LIFE IN

THE UNITED STATES, 1940–1959
SHIFTING WORLDS

The Greenwood Press "Daily Life Through History" Series

The Ancient Egyptians
Bob Brier and Hoyt Hobbs

The Ancient Greeks
Robert Garland

Ancient Mesopotamia
Karen Rhea Nemet-Nejat

The Aztecs: People of the Sun and Earth
David Carrasco with Scott Sessions

Chaucer's England
Jeffrey L. Singman and Will McLean

Civil War America
Dorothy Denneen Volo and James M. Volo

18th-Century England
Kirstin Olsen

Elizabethan England
Jeffrey L. Singman

The Holocaust
Eve Nussbaum Soumerai and Carol D. Schulz

The Inca Empire
Michael A. Malpass

Maya Civilization
Robert J. Sharer

Medieval Europe
Jeffrey L. Singman

The Nineteenth Century American Frontier
Mary Ellen Jones

The United States, 1960–1990: Decades of Discord
Myron A. Marty

Victorian England
Sally Mitchell

DAILY LIFE IN
THE UNITED STATES, 1940–1959 SHIFTING WORLDS

EUGENIA KALEDIN

The Greenwood Press "Daily Life Through History" Series

GREENWOOD PRESS
Westport, Connecticut • London

Library of Congress Cataloging-in-Publication Data

Kaledin, Eugenia.
  Daily life in the United States, 1940–1959 : shifting worlds / Eugenia Kaledin.
    p.   cm.—(The Greenwood Press "Daily life through history" series, ISSN 1080–4749)
  Includes bibliographical references and index.
  ISBN 0–313–29786–X (alk. paper)
  1. United States—Social life and customs—1918–1945.   2. United States—Social life
and customs—1945–1970.   3. United States—Social conditions—1933–1945.   4. United
States—Social conditions—1945–   I. Title.   II. Series.
  E169.K139   2000
  306'.0973—dc21   00–024843

British Library Cataloguing in Publication Data is available.

Library of Congress Catalog Card Number: 00–024843
ISBN: 0–313–29786–X
ISSN: 1080–4749

First published in 2000

Greenwood Press, 88 Post Road West, Westport, CT 06881
An imprint of Greenwood Publishing Group, Inc.
www.greenwood.com

Printed in the United States of America

(∞)™

The paper used in this book complies with the
Permanent Paper Standard issued by the National
Information Standards Organization (Z39.48–1984).

10 9 8 7 6 5 4

"Freedom from Want" by Norman Rockwell, 1943. Rockwell, best known for a lifetime of
Saturday Evening Post covers, donated his talents to the war effort in 1943 by providing
illustrations for FDR's Four Freedoms—clearly visualizing what Americans were fighting
for: freedom of speech, freedom from fear, freedom of worship, and freedom from want.
These reproductions, printed in greater numbers than any other paintings before, helped
to sell millions of dollars in war bonds when offered as gifts with bond purchases. The
Office of War Information also displayed them in schools, clubs, post offices, and railroad
stations and sent them abroad to remind Americans of their own high ideals. The paintings
became a valuable contribution to winning World War II. Printed by permission of the
Norman Rockwell Family Trust. Copyright © 1943 the Norman Rockwell Family Trust.

For the voices of the future—
Luke, Clayton, Nina, Noelle, and Sarah

Contents

Photo essays follow pages 44 and 184.

Preface

This book is designed as a series of connected essays to help readers ask questions about America during two decades that are as different from each other as the nineteenth century is from the twenty-first. By examining a broad range of daily experiences, the text should encourage speculation rather than provide neat answers to such questions. I like to think that students examining the differing moods of the 1940s and 1950s from different angles will discover much that also helps them to define the present. Although it may be impossible to come to precise conclusions about the behavior of Americans at different times, it is possible to assess the forces that shaped their lives. Students can gain a better understanding of behavior and put it into context by examining how complex are everyday aspects of the lives of ordinary people. Readers should gain a complex awareness of how difficult it is to assess any period without including an array of the details involved in daily living that reach beyond politics. We define ourselves on many levels of work and play.

In both these decades students will be compelled to struggle with the enormous question of the role of government and law in defining individual choice. How much government spending—or its absence—determines how and where people live remains worth thinking about for both the 1940s and 1950s. What is the "good life"—the pursuit of happiness—these Americans want? How do they deal with their fears as they construct new communities?

Because I see myself as a social critic of United States culture—a scholar of American studies—not as a historian, I have relied heavily on the excellent research of a number of gifted historians who have delved deeply into statistics and studied contemporary legislation to provide me with essential details. Although I concentrate on the spirit and attitudes of these decades, I could not have written anything about the '40s and '50s without a great many statistics—gathered by others—to reinforce my generalizations. The changes that took place in the United States between 1940 and 1959—the astonishing output of war materials, the mass production of housing, the overwhelming numbers of cars and television sets, the vast number of people going to college, and above all the "baby boom"—all represented an America shifting from an easily recognizable past to a multidimensional present.

What I hope readers will do is pull themselves away from the World Wide Web—for a short time at least—to go into their libraries on a treasure hunt for the many good books devoted to the 1940s and 1950s. I have tried to build an essential bibliography into the writing of each chapter so that serious students can put this text down and pursue every issue mentioned here in much greater depth in other books.

I have tried as well to call attention to different kinds of creative activities—not just journalism and political commentary, but also the fiction and drama and poetry and art and music that appeared during these decades. To study the 1950s simply in terms of political events—leaving out Jack Kerouac, Lorraine Hansberry, and Elvis Presley—is to impoverish the imaginations of the students of this period.

I have also included many references to movies—designed to take both students and teachers into video archives to search out powerful images of these times. The 1940s and 1950s remain among the great periods of film making and photojournalism. Every student of American social studies should know the movies of *The Grapes of Wrath*, *Casablanca*, *Citizen Kane*, and *Gone with the Wind* in order to enter discussions of the flaws and values in American culture such productions represent. Looking at the history contained in such films from the point of view of a new century might be doubly educational.

This text should also send students to museums and art galleries to examine the work of the many talented artists and photojournalists important in these decades. Going on-line might become essential to providing access to pictures that cannot easily be found in smaller libraries and towns. But the great proliferation of museums that took place after the war should offer research resources for readers who want to explore the United States in different ways. Most Americans are fortunate to have access to technology enabling them to find old books and illustrations many have never seen before. Learning how to use new computer resources to discover lost materials should become an educational experience in itself.

Too many clichés have been used to define these decades. I hope this book dispels some of them and provokes students to seek deeper answers to the additional questions their research may stir up.

I am grateful to the historian of education Paul A. Gagnon for reading this manuscript with care. And I appreciate the personal "oral histories" of many friends and relatives who contributed unforgettable anecdotes to enrich my own memories of World War II. I feel especially grateful to the couples and to the women of the 1950s whose definitions of the good life at that time may have had more worth than later social critics could acknowledge. My own baby boom children have taught me much about survival skills.

Without the assistance of a patient editor, Emily Birch, this book would not have survived—the independent scholar needs much support. And without the helpful searches of Margaret Johnson the photography archives included would be much less complete.

In a civilization as complicated as America's, easy explanations for historical events and daily dilemmas do not exist. I hope this text uncovers some new materials to enrich the cultural history of these two decades and make the daily experiences more convincing. Those of us struggling to describe what the United States represents need to include as much as possible of the varied energies that define the American people.

Timeline

1940	First peacetime military draft
1941	Japanese bomb Pearl Harbor
1942	Women's military auxiliaries created
	Japanese Americans interned in Western camps
	Szilard and Fermi split the atom
	Rationing of fuel oil, gas, and shoes
1944	FDR elected to precedent-making fourth term
	Congress passes G.I. Bill of Rights
1945	Atomic bombs dropped on Japan
1946	Eckert and Mauchly develop digital computer
	Cold War begins
	Levittowns started
1947	Truman institutes loyalty program
	Jackie Robinson becomes first African American to play major league baseball

1948	Truman beats Dewey
	Truman ends segregation in armed forces
	Transistor invented
1950–1953	Korean War
1950	Alger Hiss convicted of perjury
1951	Fluoride accepted to reduce tooth decay
	Video cameras with sound available
	First color TV
1952	Hydrogen bomb succeeds
1953	Rosenbergs executed for treason
1954	Salk vaccine discovered
	Brown v. Board of Education of Topeka decision orders school desegregation
	Senator Joseph McCarthy censured
	Rosa Parks arrested for refusing to move to back of the bus
1955	Martin Luther King inspires Montgomery bus boycott
	Nuclear power used for public purposes
1957	Soviets launch *Sputnik*, an orbiting satellite
	Little Rock school desegregation crisis; troops have to protect black students
1958	First commercial copying machine
1960	Birth control pill on market
	GNP reaches $500 billion

Part I

The 1940s:
The War Years
and Beyond

1

Introduction to the 1940s: An Old-Fashioned World

Trying to get at the meaning of every decade in the history of any country—even in a country with a past as short as the United States—is like trying to decide which ten years have been the most important in any

Shadows of the Depression

mature person's life. We now know that even the earliest months of infancy may be crucial in defining the way people see themselves as adults, and we have also come to recognize how extensively individuals may be shaped by broad social and economic forces. The children of parents who suffered through the Great Depression of the 1930s would always be aware that hard-working people with real skills might not be able to find suitable work even in a country as rich in resources as the United States. Many who struggled to live decently knew Ph.D.s who were grateful to find jobs teaching high school, and engineers who sold linens in drygoods stores or worked in post offices, glad for any income to support their families.

Growing up in the '30s and early '40s, children not only confronted the maimed veterans of World War I begging on street corners, but they also saw a new jobless class, hawking apples or carrying suitcases of shoelaces and dishrags from door to door, desperate for even small amounts of money. Newspaper want ads for real jobs—then divided by gender—frequently disappeared altogether during the Depression. Instead networks of church kitchens and organized soup societies emerged to help the homeless and jobless willing to wait in long lines to relieve their hunger. "Brother, Can You Spare a Dime?" was a catchy popular song many young people may have heard without understanding its economic implications. A dime in the 1930s bought a cup of coffee and a doughnut.

When President Franklin Roosevelt acknowledged in his 1937 second inaugural address that one-third of the nation were ill-housed, ill-fed, and ill-clothed, his promise to take aggressive action against the failures of the system was welcomed by most Americans eager for a "new deal" in their own lives—even if changes meant more government control. FDR's New Deal was designed to regulate money policy and generate jobs. The new administration set up a vast range of government agencies: the Works Projects Administration, the National Recovery Act, the Civilian Conservation Corps, the National Youth Administration, and the writers and artists organizations like the Federal Theater Project that created jobs for talented citizens who could not find work. In the 1930s unskilled laborers built roads and housing projects; engineers designed new bridges and dams as well as scenic waterways like Riverwalk, the famous tourist attraction in San Antonio, Texas, and the mountain road to Sabino Canyon in Tucson, Arizona. Artists painted historic murals on post office walls and in public buildings; writers prepared useful state guidebooks; and scholars of folkways catalogued the cultural resources of rural and Native Americans with subsidies from the government. Although some complained of too much bureaucracy and of government interference in the realm of art—a topic still debated—there can be little doubt that much of the work supported at this time enabled many serious artists and writers to survive. And at the turn into the 21st century the American people continue to enjoy post office murals and make use of music archives and public facilities created by New Deal expenditures. That the United States in the early 1940s had a government concerned with both the documentation and the creation of local culture—as well as with the people whose contributions to America enriched the quality of life—remains something to be proud of. The New Deal valued dimensions of America related not just to the successes of capitalism but to the greater range of human possibilities in American life.

As World War II pulled the economy back into action the need to generate jobs disappeared. By then the country needed many new workers to replace the young men going off to war. Yet the fact that FDR was elected president three times, and then for a fourth term to lead the nation through the war, suggests how strong the New Deal's "approval rating" was. Most Americans welcomed the concerned roles both Franklin and his wife Eleanor played in defining what their country could be. Children reaching adolescence in the 1940s had known no other leaders. The sense of security and stability that such an American royal couple created is now hard to imagine. Even people who came to hate the Roosevelts could not deny their vitality and their commitment to their ideals.

FDR's presence was a part of daily life. What the New Deal accomplished most successfully was the restoration of faith in the power of government to help individuals—those forgotten men and women who worked hard but could not manage to support their families. No manuscript collection is more moving than the file of letters collected in Eleanor Roosevelt's archives in the Roosevelt Library at Hyde Park from needy people asking for small loans of money until they could get on their feet again. Eleanor Roosevelt acted as Franklin's eyes and ears as she traveled all over the country to help the New Deal become synonymous with concern for human dignity. The creation of Social Security, workmen's compensation, and higher income taxes for the rich, along with guarantees that workers could strike for fair wages, demonstrated respect for the American worker, even if a number of political promises fell short of fulfillment. Called a "traitor to his class," FDR made his commitments the source of loyalty for many blue collar workers. The 31 Fireside Chats he gave on the radio made him a father figure to many who thought of the Roosevelts not as politicians but as moral leaders. Although people never saw pictures of Roosevelt in a wheelchair at the time or realized just how helpless he was (no one talked about disabilities), everyone knew about his bravery in reentering politics after surviving polio. His overpowering smile and his sense of humor won him admirers all over the world, while his aristocratic self-assurance—enriched by Eleanor's great social awareness—proved to be exactly what the country needed to inspire a national turn from provincial isolationism to global power.

In a prize-winning book, *No Ordinary Time: Franklin and Eleanor Roosevelt. The Home Front in World War II*, Doris Kearns Goodwin documents how amazingly popular FDR's radio speeches were. A May 1941 talk designed to alert the nation to the possibility of a national emergency got a 95% favorable response from the more than 65 million people in 20 million homes who listened. When popular comedians like Bob Hope and Jack Benny were thrilled to have a listener rating of 30–35%, Roosevelt was getting radio audiences of over 70%. The only other broadcast that even approached FDR's for listeners was the audience for the Joe Louis–Max Schmeling world heavyweight fight in 1938—an encounter that seemed symbolic of battles to come.[1]

The paternalism of the New Deal made it easier for many to accept the new constraints on freedom that preparation for war demanded. Price controls and gasoline and food rationing, blackouts and air raid drills, limits on travel, censorship, **Entering the War** and security clearances were all part of the war world that took over the New Deal in 1941. "Loose lips sink ships" declared a poster plastered in coastal towns, reminding ordinary people that everyone was involved in winning a war. Along both the East and West coast citizens prepared for attacks from enemy submarines or bombers. Communities set up first-aid stations, and even middle school children trained with Red Cross manuals to learn simple survival techniques. Air raid drills in schools were conducted with buddy systems so that older children became responsible for smaller ones in reaching makeshift shelters or simply hiding under designated tables. Looking back on these moments as Dr. New Deal was replaced by Dr. Win the War, old people find it hard to reconstruct that reality of fear. More often they cherish the orderliness of the daily tasks that made them feel useful to the country as a whole. The New Deal raised America's self-confidence.

In 1944 Roosevelt's State of the Union message to Congress was broadcast as a Fireside Chat because so few newspapers would print the entire message. What FDR suggested then was to extend the original commitments of the New Deal into the country's wartime role in the world. A "basic essential to peace," he asserted, "is a decent standard of living for all individual men and women and children in all nations. Freedom from fear is eternally linked with freedom from want."[2] As he went on to define America's role as one that would not repeat the tragic errors of isolationism, FDR made sure that people understood the need for firm inner discipline and well-organized government to control profiteering and social injustice.

In this speech FDR not only recommended a specific set of new laws to control the cost of living and equalize the burdens of taxation, but he also set up what he called a "Second Bill of Rights," based on the belief that "true individual freedom cannot exist without economic security and independence."[3] The rights he defined and connected with the war and with the needs of the entire world might not be as "self-evident" as FDR believed in the 1940s but they will always be worthy of serious consideration. Roosevelt wanted "all" (in his introduction he did not say "all men," but "all—regardless of station or race or creed") to have the right to a useful and remunerative job; the right to a decent home and food and clothing; and the right to medical care and a good education. He also included protection for farmers and businessmen from monopolies and unfair competition abroad, and he articulated once again the concern to provide for the economic insecurities of old age. Always the main agenda of Eleanor Roosevelt's articles, lectures, press conferences, and columns, the bill of economic rights FDR wanted to guarantee—the nation understood—also remained his wife's first priority. Wanting to clarify the dreams of the New Deal for the rest of the world, FDR concluded this 1944 Chat with a reminder that "unless there is security here at home, there cannot be lasting peace in the world."

Children who grew up in the midst of World War II gathered a sense of self-esteem from the many small roles they played to help win the peace. In Vermont, schools provided bags for gathering milkweed pods to replace the no longer available kapok fibers used for warmth and padding in jackets; in New York children collected fats to be used for making explosives. All over America young people saved tinfoil, flattened tin cans, and enjoyed squishing little yellow buttons of color in white margarine to make it look like rationed butter. Many children bought and sold ten-cent defense stamps, purchases that represented real sacrifice at the time, as ten cents could also pay for an entire matinee at the movies with short serials, cartoons, and two feature films included.

Mothers who had been convinced that being housewives was their only true profession often did both volunteer and paid work to contribute to the war effort. They labored in hospitals, knitted afghans, and helped plot and identify aircraft in undisclosed places all over American cities. Many women were proud to take jobs in defense plants doing "men's work" and finding themselves making higher wages than ever before. By the end of the war a rare group of intrepid women pilots were even flying huge bombers to destinations all over the world.

In one of his remarkable collections of interviews with Americans who lived through significant moments of American history, *"The Good War": An Oral History of World War II*, Studs Terkel recorded the impressions of a number of citizens who for the first time in their lives felt free of intense competition to survive. To a lesser extent this same experience became true on the home front. "It was the last time most Americans thought they were innocent and good without qualifications." One man noted, "It's a precious memory. . . . That great camaraderie of savin' tinfoil, toothpaste tubes, or tin cans, all that stuff made people part of somethin', that disappeared."[4]

That sense of community also developed in parts of the army where people felt what it was like to work together for the same goals for the first time in their lives. One ex-soldier told Terkel they were in a tribal sort of situation where they helped each other without fear. The absence of economic competition and phony standards created for many men a real love for the army. Although the armed forces themselves at the time were a bastion of racism, as several of Terkel's black citizens reported, and many defense industries refused to give African Americans higher paying jobs until Roosevelt issued an executive order mandating equality, people *had* to learn to work together. The dream of equal rights became part of the incentive for fighting a war against countries that made national ideals of inequality. Wartime belief in cooperation in order to win seemed more than simple propaganda. Another man Terkel interviewed remembered that the whole world seemed absolutely mad—people were in love with war.

Feeling they were "part of something" enhanced the lives of soldiers of all ages. One man recalled those moments of need when others were there to help him as the high point of his entire life. Civilians felt similar

connections. A journalist whose patriotism led him at age fourteen to lie
about his age in order to get a job in an arms plant felt that he would
have done anything for the President. When he was able to join the navy
at eighteen, he told Studs Terkel, he was sure "there was right and there
was wrong and I wore the white hat."[5]

**Shifting
Attitudes**
Over the years the "white hat" has become gray. As often
happens, time has added layers of complexity to the reasons
for war and the way individuals look back at World War II
experiences. Although some romanticize the excitement of
battle line dangers and the pleasures of sharing vegetables from victory
gardens at home, others have started to look critically at what was regarded as "The Best War Ever." Michael C.C. Adams, using this as a
partly ironic title for a book on America and World War II, surveys past
celebrations with an array of critical statistics and testimonies.[6] Students
need to recognize both the limits of statistics and the limits of mythology
in trying to understand the complexity of human aggression related to
community needs. As the century shifts, it might be possible to suggest
that scholars of Western civilization have come to evaluate all wars skep-
tically.

"There is no such thing as a just war," Terkel's older and wiser journalist concluded, adding a quote from a bureaucrat who recognized
World War II finally as the only cure for the Great Depression.[7] Indeed,
during the '40s most Americans had chosen to ignore the moral outrages
that defined Nazism. At the beginning of German aggression in Europe
many older citizens remembered the propaganda against the Germans
in World War I and appeared reluctant to believe in the atrocities we
now know as the Holocaust. Such barbarism seemed unbelievable from
the country that had produced thinkers like Kant and Goethe and musicians like Beethoven and Schubert.

In 1940 a group calling itself America First organized to keep the country out of war. Charles Lindbergh, the famous aviator—an admirer of
Germany—helped establish 450 chapters as its most prominent member.
Yet as more truth leaked out about the outrages of the Third Reich, to
remain isolationist—indifferent to what was happening abroad—posed
a political dilemma. Could people concerned with maintaining "the
American way of life" sustain a system of freedom in a totalitarian world
of atrocities? Most Americans came to accept the Roosevelts' beliefs that
we not only had to provide material help for our democratic allies but
that we would also have to send our "boys" to fight for world freedom.
When the Japanese—Hitler's allies—bombed Pearl Harbor on December
7, 1941, the day Roosevelt proclaimed would "live in infamy," they made
it easy for Americans to enter the war in the black and white terms many
fondly remember.

Life magazine, the movie critic Pauline Kael told Studs Terkel, represented the spirit of the country during the war. Americans pictured in its photos appeared clean-cut and shiny. During the war years Kael found stereotypes dominating the entire film industry: wholesome Americans, slant-eyed "Japs," and shaven-headed Nazis. But she also found something warming in the idea that, for a short time, the country believed in itself.[8] That memory of cooperation and heroism is what we have needed to cherish. But even in a "good war" the reality is more complex.

Many American children, though not separated from their families like their British counterparts, who had been sent to the countryside to avoid being bombed, nonetheless experienced a tremendous amount of upheaval as their parents moved from place to place seeking defense work in communities with inadequate housing, makeshift schools, and overcrowded daycare centers. The memories of the son of a Harvard professor who enjoyed nightly sky searches looking for enemy planes in the crystal air of Concord, Massachusetts, were bound to be different from the recollections of airplane makers' children in crowded Willow Run, Michigan.

Americans have always accepted their history in terms of movement. Immigrants and refugees, whether for material gain or for spiritual shelter, define the American way of life as "uprooted." Although the Western frontiers had closed before the wars of the 20th century, Americans have even managed to expand the vision of a country in motion by reaching back to Native American hunters and gatherers, sharpening the 20th century's new consciousness of earlier inhabitants who moved about to survive in harmony with nature. Such awareness would have been far from the attitudes expressed in the great migrations of the 1940s when huge numbers of the needy left rural quiet to pour into expanding urban areas where well-paid war work was found. But survival was also the aim of these people—and the instability remained real.

Later defined as the largest mass movement of Americans ever, this wartime upheaval involved over 30 million civil- **Migration** ians migrating in every direction. Census Bureau statistics showed that between the bombing of Pearl Harbor in December 1941 and March 1945, 15 million civilians had moved. The migration of military personnel was even larger. In the Detroit–Willow Run area, the expansion of wartime production brought 200,000 people into the area from 1940 to 1949. Half of these were children.[9]

Although some hardy American children profited from the broader social experience and the new education offered in daycare not available in the rural communities they left behind, the loss of local culture and extended family should not be labeled trivial. Important identities derived from place and ethnic connections disappeared as people put their

Americanism before all else. The huge numbers of children concentrated in small areas made even good, healthy daycare inadequate.

Some women, to be sure, acquired new skills along with the freedom to work when daycare was provided by factories and government agencies. But others continued to stay home with new babies under hard conditions. Too many young women without good jobs and without knowledge of birth control married soldier boyfriends going off to war. The baby boom was enormous. The idea that women in general had a chance to find personal fulfillment because the men were gone does not hold up well under scrutiny—particularly for the youngest women. "We were sold a bill of goods," one woman complained to Terkel.[10] Those women lucky enough to have high-paying defense jobs were warned at the beginning that they would have to give them up when the soldiers returned. Like the idea of affirmative action designed to compensate for social disadvantages and lost time, the idea of giving returning "Veterans Preference" for every opportunity was considered fair. That women too made tremendous sacrifices for their country is only beginning to be considered an issue worthy of serious historical definition.

Unlike many other nations, the United States has been reluctant to offer daycare centers for its working mothers. But during the 1940s the Federal Works Agency (FWA) managed to get funding for daycare facilities in areas of defense work. By the spring of 1944, when the FWA opened up places to care for children under two years of age, 87,406 little boys and girls were enrolled in 2,512 war nurseries and child care centers. By July 1944, over 3,000 centers served over 129,000 children, liberating many young mothers from anxiety about their families as they went off to do war work.[11] That women contributed much to the legendary production rate of the American war effort cannot be disputed.

By the end of the war the Willow Run plant was turning out one bomber every 63 minutes. In the years from 1942 to the war's end the Detroit plant produced over 8,000 airplanes, an astonishing testimony to commitment and hard work. It would be a mistake to overlook also the workers' sense of satisfaction in such achievement. The "E for Excellence" flags awarded for superior production flying over many plants inspired workers to overlook labor tensions. But the racial and loyalty questions that plagued the United States did not disappear during the war.

If most Americans were not subjected to the early inquiries of the House Special Committee on Un-American Activities run by Congressman Martin Dies of Texas in 1938 to find Communists who threatened the American way of life, the ongoing fear of disloyalty grew stronger right after the war. In 1947 Harry Truman introduced a loyalty oath for many kinds of state and government employees that cast a shadow over the idea of unity. The sense of community people had valued in wartime became more elusive; the idea of group cooperation frequently shattered into fragments.

No people experienced such shifts more clearly than the African Americans. From the individuals who fought in the American Revolution, through the heroic regiments who died for the Union during the Civil War, to the names listed on the Vietnam Veterans Memorial in Washington, D.C., no American soldiers have demonstrated greater patriotism than African Americans. Yet all during World War II these soldiers were segregated and their fighting abilities were maligned, just as they had been in previous wars. In 1940 an army of a half million had only 4,700 Negro soldiers, including only two officers and three chaplains. And there was not a single Negro in the Marine Corps, the Tank Corps, the Signal Corps, or the Army Air Corps.[12] Thanks mainly to Eleanor Roosevelt's closeness to the Negro community and her understanding of their needs, things began to change. That "separate" could not be, and never had been, "equal" became an idea that liberal minds began to confront during this period. After the war Harry Truman, a longtime Civil Rights advocate, began the final desegregation of the army. In 1948 he wrote, "I am not asking for social equality because no such thing exists, but I am asking for equality of opportunity for all human beings."[13]

Yet racism remained alive even during the war years. In 1943 alone there were over 200 racial battles in more than 45 different cities. The clashes were not just against African Americans but also against Hispanics. The famous zoot suit riots in Los Angeles in 1943 targeted Mexican Americans for simply wearing extreme baggy styles which were supposedly a threat to the men in neat uniforms—just as long hair was considered a threat to established society during the Vietnam War.

Eleanor Roosevelt worked behind the scenes to arrange the escape of European Jews, especially children. Yet except for Secretary of the Treasury Henry Morganthau, the only Jewish member of the Cabinet, she could not get the government to support her efforts to expedite their rescue. The State Department's record is embarrassing. To America's credit as a country committed to human rights, the United States Holocaust Memorial Museum, which opened in Washington, D.C., in 1993 to educate visitors about the reality of Nazi atrocities, does not hide the reluctance of the American foreign service to allow greater numbers of refugees to come here. Although a number of distinguished artists and intellectuals were aided in escaping, including the scientists who would help build the atomic bomb, the official State Department policy toward ordinary European Jews was not hospitable. What the children who did manage to get into America during the war years went on to contribute to life in the United States would make a valuable study. Students too easily forget that immigrants—and their children—often represent exceptional vitality in their pursuit of the American Dream.

Reluctance to put aside long-standing prejudice against Asians must also account in some degree for the humiliating experiences heaped on many worthy Japanese Americans at this time. Fear that connections in Japan might turn some Americans of Japanese ancestry into efficient spies precipitated the confiscation of many good citizens' properties and their incarceration in what amounted to American concentration camps. Such remote places as Rivers, Arizona; Heart Mountain, Wyoming; Topaz, Utah; and Manzanar, California; contained small prison worlds where children still pledged allegiance to the American flag and wrote letters to family members in the armed forces fighting for the United States—even as their parents wondered about who was watering their cherry trees. That the United States would much later make monetary amends to these Japanese American families must be noted, but the humiliation of loyal Americans over a period of years cannot be measured in dollars. Of the 110,000 "persons of Japanese ancestry" incarcerated, 72,000 were U.S. citizens by birth.[14]

Americans have to be grateful to the historians with unconventional points of view who keep digging up additional facts and asking new questions. Students of life in the United States need to keep enlarging their visions. They need to know how the government has measured up or failed to measure up to the constitutional possibilities that make us all so proud. The war years made people aware of many human rights that would become a challenge to the future.

NOTES

1. Doris Kearns Goodwin, *No Ordinary Time: Franklin and Eleanor Roosevelt: The Home Front in World War II* (New York: Simon and Schuster, 1994), 240.

2. Franklin Delano Roosevelt, *Fireside Chats* (New York: Penguin, 1995), 78–79.

3. Ibid., 88.

4. Studs Terkel, *"The Good War": An Oral History of World War II* (New York: Ballantine Books, 1985), 99.

5. Ibid., 159, 172, 207.

6. See Michael C.C. Adams, *The Best War Ever: America and World War II* (Baltimore: Johns Hopkins University Press, 1994), 20–42.

7. Ibid., 210–211.

8. Terkel, *"The Good War,"* 120.

9. William M. Tuttle, Jr., *"Daddy's Gone to War": The Second World War in the Lives of America's Children* (New York: Oxford University Press, 1993), 51–68.

10. Terkel, *"The Good War,"* 119.

11. Tuttle, *"Daddy's Gone,"* 82.

12. Kearns, *No Ordinary Time,* 165.

13. Quoted in David McCullough, *Truman* (New York: Simon and Schuster, 1992), 589.

14. See Page Smith, *Democracy on Trial: The Japanese American Evacuation and Relocation in World War II* (New York: Simon and Schuster, 1995). Figures on book jacket.

2

Community and Family in the 1940s

In 1938, when Thornton Wilder produced what may re-
main the best known American 20th century drama, *Our*   **Prewar**
Town, most Americans could identify with the small town **Communities**
sense of neighborhood that Grover's Corners, New
Hampshire, his mythical setting, represented. Having one character address a letter to a street in a town, in a state, in a country, in a hemi-
sphere, on the earth, in the universe, in the solar system, in the mind of
God reminded the audience of both extended human and religious connections. In the play the small town—the social unit where everyone
knew everyone else and individuals respected the power of love and
death and human loyalty—was the focus of all action.[1] The great success
of this drama—translated into many languages—emerged from a worldwide understanding of the simple human connections all people share.
Yet the outside world had already begun to change.

Before World War II most Americans did not own cars. Many families
did not have phones or radios. Different generations and adult siblings
often lived near each other. Such physical closeness was not always a
matter of choice but of economic necessity. Grandparents helped raise
children. Mixed generations and sometimes single aunts and uncles also
made up the nuclear family. Unmarried children old enough to work
brought home their salaries to share with the whole family and, more
often than not, lived at home until they married. Working class families
sometimes included boarders or lodgers, often considered family members in every sense because they too contributed to the income pool.

Although the New Deal's introduction of Social Security had begun to give more old people a sense of freedom, large-scale separation of families did not begin until the war.

In big cities closely connected ethnic groups lived in the same neighborhoods for both spiritual and material support. They functioned together in much the same way that people did in small towns like Grover's Corners. As in the 19th century, school children taught English to their immigrant parents—and some parents never learned. Even as most young people were eager to become more "American," others tried to keep and enjoy rituals connected with their immigrant origins as surely as the folks in Grover's Corners wanted to maintain their small town identity. French Canadian Catholics, for example, tried to make certain they did not get Irish or Italian priests. And although the upward mobility associated with moving into bigger houses in better neighborhoods had existed from the beginning of America, such moves required readily available cash—not accessible until the war began to alleviate unemployment. In 1940 average earnings were still beneath those of 1929, and 8 million people remained jobless.

Effects of War on Communities   Paul Pisicano, a successful Italian American architect interviewed by the oral historian Studs Terkel, noted the differences brought about by the war. Earlier, he remarked, people took their ethnic identities for granted. He described how a neighborhood group even made wine in the cellar of their Bronx apartment house. "After the war nobody used the wine cellars. The whole sense of community disappeared." When the soldiers returned, supermarkets began to replace the small groceries and bakeries that sold salami and crusty bread. Bemoaning the loss of the Mom and Pop store world where families knew shopkeepers who extended credit in hard times, Pisicano regretted the loss of struggle. Taking little comfort in the upward mobility that his professionalism represented, he concluded that the war "obliterated our culture and made us Americans. That's no fun."[2]

Others would argue that the war may have speeded up the process, but that such loss defines all Americans. The "double consciousness" the famous black scholar W.E.B. Du Bois described as the heritage of African Americans is surely the heritage of every American. People lose parts of one culture as they gain more of another. During the 1970s and 1980s, when many young people made efforts to go back to their ethnic roots, they realized that much ethnicity still existed. Families did not forget how to make crusty bread or blintzes or sing lullabies in different tongues. By then many more individuals also had the tools of education and the technical skills to extend their own knowledge. In Philadelphia the Balch Institute of Ethnicity, an example of this new consciousness, opened to help citizens learn about their roots. On entering, visitors choose among about 20 ethnic identities on a computer that produces printouts pertaining to the history and cultural offerings of the chosen group, from churches to folk festivals to restaurants. Such information, of little interest during World War II, suggests that group identities may well change and wane, but they are not completely lost. Indeed, the printouts have to be constantly updated and new groups of immigrants added. No one event—even one as tremendous as World War II—has ever been able to wipe out the defining diversity of American life.

In 1933, 12 million people—30% of working age Amer-
icans—were without jobs. The vast range of American   **Heritage of the**
religions helped comfort many through these terrible   **Depression**
Depression years. And the same bounty of spiritual
traditions also enabled loyal citizens to endure the hardships of war—to believe, as the most popular ballad then declared, that God would bless America. But just as important were the practical strengths of human adaptability. The pragmatism growing out of a past that called on many to throw over Old World traditions in favor of New World survival techniques became a necessary approach to life. Struggling through the Depression years prepared Americans on the home front for the sacrifices of wartime—modest as they were compared to those of Europeans.

During the Depression many had learned how to can vegetables as well as make wine. Socialites in one rich suburb would regularly take a thermos of martinis to drink as they dug their victory gardens, but they did manage to grow vegetables, and they shared their produce with anyone who needed it. Special cookbooks appeared to teach housewives to prepare more economical meals. Soups became popular and people learned to enjoy Jello.

The ration books of food stamps given to every individual allowed families to buy specific amounts of meat and sugar. Because family size determined quantities, few people complained about not getting their share. Gasoline rationing more often provoked protests, but automobiles were still a luxury, and those cars used for business got more fuel. For the many workers on "relief"—as welfare was called in the '30s—getting off the government dole into jobs that provided a sense of purpose in helping win the war gave meaning to their lives. Wartime activities used all sorts of ordinary skills along with new production techniques. An article by a teenager in *China Press* in 1942 described Chinese Americans in San Francisco taking first aid courses, working in shipyards, collecting cans and tinfoil, and learning civilian defense—exactly what people in the Midwest and East were also doing.

During the 1930s many middle class women made
their own clothes, darned their families' socks,   **Women, Children,**
turned over the frayed collars of shirts, and took in   **and Teenagers**
other people's laundry. Some bartered cooking and

baking skills for leftovers from farmstands or local grocers. And many men made use of their knowledge of carpentry and enjoyed the challenge of fixing new "machines," as cars were often called. Horses and wagons, still used for delivering bread, milk, and ice during the '30s, slowly began to disappear. Making what you needed—not buying it—was common during this period when people had little cash and most believed that waste made want. Because all production energies went into military items anyway, people found little to buy. It would be after the war, when "waste not, want not" turned into "waste or you shall want" that Americans made consumerism a lifestyle.

As the war created great numbers of defense jobs, middle class children felt proud to be able to earn extra money by delivering newspapers, babysitting, or mowing lawns—taking service jobs no longer done by adults who were making much more money in the factories devoted to war work. During this time teenagers began to define themselves as useful adults and to create a teenage culture. Bobby sox and saddle shoes—comfortable for jitterbugging and walking at a time when there were no silk stockings and few cars with filled tanks—made young people easy to spot. (Nylon—just perfected—was being used for parachutes.)

The special music of the war years became popular for dancing on 78 r.p.m. platters even when the leaders of the "big bands"—like Tommy Dorsey, Benny Goodman, and Glenn Miller—were either in uniform or entertaining troops. Middle class teenagers often held weekend dances with records in neighborhood homes as well as in high school gymnasiums. Some coastal towns inaugurated curfews. Although not every community had complete "blackouts," walking about at night in streets with dimmed lights was unwise. Older high schoolers, imitating many movie stars and draftees, might smoke a cigarette or two at such record parties. Often their parents gave consent to smoking. But drinking and drugs were not fashionable. Soft drinks and nonalcoholic cider prevailed. Potato chips, pretzels, and popcorn were the only junk food available.

Everyone could sing along with wartime favorites like "Don't Sit Under the Apple Tree with Anyone Else but Me," "Praise the Lord and Pass the Ammunition," and the Andrews Sisters' sensational "Boogie Woogie Bugle Boy from Company B." "Rosie the Riveter" became a particular swing favorite on the home front. Young people—themselves often lonely at home—enjoyed the yearning in sad songs of separation like "I'll Walk Alone" and "Saturday Night Is the Loneliest Night in the Week." If they went out on movie dates—usually as two-couple double dates—they sometimes treated themselves afterwards to ice cream sodas and 20-cent hamburgers. Films about the war played everywhere: *Thirty Seconds over Tokyo* (1994), *Guadalcanal Diary* (1943), and *A Walk in the Sun* (1945) were examples of the entertainment that enabled audiences—

young and old—to pretend they were taking part in different Hollywood versions of military experience.

Before the war many people came to understand the Depression from an enduring work of literature, John Steinbeck's *The Grapes of Wrath* (1939). Describing the painful journey west of Oklahoma farmers who lost their land to dust storms, the 1940s film version recorded the saga of the "Okies" with respect for their human capacity to adapt in order to endure. A number of Americans who survived the fierce trials and losses of the 1930s were grateful for such examples. And they were glad not only for rare government housing but also for the living wages that 1940s war contracts began to generate.

Studs Terkel's interviews with women war workers are especially moving. For many women the war provided the first **Women** chance ever to earn money outside the home. One woman remembered another saying she hoped the war would last until she got her refrigerator paid for. Buying on the installment plan became an option for full-time workers. Another recalled the excitement of leaving her backwoods Kentucky home at age eighteen to work in Chicago. She loved meeting "all those wonderful Polacks [*sic*] . . . the first people I'd ever known that were any different from me. A whole new world just opened up." Exposed to tetryl chemicals that turned people orange in the process of her war work, Peggy Terry was grateful at the time to learn more about human rights. She recognized that the war "taught people to expect more than they had before"—not only financially, but also spiritually. Far from romanticizing the experience, though, she recognized that her husband—a paratrooper at age nineteen—suffered throughout his life from the psychic pain of "battle fatigue." The war "brutalized him," she said, and made her lose her faith.[3]

From a statistical point of view, it is hard to generalize that the war made people's lives better. Susan Hartmann's essential text on women during this period, *The Home Front and Beyond: American Women in the 1940s*, uses many precise numbers to clarify how much more complex women's lives were than anecdotal memories suggest. To be sure, many more women were working. The 16 million men conscripted into the army—including young fathers after 1943—left many more women in positions of responsibility and power both in the workplace and in the home. General earnings for all increased from $754 a year in 1940 to $1,289 in 1944, by which time the number of people living below the poverty level dropped from over 50% to just over 33%. By 1945, when women workers had expanded to account for 50% of the work force, three-fourths were also married. Social sanctions against married women working—strong during the Depression—were relaxed because women were no longer seen as taking permanent jobs. In factories the number of women laborers increased by 460%. And women were accepted as workers in fields that had been all but closed to them: music, sports, science, and college teaching. Their earning capacities rose not simply because war work paid more than service work but also because they were gaining access to professions that had always paid men more.[4]

Middle class women who did volunteer work for the Red Cross or the Office of Civilian Defense or who acted as nursing aides in hospitals also developed a sense of pride in new found capabilities outside the home. The same legal system that created legislation to keep married women from competing with men for certain government jobs and teaching appointments during the Depression (see Section 213 of the Economic Act of 1932) even addressed the idea of protecting women from employment discrimination during the war. For the first time Congress seriously considered an equal pay bill and an equal rights amendment to the Constitution as an acknowledgment of women's contribution to the war. Such moments of appreciation—all too evanescent—were nonetheless real.[5]

To leave the impression that World War II elevated women or enhanced their social status would ignore the numbers who suffered terrible losses. Not only would many women be permanently emotionally scarred by the deaths of family members—brothers and sons—but many young brides also found themselves afterwards taking charge of fatherless families. Of the 671,000 soldiers who returned wounded, many had married in a state of wartime euphoria. Their new young brides had little experience with the sacrifices involved in dealing with extreme physical disabilities or "battle fatigue" (later called post-traumatic stress syndrome). No part of history has been more neglected than the story of veterans' wives—perhaps because it is so hard for military historians and legislators even to see such women. The Women's Army Corps and the army nurses remain more real because of their more visible professional power. Future histories examining American life beyond its military and political aspects may broaden the questions people ask about the choices in their lives. The stories of young women who simultaneously accepted the myths of patriotic duty and domesticity are beginning to emerge in oral histories such as those Studs Terkel has collected. And personal interviews have added much to Ronald Takaki's history of Asian Americans, *Strangers from a Different Shore*, making readers aware of different cultural viewpoints that also enrich knowledge beyond statistics.

Deep social changes after the war might have enabled 1940s women to enter society as equals with men to fulfill their human potential, but these did not take place. Imagine what would have happened had defense workers as well as soldiers been given the G.I. Bill to get more education. Imagine if good permanent daycare centers had been considered a right—not a favor—for women of all classes who worked. Many people at the time charged that such facilities were dangerously Communistic—that outside the home children would be brainwashed. Almost the minute the war was over, when it seemed more important to get women back into the home than to use their talents, subsidies for daycare disappeared. Too readily did women assent to the idea that their high-paying jobs were only for the duration. At the beginning of the war mothers had been castigated for making dependent psychological wrecks of their children by smothering them with too much love. After the war the prevailing orthodoxy shifted to the idea that latchkey children of full-time working mothers might end up "juvenile delinquents." Concrete evidence that showed children of full-time working mothers becoming more responsible and independent was ignored as the culture shifted from one extreme to the other in the service of the male economy.

Commitment to work that made women more interested in their jobs than in remaining "feminine" had always been suspect. The "either/or" option spelled out precisely by Betty Friedan in her 1963 classic *The Feminine Mystique*—either family or career, but not both—was a choice men rarely had to make. After the war all advertising energies went into getting women back in the home. When the economy offered first choice of jobs to returning soldiers after the war, the number of women in the work force dropped from over 19 million to about 16 million by 1946. The proportion of women in the civilian labor force dropped from 35.4% in 1944 to 28.6% in 1947.[6] No artifact makes this shift more poignant than the 1970s documentary film *Rosie the Riveter*, which records the oral histories of three women who excelled at welding and loved their wartime jobs. Although most women lost access to such high-paying work— and most were not encouraged to join unions—they did not all go back to their kitchens.

Women went back to doing the service and clerical and domestic jobs that had always been known as "women's work." There is some evidence that more men began to help with domestic chores and child care, but most of the women with jobs also took full responsibility for the care of home and family. By 1950 women remained 30% of all workers, even though many families could live on the salary of one wage earner. And newspaper ads for jobs continued to be separated by gender.

During the early years of the war, when daycare was socially acceptable and wages were high, the birthrate surged. In 1939 American women earned 62% of men's wages, but by 1953 they would again earn only 53% of what men earned. Although the war did much to demonstrate that women could do men's work, it did little to provide them with long lasting competitive money-making careers. Because "family life" had been defined as an important value to die for during the war, as the wartime economy soared the birthrate did too. The low birthrate of the Depression years disappeared. Many women chose to give full attention to families of three or four children. As more people learned about birth control and family spacing, both very large families and only children became associated with the past. The Census Bureau proclaimed the 1943 birthrate the highest in United States history.

Babies also became a consolation for the great number of young women offered no training in career alternatives. The war had weakened general standards of education in the 1940s. A poll of high school students in 1942 revealed that 44% had no idea even what the war was about.[7] Yet in 1943 Congress killed a bill to raise teachers' salaries in order to get more stimulating people into the profession. Some politicians were afraid of hot rods and comic books and the youthful hysteria for pop stars like Frank Sinatra—new and different interests that represented a separate teenage culture. Sociologists speculated that wartime easy money may have distorted the values of many teenagers who could not see how learning related to earning—and how work led to a better life.

Statistics show that crime rates and venereal disease rose among the young during the war years, but whether self-esteem also rose among those who were both working and going to school during that time needs more exploration. For every frivolous fourteen-year-old who went off with a man in uniform to later find herself permanently damaged in the ability to establish relationships, there were others who learned stability from early commitments as they felt proud to be part of a national community. During the war life in towns like Thornton Wilder's Grover's Corners remained as real as life in the Willow Run production center. A society of paradox and complexity needs to examine every event from many angles. Students may now use many historical tools: on-line statistics, newspaper reports, financial statements, diaries, letters, and "oral history" interviews with neighbors. Too often in the past scholars relied on official documents alone, ignoring the varied sociology and different visions of success that shape what Americans need and want during different times.

That World War II generated "the greatest era of prosperity in human history"—when the gross national product increased by 60%—remains the fact that diminishes the many new human problems that surfaced at the same time.[8] The huge military-industrial complex Dwight Eisenhower would warn about in the next decade began to take strong roots in the early 1940s when technical progress seemed essential to democratic survival. The peripheral problems involved with great mobility and greater urbanization got less attention.

Prejudice Throughout the 1940s the idea of racial harmony—one of our most valued myths—was pursued by extensions of rules and laws, both in the services and on the labor front. The number of "Negroes" in the army leaped from 5,000 to 920,000, the number of black officers from just 5 to over 7,000. And many new jobs for blacks opened up in both the army and the navy between 1941 and 1945. When Harry Truman issued Executive Order 9981 in 1948, ending segregation in the armed forces, he made such changes a matter of legal rights. Doris Kearns Goodwin noted that one historian, Carey McWilliams, saw more improvement in race relations during the 1940s than had occurred in the entire span of years from the Civil War to 1940.

The need for workers also extended opportunities to Asian Americans long denied the rights of naturalization. Filipinos, Indians, Koreans, and Chinese, previously limited to "ethnic jobs" such as work in laundries and restaurants, found new opportunities just as women had. Allowed in the army for the first time, and allowed to buy some of the farms confiscated from Japanese Americans, Filipino Americans felt especially grateful and eager to fight to free the Philippines from Japanese occupation. But Filipino soldiers in uniform were still refused service in "American" restaurants. And like Chinese and Korean Americans, they often chose to wear big badges so that people would realize that they were not the hated Japanese. On December 22, 1941, *Time* magazine published an anthropologically questionable article on how to distinguish your Chinese friend from your Japanese enemy by physical traits.

In 1941 Roosevelt also signed Executive Order 8802 asking that both employers and labor unions "provide for the full and equitable participation of all workers in defense industries without discrimination because of race, creed, color or national origin." A commission was established at the same time to investigate grievances. Many Americans might have agreed with lawyers who saw this moment as the most significant government action on behalf of equal opportunity since the Emancipation Proclamation. But good laws do not always bring about immediate results. Unbelievable numbers of workers had crowded into small areas where war production flourished. And many people did not want to share jobs or housing with migrants—black or white. Detroit, with $11 billion worth of war contracts, extended its boundaries to include Willow Run, a subsidiary town that grew from 15,000 people to 47,000 during the war years, bringing in what one native in a Studs Terkel interview saw as an influx of riff-raff.

African Americans forced out of the South by the inven- **Migration** tion of mechanical cotton pickers were particularly vulnerable to hostility because they came North in such tremendous numbers. Nicholas Lemann's fine book, *The Promised Land: The Great Black Migration and How It Changed America*, shows just how extensive this migration was. In 1940, he notes, 77% of all black Americans lived in the South. After that year 5 million headed north, making the exodus larger than that of any other ethnic group. At one point during the '40s, over 2,000 black people were moving into Chicago every week. Because these African Americans often moved as families, the housing situation became critical. In Detroit in 1942 a federal housing project segregated for African American workers was attacked by Polish Americans even as it was being built. The police—at least one participant reported—were on the side of the whites. In June 1943 massive racial violence erupted in Detroit. Thirty-four people died, 25 of whom were black, and over 700 were injured.[9]

Although it is hard to imagine what impact such confrontations had on both black and white children in terms of education, hostility, and bitterness, books like *The Autobiography of Malcolm X*, which describes growing up black in the 1930s, suggest how a child's spirit may be shaped by confrontations with violence and injustice. Yet even in a decade when Jim Crow laws were firmly in place in many states, slow integration began to occur in a number of northern restaurants and restrooms.

In localities where war production boomed, the huge numbers of migrants—black and white—destroyed any sense of community connections. The new people had not only lost their own homes, but they were also seen as intruders. Living conditions disintegrated as more and more people moved in. By 1945 pressure to maintain decent standards of living and minimal education often seemed hopeless. One Willow Run mother wrote in her diary over and over, "A Trailer Camp is no place for a child."[10] The loss of stability that constant moving and poor physical conditions represented between 1941 and 1945—when 30 million were on the move—is hard even to imagine. Fortunately another fiction writer later emerged to convey these historic moments with eloquence. Better than any statistics, Harriette Arnow's 1954 novel *The Dollmaker* communicated the depth of personal loss one Appalachian family experienced migrating north. Like *The Grapes of Wrath*, this novel remains a testimony to survival.

Army "brats," children of professional soldiers used to moving about, experienced even more environmental variety and instability during wartime. One child mentioned attending five schools in one year; another attended thirty-six schools in six years.[11] Such examples represent patterns of instability in American life that educators still deplore. Yet strengths as well as weaknesses sometimes emerge from such forced adaptability. The Census Bureau took note of the count of ration books during the war years, concluding that cities everywhere were growing at the expense of farms. One out of eight rural families during the '40s left the family farm forever.

California grew spectacularly during the war years. Richmond, a small city near the San Francisco shipyards, grew from a population of 23,000 in 1940 to over 135,000 in 1943. Teachers there were so busy registering new students they had no time to hold classes. There was as much hostility to "Okies" and "Arkies" in Northern California as to blacks in

Detroit or to Hispanics in the Los Angeles area. The 1943 race riots in Southern California led not to the protection of the minority but to the outlawing of wearing baggy zoot suits, defined as an act of "vagrancy" by a city council offended by styles that challenged traditional white values. That young children and teenagers growing up in this world of constant change might become unusually sophisticated should not be surprising.

Generalizations—easy when they involve migration numbers and work statistics—are harder to make when they involve creativity and spiritual growth. Scholars know that the population of blacks in Chicago increased by 77% in the 1940s, going from 278,000 to 492,000. Nicholas Lemann's history of this great migration offers both political and personal details to document the amazing changes. Such changes could also be measured in cultural terms. Chicago provided a setting for some remarkable musicians and talented black writers as their audience grew. Pulitzer Prize–winning poet Gwendolyn Brooks and gifted playwright Lorraine Hansberry were able to extract material for their work out of the social inequities that defined the changing urban scene. Hansberry's play *A Raisin in the Sun* became an example of a drama deeply rooted in social reality that also managed to create lasting characters rather than stereotypes. The blues traditions of such artists as Muddy Waters, Howlin' Wolf, and Koko Taylor, to name but a few, continued to flourish in the Chicago environment that did little to encourage the upward mobility of most other African Americans.

Unfortunately, Executive Order 9066, signed by FDR on February 18, 1942, remained the most embarrassing law at the end of the century, when it was hard for most Americans to realize that wartime political decisions were sometimes based on fear rather than on reason. The idea to put **Japanese American Internment** over 120,000 West Coast Japanese Americans—most of whom were born in the United States—in internment camps will remain a blemish on the history of American civil rights. Here was an instance where Eleanor Roosevelt's pleas for humane consideration went unheeded. Though fear of espionage was the rationale for the procedure, 40 years later not one spy had been exposed.

The art and poetry created by those who were incarcerated, however, remain a tribute to their strength of character. Some Japanese American writers, among them Janice Mirikitani, John Okada, and Hisaye Yamamoto—who were children at the time—continued to write after the war, enriching the American literary tradition with the consciousness of a new community of Americans. Hustled onto trucks, made to live in barracks, forced to share latrines—deprived of their individualism in every way—these Japanese Americans managed to lead dignified, creative lives. They published magazines and newspapers in addition to producing creative writing and paintings. Ironically, many of their relatives in the U.S. Army proved their loyalty by being among the most decorated fighting units the country produced during the war.

Perhaps jealousy also played some role in getting the internment order passed. Whites at the time openly admitted envy of the frugal farmers who produced 40% of California's crops on 1% of the land. People lined up to take over the confiscated properties and carefully cultivated lands the Japanese Americans had left behind. *Fortune* magazine pointed out that our Japanese enemies were using the incarceration of Japanese Americans in a propaganda campaign to "convince all Orientals that the war in the Pacific is a crusade of the white man's racial oppression."[12]

Younger Japanese Americans—including lawyers—later began to rely on the Constitution to pursue the civil rights of this American-born group of good citizens. But it was not until 1988 that Congress voted an apology and offered each person interned $20,000 in reparations. To many this money seemed small recompense for all the humiliation. Oral history, films, art exhibits, and literary records of this dark moment in history enable students to understand the wartime reality more precisely. Particularly good is the Public Broadcasting Network's documentary *A Family Gathering*, produced as part of a series called "The American Experience." Invaluable as a record of one Japanese American family that thrived in Oregon from 1900 until the moment of their 1941 internment, the film reaches beyond all their successes and sorrows to address what it means to be an American from both first and second generation Americans' viewpoints. The film extends the wartime anger captured by such writers as Jeanne Wakatsuki Houston in *Farewell to Manzanar*, a young person's memoir of the world of incarceration, to a more philosophical vision of America. The pain is there; Masuo Yasui, the grandfather who cannot overcome his final sense of shame, commits suicide. But the constitutional triumph of his children is also real. The warm sense of success and cohesion in his large Japanese American mixed-marriage family transcends the war with the power to touch everyone. By the end of the 1940s it was possible to find Asian war brides all over America, even in places as small as Grover's Corners.

NOTES

1. Thornton Wilder, *Our Town* (New York: Harper and Row, 1938. Reprint, Perennial Library, 1985). Available in many anthologies as well.

2. Studs Terkel, *"The Good War": An Oral History of World War II* (New York: Ballantine Books, 1985), 139, 140.

3. Ibid., 107, 109.

4. Susan M. Hartmann, *The Home Front and Beyond: American Women in the 1940s* (Boston: G. K. Hall, 1982), chap. 1, 2–9.

5. Ibid., chap. 2, 15–24.

6. Ibid., 24.

7. Cited in Michael C.C. Adams, *The Best War Ever: America and World War II* (Baltimore: Johns Hopkins University Press, 1994), 126.

8. Ibid., 114.

9. Nicholas Lemann, *The Promised Land: The Great Black Migration and How It Changed America* (New York: Vintage Books/Knopf, 1991), 71–76.

10. William M. Tuttle, Jr., *"Daddy's Gone to War": The Second World War in the Lives of America's Children* (New York: Oxford University Press, 1993), 50.

11. Ibid., 51.

12. *Fortune*, April 1944, 47.

3

Movies Define Wartime America

"Say it, no ideas but in things," repeated William Carlos Williams in his long poem, *Paterson*. Williams, a pediatrician who remained a quiet poetic presence on the American scene from the 1920s until his death in 1963, was not valued in the university poetry courses of the 1940s, although the first volume of *Paterson* was published in 1946. It was not until the 1960s, when Williams' concern for ordinary experiences became as important as his images, that the practicing doctor gained academic esteem. But helping people understand the value of the common things that stood for ideas became an important contribution to the way Americans looked at their everyday lives. William Carlos Williams reasserted the importance of daily living in his descriptions of one community—Paterson, New Jersey—writing in a style connected to the rich culture of Walt Whitman and the ongoing humanity of American ideals. His poetry, designed to be accessible to everyone, helped readers discover beauty in ordinary surroundings and to cherish the meaning embedded in a vast range of common things.[1]

A 200-year-old culture—young by the measures of other civilizations—tries in different periods to shape itself by listening to the past with only one ear. Americans have had to make much of the symbols—the "things"—that define the present, even as they observe that all human beings struggle to understand their own cultures by examining the artifacts people leave behind. People cannot ignore such gigantic images as the Great Wall of China, or the Egyptian pyramids, or Chartres Cathedral, or—in the case of 1940s America—the atom bomb. Although the gigantic scars the bomb left may seem the most overwhelming remnants of its power, tourists now also go to the desert of Los Alamos to read a tablet that commemorates the burst of the first incredible mushroom cloud in 1945. And travelers to Japan today can visit a tower of paper cranes made by Japanese children to remind people of the common humanity that should control the fierceness of such power in the future. The 50th anniversary of the great explosion, 1995, saw different intellectual artifacts appear—symbols in the form of new books and catalogued museum displays to mark and question the meaning of this overwhelming moment in 20th century history when human beings began to reassess the future as the "Atomic Age."

The details of human experience related to the daily reality behind the creation of such tremendous artifacts are often less available for study. But the kinds of forced labor that created the Great Wall of China and the pyramids of Egypt must be a part of their history as much as religious fervor was essential to the creation of Chartres Cathedral. Similarly, the freedom of expression that characterized America and made it a sanctuary for victims of political oppression during the 1940s contributed to the creation of the atom bomb. Had the United States not provided a refuge for many of the intellectuals fleeing fascism in Europe, the United States might not have been the first nation to herald the Atomic Age. Nor would the democratic institutions Americans cherish have survived defeat by the totalitarian states of the Germans and Japanese. Ideals at that moment became quite practical. That a country in the midst of the Depression, on the verge of class, and race, and ethnic disintegration, managed to discard its isolationism—its selfish desire to put "America First"—and organize its resources to win a terrible war fought in every part of the world remains a testimony to the 1940s unity many people remember fondly when they think of the war.

What were some of the "things" that contributed to the sense of unity that emerged in wartime? How did the people in the United States find strength to fight a war that involved the whole world and forced them to redefine themselves as Americans? How did they come to describe World War II, as it pulled the country out of economic disaster, as "the best war ever"? Few would deny that for the first time in history the media played a tremendous role in creating and unifying national values with workable myths that spoke to all America, not just as a country but as a community, standing above the divisive tensions of daily life. Another poet, Archibald MacLeish, director of the Office of Facts and Figures during the 1940s, commented that the principal battleground of the war was "American opinion."

Radio   In the present world of instant telecommunication with excesses of information in every space, it is hard even to imagine the 1930s, when not every American family owned a radio. When

Franklin Roosevelt gave his fireside chats, often more than one household joined together to listen. During this period rural electrification had just begun to extend airwaves to allow farmers to hear stand-up comedians like Jack Benny and Fred Allen and sitcoms like *Fibber McGee and Molly* and *Amos 'n Andy* (stories of blacks played by whites—not heard as racist at the time). Daytime soap operas (which really advertised laundry soap) like *Ma Perkins, My Gal Sunday*, and *Pepper Young's Family* enabled the homebound to imagine that other families' problems could be worse than their own.

A popular radio demagogue and Catholic priest, Father Charles Coughlin, used *The Golden Hour of the Little Flower* to attract as many as 40 million listeners. His original belief in the New Deal turned into hatred for FDR and support for European fascism, causing his audience to drop away before he left the airwaves in 1940. And one sensational reporter, Walter Winchell, broadcast gossipy versions of news like the items printed in the *National Enquirer*—even as a few serious journalists, like Edward R. Murrow and H. V. Kaltenborn, felt free to express personal liberal opinions. Lowell Thomas, a daily newscaster, used broadcasting to help isolated families visit remote places like Arabia and Tibet, making more convincing the "One World" advocated by Wendell Willkie, FDR's 1940 Republican opponent, in a bestselling book. In trying to solidify new ideals, Americans have often found it difficult to imagine the vast range of cultural experiences others have had to put aside to become citizens of the United States. More than books or magazines, the radio became a source of "public relations" for unifying a frequently fractured society. Just as talking pictures took over from the silent films of the 1920s, movies replaced radio as a means of communication and entertainment, becoming one of the few American businesses that flourished in the 1930s.

During the 1940s sales of movie tickets soared to 3.5 billion a year. By then movies would be the "things" that embodied American ideas—not just for Americans, but for the whole world. Entertaining, in- **The Role of Film in Entertainment** formative, and relatively cheap, films reinforced the values this country wanted to honor, the ideas people would be willing to make sacrifices for. A 1940s classic, *Mrs. Miniver*, created to glorify the bravery and ingenuity of our British ally—personified by the charming Greer Garson— could be seen in New York along with the famous Rockettes' precision dancing stage show at the elegant Radio City Music Hall for 75 cents. The film broke all attendance records for the time, grossing over a million dollars.

One anthropologist, Hortense Powdermaker, referred to Hollywood as a "dream factory," while Robert Sklar, an historian, defined the whole country as "movie-made America." The power of the motion picture industry to influence how Americans saw themselves, to turn myths into live traditions, would become more and more apparent. When we elected our first movie star president, critics remarked that Ronald Reagan sometimes seemed to confuse his World War II movie roles with what actually happened. In the 1940s the social and cultural makeup of the movie industry reflected the values of an America concerned with helping people recognize what was worth fighting for.[2]

Hollywood's representation of the American Dream has been definitively described by the television movie critic Neal Gabler in a social history of the film industry, *An Empire of Their Own: How the Jews Invented Hollywood*. Examining the lives of Hollywood tycoons as symbolic American successes, Gabler reveals the anxieties of the movie moguls' world as suggestive of the values of most new Americans. In articulating on film their own immigrant dreams of the good life available in America, the film makers helped influence how other Americans defined their identity. Most convincingly, Gabler records the intense and often uncritical patriotism that shaped the movie makers' attitudes toward foreign ideologies, like the Nazism so many in the industry had fled and the Communism that others believed was a threat to American life.[3] In the 1940s the movie empire demonstrated unquestioning patriotism—a wholehearted commitment to the war effort that would help both to educate soldiers and to stir up civilian support for the war. Films like *This Is the Army* (1943), *Yankee Doodle Dandy* (1942), *The Fighting 69th* (1940), and *Lifeboat* (1944) attempted to revitalize the American myths of ethnic success and integrated culture. All groups needed to believe that individuals could do well working together in a pluralistic society for a common goal.

During the war years attendance at local theaters mounted to over 90 million viewers a week. Commitment to the war effort by the film industry extended to many different levels. Movie houses—palaces of imagination in the 1930s—were used in the 1940s as community centers. In their spacious lobbies people gathered to buy and sell war bonds and to collect flattened tin cans and aluminum pots as well as surplus fats for making munitions. Even youngsters worked at selling defense stamps at small tables set up near the ticket takers to remind people of their civic responsibilities. When movie stars joined in the sale of government bonds at American theaters everywhere they sold over $350 billion worth. People did not hesitate to lend their savings to the government.

Teenagers also collected money in movie lobbies to boost the canteens of the United Service Organizations. Many young soldiers stationed all over America in army training camps far from their homes needed "wholesome" places for entertainment on weekend leaves. Members of the film industry worked with local volunteers to make these Stage Door Canteens represent homey refuges of warmth and hospitality for young strangers. Even though the armed forces were racially segregated during World War II, the canteens for relaxation often made a point of being integrated. Actress Bette Davis, one anecdote records, threatened to sever connection with her local canteen when some officious volunteers questioned the interracial dancing that took place there. Although most of the elegant theaters where such community activities could happen were torn down in the 1960s when television became a more socially isolating way to view movies, a film called *Stagedoor Canteen* (1943) remains a tribute to the idea of innocent entertainment and welcome for out-of-towners under supervision of the movie industry. The Hollywood Canteen, sponsored by 42 craft guilds including both white and African American musicians' locals, fed thousands of meals to eager soldiers and sailors during its first two years. Yet it is the movies themselves—the "things" that embody the ideas of the 1940s—that students will continue to consider the most important social artifacts of the war. Almost every film made during the war years reveals some social aspect of wartime America.

On the most obvious level Hollywood film makers offered the government their resources to create training films for the army—telling soldiers about our allies and introducing our enemies. The public would be offered similar fare. Propagandistic work like *A Yank in the R.A.F.* (1944) and *Journey for Margaret* (1942), about an evacuated English child, were meant to demonstrate our deep connection with the British. Ideological films like *Hitler's Children* (1943) or Charlie Chaplin's *The Great Dictator* (1940) made it easier to dislike Germans. Exaggerated features of treacherous Japanese film characters helped Americans accept the necessity to incarcerate patriotic fellow Americans. Not until after the war, when Japan had become an American friend, was a film made to expose the injustice of the internment camps. Made out of Jeanne Wakatsuki Houston's memoir, the film *Farewell to Manzanar* in 1976 captures one Japanese American's story of the humiliations of displacement. Other movies created during wartime to familiarize the American people with our new allies, the Russians—like *Mission to Moscow* (1944)—would haunt their Hollywood producers and writers after the war when the relationship with Russia disintegrated and a blacklist labeled the creators of such sympathetic scripts Communist sympathizers.

That distinguished writers like John Steinbeck joined the war effort with *The Moon Is Down* (1943) and *Lifeboat* (1944) suggests the extent of involvement of serious writers and artists in wartime propaganda. A list of Hollywood producers, writers, directors, technicians, and stars who put personal preferences aside to do what was most helpful for their country in fighting the war would fill a small book. Two favorites—the witty movie star Carole Lombard and the band leader Glenn Miller, who traveled as an enlisted army officer entertaining troops—lost their lives in military air crashes. No one in the movie community criticized the government or questioned the need to get behind the war. A rare pacifist, star Lew Ayres, emphasized his opposition to killing by joining the medical corps. Newsreels—shown in Translux theaters for short subjects were also included with feature films, recording ugly realities just as TV news did during the Vietnam War. There were honest journalists like Ernie Pyle who described what continuous fighting did to people, but there was also protective censorship. People on the home front complained if too much brutality was exposed. Movies were constructed to show the enemy—not American young men—being blown to bits. Students might consider how much such attitudes shift in different decades by looking at the 1998 film *Saving Private Ryan*, an effort to depict the invasion of Europe with utmost accuracy.

Glorification of the war experience became essential while the war was being fought. Although films like *The Story of G.I. Joe* (1943), *A Walk in the Sun* (1945), and *Pride of the Marines* (1945) stressed a wholesome distaste for war as human activity, they made a point of demonstrating the surprising courage of the ordinary individual in the multicultural foxhole. Critics tend to make fun of the Hollywood melting-pot group: black-white, Catholic-Jew, slum kid–stockbroker dependent on each other in submarine or fighter plane; but the need to nourish the myth of equality for those willing to die for it brought about a more realistic exploration of American prejudice in films after the war. A 1939 movie like *Gone with the Wind* could get away with showing blacks to be dully loyal or simply silly. In the name of the national unity forged out of the Civil War, this famous classic praised only the individual spunk of whites enduring social disaster—slavery was not an issue in the film. After World War II African Americans would be taken more seriously in films, and American prejudice would be discussed in the open. Such movies as *Crossfire* and *Gentleman's Agreement* (both 1947) would also help to alert many to the reality of American antisemitism. *Intruder in the Dust* (1949) allowed viewers to appreciate the intelligence of a black hero. In 1948, acknowledging the need for equality of opportunity in an important section of American life, Harry Truman integrated the army. In 1945, during Roosevelt's brief fourth term, the government repealed the 1882 Chinese Exclusion Act, which set quotas on Chinese immigration and denied citizenship to the Chinese.

The 1940s film industry's contribution to pure entertainment to help people escape the tensions of war and the problems of reshaping postwar life also included such classic musicals as *State Fair* (1945) and *The Harvey Girls* (1945). "Black film" masterpieces such as *The Maltese Falcon* (1941), *Laura* (1944), *Double Indemnity* (1945), *The Postman Always Rings Twice* (1946), and *Spellbound* (1945) made distraction exciting. Westerns like *The Ox-Box Incident* (1943) and *My Darling Clementine* (1946) extended the mythology of the West with greater compassion.

What role the motion picture industry played as an edu-
cation in possibilities for those who experienced daily prej-   **Film as**
udice in real life is hard to evaluate. Hollywood, for instance,   **Education**
often produced mixed messages concerning women. During
the war movie heroines were frequently depicted as self-effacing nurses.
But many younger women who never knew any women professionals
could also relish the feisty characters played by Katharine Hepburn and
Rosalind Russell. Even in marriage these women did not submerge their
individuality. And Scarlett O'Hara, the assertive Southern survivor of
the Civil War in *Gone with the Wind* (1939) more often defined the American woman to the world than her self-effacing friend Melanie Wilkes.
Ginger Rogers, Fred Astaire's dancing equal, appeared on the assembly
line in *Tender Comrade* (1943) to make aircraft factory work seem glam-
orous. Much later, as the 1970s documentary *Rosie the Riveter* demonstrated, the equal skills of women doing men's jobs during World War
II could not be challenged. Many women disliked being urged back into
the home. But by the '70s, when women had long been out of high-
paying hard-hat jobs, they also found some labor unions more welcom-
ing. Almost the minute the war was over, as this detailed documentary
also demonstrates, subsidized daycare was taken away from working
mothers, and women were made to feel guilty for neglecting their children as well as for taking good jobs away from returning heroes.

Specific war documentary films made for the public also helped all
Americans better understand the democratic processes they were fighting for. The Office of War Information offered *Tuesday in November* on
the importance of voting and *A Better Tomorrow* about the value of public
education. *The Cummington Story* told of an immigrant's acceptance in a
conventional New England town. Such film experiences contributed to
the better informed electorate essential to any well-run democracy. The
lost civic awareness that people mourned in peacetime did not come to
citizens instinctively. During the 1940s such awareness was consciously
cultivated by the government as propaganda essential to wartime unity.
Patriotism was aroused by films that kept reminding viewers of what
was good about American life.

Other government documentaries were available on such topics as
public health, the Tennessee Valley Authority, the Library of Congress,
medical education in America, and—after the war—the founding of the
United Nations. All such films were offered to schools at the cost of
printing. Experts teaching soldiers demonstrated that people could master a process a third faster if they saw it first in motion pictures, a valuable discovery for a war effort of conversion and retraining. Films of
all kinds would become a primary tool in American education. The commitment to community that included informing people about the best in
national life—not just the political process—also produced a series of

biographical documentaries about elder wise men like Frank Lloyd Wright, Robert Frost, and Pablo Casals. More direct educational documentaries on training "Negro midwives" or studying disturbed children at the Wiltwyck School were made to extend social awareness after the war, enabling large numbers of people to appreciate different kinds of community experiences.

The sense that Americans had a stake in each other's lives lingered only for a short time after the soldiers were out of the foxholes and onto the streets. No Hollywood film demonstrated the change more clearly than *The Best Years of Our Lives* (1946) about returning G.I.s in a society that had no understanding of how the war experience had shaped the veteran's consciousness of what really mattered.

Artistic Aspects of Film

Film makers of the '40s cared about the artistic quality of their work. Some of the artifacts that made ideas into things were often beautiful. America's most influential film reviewer, Pauline Kael, asserted, "I don't have any doubt about movies being a great art form."[4] Few movie lovers at the time would have had any doubt that our most famous artistic film was also a product of the 1940s. Orson Welles' *Citizen Kane* became available to viewers in 1941 as a document of social criticism and an exploration of American success. Welles' film suggests the pain of an extremely rich American's life that disintegrates as he loses the relationships that support most people. It also remains a triumph of the artistry of black and white cinematography. The images that Orson Welles created—the sled, the picnic parade, the castle, and the long library table—stick in the mind as classic examples of what William Carlos Williams meant by the phrase "no ideas but in things." Almost every moment of *Citizen Kane* strikes the visual imagination. In a reversal of the wartime emphasis on co-operation and community, Welles' film gave his fellow citizens an example of the prewar self-indulgent individualism so important to the ongoing American mythology of success. As Citizen Kane loses his commitment to his high ideals of journalism, his indifference to his family drives him toward another woman. He loses the humanity identified with the simpler America of his youth. That such ego indulgence could also be measured in wartime by greed and profiteering, Arthur Miller explored in depth in the stage play *All My Sons*, safely turned into a film for a larger audience after the war in 1948.

Casablanca: The American Experience and the American Dream

Although as a society Americans remain more committed to individual fulfillment—to "the pursuit of happiness"—than to action for the common good or the pursuit of social responsibility, the preparation for war in the 1940s demanded a modification of such values. While a story like *The Wizard of Oz*, emphasizing each individual's capability to shape the self in terms of personal needs, could be celebrated in the 1930s as an example of the myth of self-reliance essential to help overturn the economic Depression, the 1940s had to offer the country a different kind of myth that provided examples of both capability and self-sacrifice. The great British inspirational classic of the war years, Laurence Olivier's version of Shakespeare's *Henry V*, emphasized the concealed kingliness of the once wanton prince as well as the superhuman strength of his common followers. In America filmmakers offered audiences a convincing tale about the heroism of a rootless saloon owner willing to sacrifice his personal love and even to kill for the allied cause: *Casablanca*.

The Warner brothers, who produced *Casablanca*, were famous for their 1930s stable of gangsters, underdogs, and outsiders. Theirs were not the movies that reinforced the immigrant dream of small town family happiness and modest domestic success—theirs were the films that admired guts and assertiveness in a competitive world. The American experience they validated acknowledged the deep divisions in everyday life during the Depression and the frequent discrepancies between action and reward. Their film repertory celebrated an indifference to law and conventional behavior that had defined the heroic underdog in American literature from Natty Bumppo to Huckleberry Finn and Jay Gatsby. In films of the '30s and '40s such independent spirits found expression in both Western and gangster films. More often than not audiences—like readers—learned to appreciate loners who stood for vigilante justice rather than community law and order. Our mythology has often insisted that the individual conscience is more reliable than the group's.

To film critic Neal Gabler, the Warner brothers themselves were fringe members of the Hollywood studio community, examples of the outsiders they seemed to define. By "mythologizing the qualities of the poor and the marginal," they forged a community of energy to mount an artistic challenge to the insiders.[5] In a peculiar way this community, making the film *Casablanca* entirely on a Hollywood set, managed to suggest all the experiences of wartime America. Not only did the outsider hero—almost against his will—become an example of the turn from self-indulgence to commitment, like Henry V, but the entire studio involved in the making of the film seemed also to represent rare selfless American values. Unlike the earlier hero-outsider Rhett Butler, who was enriched both emotionally and financially from profiteering during the Civil War, the character Rick stands to lose everything by doing the right thing in helping the leader of the Allied underground escape.

Made in the darkest early moments of the war, 1941 and 1942, and released in 1942, *Casablanca* won an Academy Award in 1944 as an example of the film industry's wartime best. Jack Warner, always sensitive to antisemitism, had made earlier films about important Jews like Benjamin Disraeli, Alfred Dreyfus, and Dr. Paul Ehrlich, whose "magic bullet" was a cure for syphilis. He had been the first film maker to challenge Hitler. Often personally offensive as moguls, the Warner brothers demonstrated a commitment to the war effort that was consistent and self-sacrificing. They gave all the profits from films made for Great Britain's Ministry of War Information, for example, to buy Spitfire planes for the British air force. In 1941 the Ku Klux Klan expressed pro-German sympathies by vandalizing a number of Warner-owned movie houses. Other producers were much less concerned about Nazi ideology. Movie mogul Sam Goldwyn, characterized by memorable sayings, remarked that movies were first and always entertainment: "If anyone wants to send a message," he said, "let him hire Western Union." The Warner brothers' belief that movies could play an important role in "the cultural and educational development of the world" was new.[6] Jack Warner also understood the propaganda needs of wartime America.

Casablanca became one of America's most successful films both in terms of entertainment and in terms of creating stars. And it also managed to realize Jack Warner's serious goals. Not only did the film capture a wartime moment rich in personal complexity and high idealism, but its entertainment value extended its influence as an emblem of America through the remainder of the 20th century. On many levels and in many ways the film captured the nuances and the riches of the best aspects of the American Dream. The spirit of the foxhole melting pot and the brains of the Los Alamos intellectual refugees came together on the level of creative experience to make a propaganda film which was also a work of art. In the 1990s *Casablanca* would be called an American icon.

The film became an embodiment of American idealism to younger generations who knew hardly anything about World War II but knew the lines of Ingrid Bergman and Humphrey Bogart by heart. Bogart in the role of Rick, embittered by betrayal in love, boasting that he will stick his neck out for no one, appeals to everyone's sense of what human beings can be when called to act for a higher cause. Even the most cynical, the film suggests, will put aside personal interests to do the right thing. To be sure, the film sets the audience up to know that Rick's "profiteering" has always been on the side of the underdog—first as a gun-runner against fascists in Ethiopia, then active in the war against Franco in Spain.

In a remarkable book connecting the making of *Casablanca* to the social and cultural forces that shaped the 1940s, *Round Up the Usual Suspects: The Making of Casablanca—Bogart, Bergman and World War II*, Aljean Harmetz notes that Rick's personal past would have put him on the blacklist of the House Un-American Activities Committee.[7] Yet throughout the film Rick feigns indifference to moral purpose. In spite of the hints about his moral decency, viewers cannot be sure until the very end how Rick, the classical American outsider, will behave. Todd Gitlin, who was born in 1943 and who chronicled his own life in a period of high commitment in *The Sixties: Years of Hope, Days of Rage*, wrote that as a student he found *Casablanca* an overpowering experience. In the film he saw his own "personal melodrama," his own "personal rite of passage" as a member of a peace group. Articulating once again the tradition of individual morality made so clear by Huckleberry Finn, Gitlin ponders the idea that some actions must matter more than others for social good. He praises *Casablanca* for offering audiences an archetype—in the character of Rick—of the imperative to "move from disengagement and cynicism to commitment."[8]

In *Casablanca* the heroine as well as the hero is able to make a social choice to do the right thing. The belief in public good that seemed to fade from consciousness during the self-indulgent decades after World War II appeared restored by the complex memories the film evokes. Although focused on the easily distinguished good and evil historical forces during World War II, the film's propagandizing is not entirely simpleminded. The settings and the vast number of minor characters (75) make it a triumph of variety and persuasive nostalgia. The resonance of the writing, as Gitlin's enthusiasm suggests, carried it beyond its own time and place. In 1977 *Casablanca* was still the most frequently shown film on television. It has been voted, along with its near contemporaries, *Citizen Kane* and *Gone with the Wind*, one of the three best American films. A British group of film critics in 1983 called it the best film ever made. In 1987 Joyce Carol Oates titled a novel *You Must Remember This*, suggesting the lasting power of the song the film made immortal. *Play It Again, Sam* (1972), a Woody Allen spin-off film, assumed that audiences would be familiar with Bogart's special charms. A British sitcom about an older couple who had been separated by the war is called *As Time Goes By*. New books continue to appear. The title of Harmetz's book (itself a valuable cultural artifact), *Round Up the Usual Suspects*, suggests—perhaps unconsciously—that one of the film's final lines reached beyond police jargon into surprising relationships between unlikely comrades.

The making of *Casablanca*, as Harmetz describes it, also became a metaphor for American behavior in the 1940s—when both consciousness and conscience were forced to reach beyond the United States for collective identity. Even the making of the film suggested the idea of a working democracy so essential to winning the war. During World War II Americans began to understand more clearly that we were both a nation of immigrants and citizens of a much larger world. A glance at any map charting the war zones involved in World War II makes clear how much more of the world's surface the action covered than did World War I. On the home front we were just beginning to accord African Americans the dignity on screen that Dooley Wilson represented in the role of

Sam—talented musician and wise companion who accompanies Rick as an equal through the pain and choices of life.

Racism and the Rising Threat of McCarthyism. Although the Office of War Information had recommended that film makers upgrade the roles of black actors during the war to make African Americans more acceptable as fellow workers in defense industries, as late as 1944, 75 out of 100 films still used black actors only as stereotypical janitors and butlers. Dooley Wilson's role in *Casablanca* represented a larger vision. Although the song "As Time Goes By" will forever be the music that identifies the film, Wilson played a good bit of other popular American music in it, demonstrating obvious musical skills. Talent, however, was no protection against 1940s racism. Even the distinguished African American singer Lena Horne had trouble buying a house in Humphrey Bogart's neighborhood. He rose to her defense when other neighbors tried to evict her. Like Rick, the star himself had a history of supporting the underdog. Outraged by the anti-Communist blacklist that would grow after the war, keeping many writers and stars jobless (eventually even *Casablanca* co-star Paul Henreid), Bogart joined the Committee for the First Amendment in 1947 to protect the rights of writers and artists to express unpopular opinions. Congress continued to believe that media people were especially dangerous because their influence was so broad.

It would be the film media, the cameras that televised the Congressional hearings of the '50s, that would devastate the crude anti-Communist tactics Senator Joseph McCarthy used against the Army. Seeing McCarthy in action made many viewers eager for his 1954 downfall. The senator's vindictive style would also be captured in a documentary film, *Point of Order* (chapter 6), revealing the fear and the hostility to Communist ideas that seized the American imagination as early as 1947 when Harry Truman sanctioned invasions of human rights if necessary to protect democracy. The documentary remains an important artifact—a thing that clearly reveals an idea. But no film clarifies the offensiveness of these times better than Woody Allen's black comedy *The Front* (1976), made at a time when it was safe to use blacklisted artists to explore their own earlier cultural anxieties. Students must ever be grateful that such carefully crafted films exist for speculation and analysis. Every democracy has a responsibility to exhume and explore the behavior of other eras from different angles of vision, even as we honor our myths. Movies looked at critically can contribute valuable insights into the past.

The world connected with the making of *Casablanca* was a world of honor. It represented the American dreams of all sorts of people working together toward an important goal. The necessity of winning the war made viewers believe that the hero and heroine could each renounce personal desires for a higher cause. If any American thought for a moment that a good woman would leave a heroic freedom fighter to follow her heart, the audience knew unconsciously what such a message would represent to all soldiers separated from their wives. The historical moment demanded renunciation and sacrifice as surely as it did in the time of Homer's *Iliad*. Without even seeming sentimental, *Casablanca* managed to convey this idea because the huge number of refugees working both on and in the film made the story so convincing.

The Immigrant Involvement in Casablanca. With a few exceptions—from the Warner brothers on down the entire production was the creation of immigrants. The minor roles are so persuasive because so many of those involved in the film were responding to their own personal experiences. Film critic Aljean Harmetz noted that in California at this time there were over 1,500 German film industry exiles alone—too many to be supported by real work, especially as German immigrants were subject to 8 P.M. curfews during the war. Following 19th century American immigrant patterns, those who worked helped their jobless countrymen. From 1938 until 1945 a European film fund existed to collect 1% of workers' wages to help the unemployed.

The subplots involving resonant minor parts in *Casablanca* were all played by immigrant actors who had been stars in their native countries before exile. "If you think of *Casablanca* and think of all those small roles being played by Hollywood actors faking accents," Pauline Kael remarked, "the picture would not have anything like the color and tone it had."[9] She pointed out that in the great scene when Rick gets the band to drown out the German anthem with the "Marseillaise," many of those crying on screen were refugees who had experienced similar loss. The cast included at least 24 Nazi escapees, including both Jews and homosexuals. Helmut Dantine, who plays a Nazi on screen, fled his native Austria because he openly opposed the German takeover—a moment in history immortalized in a later American-made film, *The Sound of Music*.

Only three members of the entire cast of *Casablanca*—Humphrey Bogart, Dooley Wilson, and Joy Page—were born in America, suggesting again the wealth of immigrant talent that enriched the film industry during this period. That immigrants and exiles continued to give as much as they took from our society remains clear. Michael Curtiz (Mihaly Kertesz), the director of the film, lost his sister, his brother-in-law, two nephews, and a niece in the concentration camp of Auschwitz.

The humanity of the minor characters as refugees enhances the plot by underlining the choices human beings must make in extreme situations. War means sacrifice. Laszlo, the heroic freedom fighter who has always put ideals first, salutes Rick at the end: "Welcome back to the fight."

But Rick's personal moral decision becomes just one of many against the background of war. Even the character of the corrupt bureaucrat

Captain Renault, played so artfully by Claude Rains, makes a decision to reach beyond selfish ends when he symbolically throws away his bottle of Vichy water, separating himself from the Vichy collaborators with the Nazis. He and Rick, in choosing each other for the beginning of a long friendship, enter that long tradition of male bonding in American mythology—as in the case of Huck and Jim or Natty Bumppo and Chingachgook—that suggests the extended possibilities of an unconventional good life—a representation of collective conscience. Some critics saw the two eccentric characters as America and Europe—lawless freedom and corrupt bureaucracy—working to save democracy.

The Merging of Individual and Collective Consciousness. In *Casablanca* Rick grows up in a way that Citizen Kane never could. World War II forced maturity on many young people, turning them away from material pursuits toward the transcendent human qualities needed in times of sacrifice. "We'll always have Paris," Rick says to Ilsa as he also says good-bye, reminding viewers that American culture, in spite of its materialism, has often honored noble ideas as much as concrete realities. The idea that is also the "thing" in this film stresses the individual's capacity to give up pleasure when necessary; but it lingers also in the strong satisfactions of the mind—in moral choice and in memory. Compared to the experiences of Europeans, of course, the actual sacrifices most Americans made during the war were trivial. Gasoline, sugar, and meat rationing, margarine instead of butter, shoe rationing and baggy stockings replacing silk—such hardships along with disintegrating artificial rubber tires did not add up to much deprivation. Blackouts and air raid drills prepared people for bombing, but bombs did not fall on American homes as they did on much of the world. Still, it is essential to honor the 405,399 soldiers who lost their lives fighting for American ideals and important to remember as well the 671,846 Americans who returned home wounded.[10]

Casablanca did more than help people in the United States address the loss of loved ones and respect the freedom to choose causes over personal gratification. The film also clearly recorded a specific moment in world history. That America produced such an artifact, providing insight into what was exemplary in the American century, should remain a source of pride. *Casablanca* may still be the best on-screen example of the merging of the individual and the collective consciousness. By the end of the century most historians would accept the use of movies as tools to implement the understanding of ideas about what is both rich and shallow in American life. As *Casablanca* the thing becomes *Casablanca* the idea, it suggests even to new viewers the moment of community and commitment that represented the best of America's role in World War II.

NOTES

1. William Carlos Williams, *Paterson* (New York: New Directions, 1946), 9.

2. See Hortense Powdermaker, *Hollywood: The Dream Factory* (New York: Universal Library, 1950); Robert Sklar, *Movie-Made America: A Social History of American Movies* (New York: Random House, 1975. Reprint, Bantam, 1987).

3. Neal Gabler, *An Empire of Their Own: How the Jews Invented Hollywood* (New York: Doubleday-Anchor, 1988), Introduction, 342–374.

4. Pauline Kael, *Deeper into Movies* (Boston: Atlantic Monthly Press, 1973), 237.

5. Gabler, *Empire* 197ff.

6. Ibid., 195.

7. Aljean Harmetz, *Round Up the Usual Suspects: The Making of Casablanca—Bogart, Bergman and World War II* (New York: Hyperion, 1992).

8. Todd Gitlin, *The Sixties: Years of Hope, Days of Rage* (New York: Bantam Books, 1987), 103; discussed in Harmetz, *Usual Suspects*, 345, 349.

9. Quoted in Harmetz, *Usual Suspects*, 212.

10. Statistics cited in James T. Patterson, *Grand Expectations: The United States, 1945–1974* (New York: Oxford University Press, 1996), 4. An excellent detailed summary of these years.

August 1942, Chrysler-Dodge factory. African Americans and whites work together on hand assembly of experimental Dodge trucks. Library of Congress, Prints & Photographs Division

United Auto Workers election at Ford River Rouge Plant; 80,000 voted, both black and white. Library of Congress, Prints & Photographs Division

Women building gliders for the war in what appeared to outsiders as a Heinz pickle factory in Pittsburgh. Owned and reprinted by permission of H. J. Heinz Company.

1942, Williston, North Dakota. Farmers organize to protest the sale of family farms to big corporations. Library of Congress, Prints & Photographs Division

1942, Detroit. African American defense workers needed police escorts to enable them to move safely into new housing. Library of Congress, Prints & Photographs Division

1942. The Sojourner Truth Housing Projects, ironically, did not welcome blacks. Library of Congress, Prints & Photographs Division

1942, East Montpelier, Vermont. One family salvaged more than a ton and a half of steel, including 50 pounds of license plates. Library of Congress, Prints & Photographs Division

East Montpelier, Vermont. Conrad Ormsbee, age 11 and member of local 4-H Club, raised a Jersey calf as his war project. Library of Congress, Prints & Photographs Division

President Franklin Delano Roosevelt. Library of Congress, Prints & Photographs Division

Harry S. Truman campaigned from trains, stopping at many small towns to win the votes that made him president in 1948. Library of Congress, Prints & Photographs Division

Air raid wardens meet to discuss roles in emergency. Photographer: Gordon
Parks. Library of Congress, Prints & Photographs Division

July 1942, Frederick Douglass Housing Project. "Victory Through Good Health"
programs targeted black communities and schools. Dance group. Photographer:
Gordon Parks. Library of Congress, Prints & Photographs Division

October 1942, Silver Spring, Maryland. Young men made model planes according to Navy specifications to train military and civilian personnel to recognize them. Library of Congress, Prints & Photographs Division

Federal Workers' integrated Service Canteen. Here Pete Seeger in uniform entertains Eleanor Roosevelt. Library of Congress, Prints & Photographs Division

Washington, D.C. victory garden being prepared by gardener still wearing hat and tie. Library of Congress, Prints & Photographs Division

Japanese internment, 1942. West coast fear sent many loyal American families into detention camps. National Archives

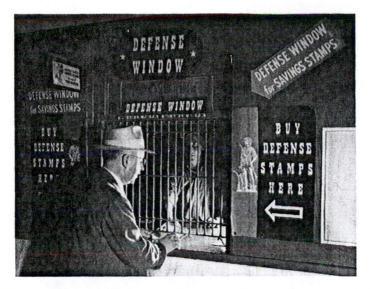

May 1942, Southington, Connecticut. People bought defense stamps and bonds at post office windows. They could also buy them in movie theaters and five-and-tens. Library of Congress, Prints & Photographs Division

June 1945, Oswego, New York. Many contributed blood to wounded soldiers. The blood donor clinic at this Elks Lodge was run by 1,000 volunteers for several days each month. The Red Cross could handle ten people every fifteen minutes. Library of Congress, Prints & Photographs Division

June 1942. At a time when trousers had their cuffs cut off in order to save wool, women also collected scraps for reprocessing as usable warm material. Even incompetent knitters made squares for hospital afghans. Library of Congress, Prints & Photographs Division

1944. Teenage volunteers at Greenwich Hospital, New York, instruct younger children while their mothers work in war production. Library of Congress, Prints & Photographs Division

1944. Manhattan schoolchildren's victory garden. Library of Congress, Prints &
Photographs Division

December 1942. Garment worker in Daniel Boone hat contributed by a hunter.
The War Emergency Board of the fur industry donated one day each week to
making fur-lined vests for Merchant Marines. Library of Congress, Prints &
Photographs Division

1943. "Italian American" boys at Sullivan Square depot contribute scrap to help defeat Italy. Library of Congress, Prints & Photographs Division

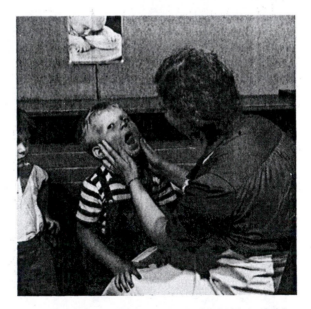

1943, New Britain, Connecticut. Daycare center kept thirty children ages two to five from 6:30 A.M. to 6 P.M. Daily visiting nurses, monthly physicals, and doctors on call comforted mothers' anxieties about leaving children at a time when polio was a reality and few vaccines for other childhood diseases existed. Library of Congress, Prints & Photographs Division

1943, Buffalo. Mother picking up children from daycare provided by the Board of Education for $3 per week. Library of Congress, Prints & Photographs Division

1945. The hydrogen bomb—the beginning of a new age. Library of Congress, Prints & Photographs Division

4

Science and Technology

Many historians see the 1940s defined as much by social struggle—vast internal migration and racial tension—as by astonishing productivity and deep spiritual commitment to winning the war. For a few days in 1945 after Franklin Roosevelt's death on April 12, a great mix of people demonstrated—perhaps for the last time—the sense of national unity their aristocratic president had helped establish during the war. "A soldier died today," reported James Agee in the April 12, 1945, issue of *Time* magazine: "Everywhere to almost everyone, the news came with the force of a personal shock."[1] The eminent and humble mourned together the leader who had been America's president for twelve hard years. Because no broadcast television then existed citizens relied on the power of radio to recreate the details. No one who listened has ever forgotten the broken tearful voice of the radio announcer Arthur Godfrey describing the quiet lines of mourners. Along the railroad tracks that guided FDR's body home to Hyde Park stood hordes of silent working-class people who believed that his New Deal had restored their dignity by giving them work. Although some revisionist scholars label the New Deal an economic failure, most historians concede that Roosevelt's domestic policies helped many "forgotten" men and women to recognize their rights. They trusted their government.

The love of these people for her husband also helped Eleanor Roosevelt conquer her complex grief at that moment to continue as an American leader on her own. If the country neglected the social programs she deemed so important in favor of the rituals of war, Eleanor Roosevelt still used the time of emergency to put forward modern ideas on exercise and healthy diet for every woman and child. And she also helped a few industries—such as the Kaiser shipyards—to become aware that daycare was as important for workers as cafeterias were. The Swan Island Center for Children in Portland, Oregon, a result of Eleanor's persistence, became a technical example of just how good daycare could be for children at the same time that their mothers' worker productivity increased. By the end of 1945, more than 1.5 million previously ignored children would be cared for in such centers. As a journalist with a daily syndicated newspaper column and a monthly question and answer page in the *Ladies' Home Journal*, Eleanor Roosevelt cultivated a huge audience for the range of her social concerns when few politicians were listening. As FDR's scout she was use to traveling all over America, digging out and describing unpopular problems. A rare example of a truly active First Lady, Eleanor Roosevelt continued after FDR's death to play the role of moral witness on behalf of many groups with inadequate Congressional representation. Native Americans, Japanese Americans, Holocaust children, overworked and underpaid laborers, women, and especially African Americans profited from her concern. She lobbied Congress and exerted pressure on influential friends to make New Deal social commitments realities.[2] When Harry Truman gave her some real power—extending her influence to the rest of the world by making her Ambassador to the United Nations—she proved openly to be an astute politician. She remained as valuable to the United States at the end of the 1940s in her dealings with the Russians as she had been in the White House in the early days of the New Deal. It was not surprising that the people who loved, and trusted the Roosevelts did not question FDR's decision to develop atomic energy.

Harry Truman, president for the last half of the decade, had offered the American people little of the sense of confidence the Roosevelts inspired when he moved into the Oval Office at the tail end of the war. Known for his political talent, he was mocked as a failed haberdasher whose experience did not suggest the feisty leader he would become. Indeed, Franklin Roosevelt had not even told him about the Manhattan Project—the code name for the creation of an atomic bomb. "The buck stops here" was the slogan Truman kept on his desk, but the enormity of the responsibility he had inherited was hardly imaginable. Not only would he have to pursue Roosevelt's intention to drop the bomb, but, with little diplomatic experience, he would also have to redefine America's enemies as he shaped a new kind of war—a "Cold War" that created an entirely different range of problems. Under Truman the fear of Communism would again enter American life as disproportionately as it had in the 1920s.

The $2 billion—an enormous sum at the time—invested by the U.S. government in the atom bomb to prevent the Germans from getting it before the United States did seemed to make its use inevitable. That many of the European scientists who worked on the bomb in America had fled Hitler's persecution with knowledge that could be used against him remained a satisfying irony. Indeed, Albert Einstein was the first to alert Roosevelt to the Germans' intentions to get the powerful bomb first. Imagine what the world would be like had totalitarian countries like Italy, Japan, and Germany succeeded in taking over the democracies of France, Great Britain, and the United States by successfully harnessing atomic energy. The secrecy and the incredible unity of effort that produced the atomic bomb also suggested great discipline and energy on the part of all the workers involved: scientists, soldiers, engineers, and construction workers. The sacrifices made by their families, many of whom lived confined lives in remote places, are often overlooked and must be commended.

The Atomic Bomb

Almost overnight 7,000 workers and their families settled in Los Alamos, New Mexico, as they did in a few other places like Oak Ridge, Tennessee, another community dedicated to creating components for a bomb the inhabitants knew nothing about. Just as the astonishing increases in the production of tanks and airplanes seemed to prove what a hard-working, committed democratic work force could achieve on a material level, so the building of the bomb similarly represented a different kind of democratic intellectual accomplishment. Never before, one scientist remarked, had so much brain power been focused on a single problem. Italian and Danish physicists Enrico Fermi and Niels Bohr played essential roles in building the bomb, as did the Hungarians Leo Szilard and Edward Teller, the Austrian Lise Meitner, and the German Hans Bethe. Using the knowledge of a British scientist, Ernest Rutherford, Californians Ernest Lawrence and J. Robert Oppenheimer and Bostonian Kenneth Bainbridge shaped the project. Oppenheimer, as director of the entire enterprise along with U.S. General Leslie Groves, led the first group who witnessed the successful mushroom cloud explosion at Alamogordo, New Mexico, in July 1945. Such moments of achievement made it possible to imagine a world of international cooperation. *Time* magazine praised the creation of the bomb as a symbol of how all sorts of Americans could work together: "Professors, including Nobel prize winners, deserted their campuses to live in dusty deserts. Workers trekked in their trailers—careful New England craftsmen, burly Southern Negroes, all the races and types of the great United States."[3]

Few Americans on August 6 that same year, the day the first atomic bomb was dropped on Hiroshima, would have questioned the use of any new weapon to speed up the end of the war. People rejoiced in the idea of a secret weapon that would finish all battlefield suffering. Almost no one had any appreciation of what atomic energy was or any knowledge about how destructive it could be. Kept in the dark about the bomb for so long, Harry Truman certainly believed it would save the lives of many American soldiers scheduled to invade the Japanese islands and put us in a position to dictate the terms of peace—not just with Japan, but also with our ally Russia. Yet the dropping of the bomb that represented the world's entrance into the Atomic Age also represented the end of the American vision of unity that characterized the war effort. Since Truman's decision to drop not only one bomb on Hiroshima, but also a second one on Nagasaki, historians have had to confront these events as an ongoing source of political and moral debate, culminating in a public dispute in 1995 about an exhibit in the Smithsonian Institution to commemorate the 50th anniversary of the use of the bomb. Trying to weigh the 1940s evidence involved in such decisions becomes the responsibility of well-informed citizens—the reason students study history to shape their judgments.

In peacetime the buck stops with every voter as much as with the president. Gar Alperovitz, along with seven research assistants, produced a book of 847 pages, including 1,200 documents, called *The Decision to Use the Atomic Bomb* (1996), to provide readers with a vast array of impartial materials on both sides.[4] Teachers and museum curators need such collections to help students and visitors weigh the complex moral viewpoints that shape political decisions at different times. On the other side of the world visitors to the Peace Museum at Hiroshima in 1996 would also find new mention—missing in earlier textbooks—of the aggression and militarism of the Japanese as partly responsible for the city's destruction. Trying to understand such overwhelming historical moments as the dropping of the atomic bomb cannot be confined to one time or place.

The 1995 debate over the Smithsonian's plan to exhibit the *Enola Gay*, the plane that dropped the first atomic bomb, made Americans aware of how different decades may represent contrasting attitudes toward war. The planners of this display, influenced by the complex attitudes toward war that had emerged since the conflict with Japan and Germany, attempted to create a balanced exhibit. But to many World War II veterans, showing the results of the bombing diminished the outrages American soldiers had endured at the hands of the Japanese. They felt that the exhibit did not communicate how eager everyone was in the '40s to prevent further loss of American life. Even more than the civilians at home, the men fighting saw the bomb as their salvation. At the time a reporter flying on the plane that bombed Nagasaki wrote, "Does one feel any pity or compassion for the poor devils about to die? Not when one thinks of Pearl Harbor and of the Death March on Bataan."[5]

More than once Harry Truman declared he had no hesitation at all about making the choice to use the bomb. By the 1990s many young Americans could not imagine how important it was in the 1940s simply to end the brutal war that had gone on for over four years. By the end of the 20th century, Americans had also begun to see the Japanese as ordinary human beings, not as vicious enemies. An opinion poll reported in a 1995 letter to the *New York Times* revealed that 50% of all Americans believed that some alternative should have been used before dropping the bomb. Because the planners of the Smithsonian display wanted to explore the ethics of atomic warfare as much as the horrors of World War II, they appeared to many survivors to trivialize American bravery. Powerful veterans' groups succeeded in having the exhibit dismantled. But the controversy also awakened a new awareness about the decision. Looking at the collection of Alperovitz documents should stimulate on-going debate.

Earlier in the 1970s in a similar display of the changes time can bring about, the Smithsonian also offered an exhibit on the Japanese American internment camp at Manzanar, using many artifacts to demonstrate the injustices of the 1940s. But it would not be until Ronald Reagan's Administration in the late 1980s that restitution would be offered to these wartime incarcerated Japanese American citizens.

Since World War II, museums have also become a responsive source of education about such historic moments, subject even as textbooks are to the protests of special interest groups. Organizing exhibits representing shifting or conflicting attitudes without stirring up ideological prejudices becomes a challenge to curators trying to extend the public's critical intelligence with material objects as well as words. Museum displays are a new way to examine history from different viewpoints. What ideas do people take away when they look at the Enola Gay? What might they realize when they read the newspapers that appeared the day after the first bombing? Museum visitors from different parts of the world can find many strands of American life represented in such visual displays. And students may be inspired to look for wartime artifacts in the homes of their own families or to seek out World War II veterans to interview as oral history.

A new complexity of attitudes toward the bomb appeared almost at once after the war through the scientists who helped create it. Many theoreticians who worked so hard together to turn nuclear fission into destructive energy had grave doubts about continuing to produce such bombs. Seven months after the end of the war the Federation of American Scientists published *One World or None*, an 86-page paperback available for $1 that sold a hundred thousand copies. Samuel K. Allison, head of the University of Chicago's Institute of Nuclear Studies, described the opinions of fellow scientists who had worked on the project: "All of us had a momentary elation when our experiment met with success, but that feeling rapidly changed to a feeling of horror and a fervent hope that no more bombs would be dropped. When a second bomb was released, we felt it was a great tragedy."[6]

The organized movement of scientists that grew out of this moral concern represented an entirely new kind of social involvement on the part of a research community. Political theorist Sydney Hook remarked that it was no exaggeration to say that "American atomic scientists molded the opinions of the entire Western world on the subject of nuclear energy."[7] The men and women who worked on the bomb, having a clear grasp of the dangers of an atomic energy, attempted to exert their influence on politicians. In 1945 the *Bulletin of Atomic Scientists*, inspired by Eugene Rabinowitch, another German refugee, became accessible to lay readers everywhere. With an unforgettable clock on every cover measuring the world's closeness to 12 o'clock doom, the publication had "an influence out of all proportion to its circulation."[8] At this moment in the late '40s the debate on whether to build the 1,000 times more powerful hydrogen bomb found the scientific community openly split.

Life magazine in October 1945 exhorted American scientists to help everyone understand the menace of an atomic holocaust. But it was a writer of imagination who finally brought the reality of the first atomic bomb into the consciousness of most Americans. Novelist John Hersey, in an article filling the entire August 31, 1946, issue of the *New Yorker*, focused his account of the bombing of Hiroshima on the lives of several individuals who survived the blast. Like *The Diary of Anne Frank*, John Hersey's *Hiroshima* implied the unspeakable through the details of everyday life. Subsequently published as a book, it became an immediate bestseller. The Book-of-the-Month Club also awarded *Hiroshima* as a gift to every one of its 848,000 members. ABC had the entire text read aloud over the radio.

As John Hersey described the atomic blast, an overwhelming sense of humanity measures its wonder. His classic did not diminish the vast physical suffering or the geographical extent of the fiery destruction of one bomb. He visualized the melted eyes and the skin slipping off like gloves. Speculating on the horrors imbedded in the minds of the children who lived through the day of the Hiroshima bombing, Hersey reminded Americans that thousands of people like us had nobody at all to turn to for help. In describing the struggles of the small lives and experiences of ordinary individuals who survived, he made Americans imagine their daily worlds in similar chaos. Yet grasping the full dangers of radiation took more time. Not until after the 1946 destruction of Bikini Atoll could people come to grips with the horrors of spreading radiation poisoning. In 1948 David Bradley, a doctor who had served with the Bikini radiology unit, sold his journal *No Place to Hide* to the Book-of-the-Month Club. On the *New York Times* bestseller list for ten weeks, Bradley's book had sold 250,000 copies by the end of 1949. He believed the diary's power came from the contrast between the innocent, beautiful paradise that had been Bikini and what it became after atomic tests changed it for generations to come. The idea that President John F. Kennedy later used to describe the aftermath of a nuclear holocaust—a world where the living would envy the dead—began only slowly to invade the consciousness of the 1940s.

Time named Harry S. Truman its Man of the Year for 1945, remarking that the world would remember 1945 for the mushroom clouds over Hiroshima and Nagasaki. By July 1985, when a new mood had seized the nation, *Time* featured a cover photo of the mushroom cloud rising over Hiroshima with the exclamation of the *Enola Gay*'s co-pilot: "My God! What have we done?" A nation with an apocalyptic tradition extending back to the Puritans did not need goading to make atomic fears the focus for the Cold War against the Russians. All sorts of isolationist anxieties about America's need to remain in control of atomic power sprang up. The discovery that the Russians had their own atomic bomb in September 1949 meant that public decisions in Cold War strategy from that moment on would be built around the fear of the bomb.

Yet at the same time that science created weapons of destruction, many scientific and technological discoveries with civilian use grew out of World War II. Gone forever was the 19th century world of horse-drawn milk wagons, party-line telephones, and porch swing entertainments. The huge amounts of government spending on technology and **Wartime Discoveries and Inventions** research during the war continued to produce new products such as frozen foods, synthetic materials, and plastics demanded by both civilians and the military.

No one feared a military-industrial complex that improved everyone's standard of living. The utopian "World of Tomorrow" imagined at the New York World's Fair in 1939 became an overnight reality. As one historian put it, "Technology seemed a far sturdier and more efficacious instrument of progress than the various panaceas proposed by . . . utopians: taxation, socialism, religion, communitarianism, or revolution."[9] After the war the fruits of production were available to all workers; progress seemed undeniable.

In 1945 two issues of *National Geographic* magazine celebrated discoveries developed during the war that could be used afterwards to extend human well-being. First among these was **Uses of Atomic Energy** atomic energy—to be valued as a new source of power. The government created the Atomic Energy Commission (AEC) in 1946 to regulate atomic energy and to help Americans understand how atomic power would work. During 1947 and 1948, along with a number of corporate contractors such as Westinghouse and General Electric, the AEC sponsored a series of exhibits—viewed by more than 4 million people—that attempted to dispel fear about the mystery of atomic power. One New York Central Park display called "Man and the Atom" gave out 250,000 comic books titled "Dagwood Splits the Atom." Dagwood, husband of comic heroine Blondie, was famous for his enormous sandwiches, not his wit. If he could deal with atomic energy, anyone could. Exciting new uses for atomic energy included power plants, radiated agriculture, and medical labs and ships. In August 1945 *Newsweek* offered pictures of atomic cars and planes, ocean liners and working kitchens, all energized by power sources the size of a tiny dot. General Groves who, with Oppenheimer, had headed the Manhattan Project, took on a new role for the government persuading people to forget the past and to concentrate on the future. In 1949 he urged Americans to regard atomic energy just as they would fire and electricity. A 1947 radio show called "The Sunny Side of the Atom" talked about the possibility for cancer cures with radioactivity, while *Collier's* magazine in May of that same year imagined a paraplegic leaving his wheelchair behind in an atomic cloud of hope.

New Technologies in Communications and Travel

National Geographic went on to include a celebration of the electron microscope as part of the research developed during the war to make entirely new realms of science possible, such as more precise work with viruses. It also praised the technological advances that extended vision into the sky—the great telescope on Mount Palomar in California was set up in 1948. As the transistor replaced the quaint prewar radio tube, television's instant communication became part of the excitement of the future. Radar developed to intercept enemies started to enhance the safety of commercial flying. Since the first commercial flight to cross the Atlantic had not taken place until 1939, it was also easy to label World War II the beginning of the age of air travel. The first supersonic flight took place in 1947.

In 1944 the extensive first-time use of helicopters in war also enhanced the possibilities of air travel within small urban corridors. And the wartime development of specifically targeted rockets and gigantic computers for solving military problems could be turned toward the civilian conquest of outer space after the war. The Space Age grew out of the research and discoveries of World War II as surely as the Atomic Age had.

New Technologies in Health and Medicine

The huge budget allotted for war—$321 billion from 1941 to 1943—was not solely focused on the creation of weapons. Americans' payroll deductions and defense bonds also went into research that would eventually contribute to the better health of humankind.

First in this research was the massive production of antibiotics. Although Sir Alexander Fleming had discovered penicillin in 1928, it was hardly available until a number of scientists and facilities pooled their energies to meet the needs of war. The federal government, using the Department of Agriculture's regional laboratory in Peoria, Illinois, combined the talents of more than 21 companies to produce more than 650 billion units of penicillin a month by 1945—enough to include even some civilian needs. The discovery of streptomycin by Selman Waksman in 1943, subsequently produced by private pharmaceutical companies, demonstrated that industry and government cooperation remained important during this period, as it had been before in the history of American science.

Since private laboratories rarely had adequate money for complex research, government funding given to university laboratories enabled rapid and important discoveries to take place.[10] One historian of medicine commented that the cooperation among university researchers, government support groups, and private industry seemed to be a unique American phenomenon leading to extraordinary productivity. Other antibiotics produced during this decade included bacitracin, chloramphenicol, polymyxin B, chlortetracycline, and neomycin. By the end of the 1940s almost all bacterial illness appeared to be under control. By 1950 John Enders had also succeeded in isolating viruses in tissue culture that would lead to the successful creation of vaccines against polio and other dread viral childhood diseases.

Another concentrated wartime effort, the search for synthetic quinine to combat malaria—essential because the Japanese had cut off areas of natural production—also proved successful. Many American troops taking part in the Pacific war were completely disabled by the mosquito-borne illness. One survey from Guadalcanal reported three entire divisions inoperative with malaria. The discovery of the synthetics Atabrine and Chloroquine alleviated much physical suffering in the South Pacific. Just as important at the time was the mass production of insecticides like DDT and insect repellents for personal use that wiped out the plague-carrying mosquitoes and body lice. A typhus epidemic was said to have been averted by these new vermin destroyers. No one thought about disturbing the balanced life cycle involving the other creatures who survived on such insects. Nor was there any awareness of other illnesses that human beings could develop from pesticides. What mattered most was saving the lives of soldiers and making their national service as comfortable as possible. Perhaps one of the most important areas of study to emerge from World War II has been the examination of secondary effects of goal-oriented knowledge. The realization that unforeseen results often arose from the pursuit of narrow purposes would become a challenging and legitimate field of study, as well as a source of popular fear—a favorite theme of science fiction.

Along with the antibacterial drugs that for a time ended pneumonia and tuberculosis came the extensive use and production of blood plasma. Death from infection became so rare that between 1945 and 1951 mortality from flu and pneumonia fell by 47%. Mortality from diphtheria dropped 92% and that from syphilis 78%.[11] During World War II, research on steroids to relieve arthritic pain was also intensified. The discovery of cortisone led to the production of the most complex drug yet manufactured on a large scale. A detailed study of postwar science and technology could document how extensively wartime managerial and production skills became part of the nation's overall approach to health. Along with the 1948 expansion of the National Institute of Health came the establishment of smaller foundations dedicated to research on specific problems. Only a few days after the bombing of Nagasaki, for example, General Motors—in the names of its directors Alfred P. Sloan and Charles Kettering—gave $4 million to set up a cancer research center in New York City. Certain kinds of childhood leukemia would be eradicated before the end of the '50s. Elsewhere new drugs were being discovered to alleviate severe allergies and anxieties, and most important, to combat certain forms of acute mental illness. Chlorpromazine, produced in quantity after the war by Smith, Kline and French, liberated many individuals who might have spent years in custodial care in mental hospitals.

The rapidity of change can be imagined in the assertion of historian James Patterson that by 1956, 80% of all the drugs being prescribed had reached the market only within the past fifteen years. These "miracle drugs" had an immediate impact on the longevity of Americans. Life expectancy reached an average of 69.7 years by 1960, in contrast with 62.9 years in 1940. Women would continue to live longer than men, and whites to live longer than blacks, but wartime medical research unquestionably produced healthier lives for most Americans.[12]

Rise of Consumer Culture

Unlike most of the world, the United States did not have to clean up messes of debris and destruction in order to rebuild the country. Nevertheless, the American people continued to have an enormous need for every kind of housing. Possibilities for work for returning soldiers expanded as the new world of highways and suburbs developed. The internalized frugality of the Great Depression and the discipline that grew out of living with wage and price controls during the war lasted but a short time. In 1945 *National Geographic* magazine headed every issue with "Buy United States War Savings Bonds and Stamps." After the war ended its heading changed to "Buy United States Victory Savings Bonds and Stamps." Children during these years were conditioned to buy 10-cent stamps not just to help their country but also to save for future needs. When they turned in booklets with $18.75 worth of pasted stamps they would get $25 bonds. But by 1947 the magazine headings disappeared. The world of consumer satisfaction began to replace the world of wartime contribution. Although there would be no plastic credit cards until the mid-'50s, department store charge cards existed, and people could buy large items on the installment plan, paying interest monthly. Credit was available for instantly unrationed gasoline. Car ownership—usually managed by low-interest loans—came to signify both freedom and prosperity.

Statistics on the postwar purchase of automobiles are almost unbelievable. In 1945 new car sales totaled 69,500; in 1946 they **Cars** leaped to 2.1 million, and in 1949 to 5.1 million. By 1950 sales reached 6.7 million, and by the middle of the next decade they hit 7.9 million. As railroads and trolleys were dismantled, Americans defined themselves clearly as a car culture. The elegant, capacious, gas-guzzling chariots of the postwar period were expensive—even Fords and Chevrolets cost $1,300 dollars, about two-fifths of the median family income at the time.[13] By 1950, nevertheless, 39.9 million families had registered 40.3 million automobiles. What becoming a car culture meant to the centers of America's cities and to the idea of public transportation was not yet apparent. What was visible was the great number of new jobs connected to the automobile boom. The oil business, the trucking industry, and the highway construction crews needed more and more workers. Motels for easy traveling and shopping malls designed for easy loading of consumer goods from shop to car to home sprang up all over America. In 1946 there were only 8 malls, but by the end of the 1950s there were 4,000! A new American lifestyle evolved as cornfields were covered with asphalt and cars allowed people greater choice of where to settle. Suddenly the family car also became an important source of recreation, not just for vacation trips for boating and fishing and skiing, but also for local entertainments like drive-in movies and teenage dating.

The demand for housing to fit new lives—to accommodate all the Americans who moved during the war or needed a **Housing** place to put a new family—was again eased by financial help from the government. In 1949 Congressional subsidies helped build low income urban housing even as many universities built temporary housing for the huge number of new students the government was also sending to school. The G.I. Bill helped returning veterans get mortgages as well as educations. A great variety of developments in single-family homes appeared in the suburbs. Between 1945 and 1955 some 15 million housing units were constructed in the United States, leading to historic highs in home ownership. Before World War II would-be homeowners often had to offer down payments as high as 50% to buy a house, promising to pay the rest in periods as short as ten years. With the G.I. Bill some veterans put down nothing at all, and others were offered a token one dollar down payment with long-term mortgages.

After 1947 changes brought about by the Federal Housing Administration, working with the Veterans Administration, made available mortgages of up to 90% with interest rates as low as 4%—and with periods as long as 30 years to pay off the debt. By 1960, 60% of all Americans owned their own homes.

And by 1950 these two government agencies were also insuring 36% of all new nonfarm mortgages; by 1955 they handled 41%. The suburbs that grew out of governmental generosity became the market for the new consumerism, demonstrating once again the interdependence of public and private forces shaping the lives of every class. Taxes—withheld from salaries for the first time in 1943—continued to be deducted during the postwar period. People gladly maintained the New Deal tradition of tax-provided public services, such as twice a day mail deliveries and street cleaning.[14]

Material Abundance   The material abundance that began to deluge America after the war included many wartime discoveries like nylon and Dacron, frozen foods, and plastic wrap. And the inventive imagination continued to flourish. In 1947 Edwin Land invented the Polaroid camera; C. F. Carlson developed the Xerox machine in 1948. And Buckminster Fuller perfected the geodesic dome for possible use in constructing ready-assembled housing during this period. An example of American ingenuity, a gigantic example of the dome was used as the center of a U.S. trade exhibit at the Montreal, Canada, world's fair in the '60s. Some sincere citizens jested that instead of dropping bombs on our Communist competitors we should drop Sears, Roebuck catalogues to show off the vast array of goods—mostly made in the United States—available at reasonable prices to most Americans at the time.

Nothing could be more striking than the amount of consumer goods defining America between 1945, when only 46% of all Americans had telephones, and 1960, when middle class America seemed to epitomize consumer paradise. Historian James Patterson tells the story neatly in his list of what Americans took for granted in 1960 that didn't exist at all in 1945: supermarkets, malls, fast-food chains, residential air conditioning, ranch-style homes, freezers, dishwashers, dryers, detergents, ballpoint pens, electric razors, power mowers, hi-fis, tape recorders, long-playing records, Polaroid cameras, computers, and transistor radios.[15] The number of technical additions to cars—such as power steering and other automatic transmissions, air-conditioning, and directional signals—continued to grow. And the number of television sets, like the number of automobiles, grew astronomically. In 1950 only 10% of all people polled had television sets, and 38% had not even seen a TV program. In 1945, in fact, 52% of all farms still had no electricity. Astonishing changes in lifestyle—and in expectations—took place in a remarkably short period of time.

As America as a whole became more urban and, specifically, more suburban, it became easier to record material changes in terms of statistics. More complicated is the question of how these changes reflected changes of spirit. How did people feel about themselves as they adapted to all sorts of new appliances and technologies?

NOTES

1. Quoted in *Reporting World War II: Part Two, American Journalism, 1944–1946* (New York: Literary Classics of the United States, 1995), 697.

2. Doris Kearns Goodwin, *No Ordinary Time: Eleanor and Franklin Roosevelt. The Home Front in World War II* (New York: Simon and Schuster, 1994), 417–418.

3. Quoted in Paul Boyer, *By the Bomb's Early Light: American Thought and Culture at the Dawn of the Atomic Age* (1985; new ed., Chapel Hill: University of North Carolina Press, 1994), 138–139.

4. Gar Alperovitz, *The Decision to Use the Atomic Bomb* (New York: Random House, 1996).

5. William L. Laurence, *Part Two*, "Atomic Bombing of Nagasaki, told by Flight Member," 769

6. Boyer, *Bomb's Early Light*, 49.

7. Ibid., 62.

8. Ibid., 64.

9. Howard P. Segal, "The Technological Utopians," in *Imagining Tomorrow: History, Technology and the American Future*, ed. Joseph J. Corn (Cambridge, MA: MIT Press, 1986), 122.

10. C. Barroughs Mider, "The Federal Impact on Biomedical Research," in *Advances in American Medicine: Essays at the Bicentennial, Volume II*, ed. John Z. Bowers and Elizabeth F. Purcell (New York: Josiah Macy, Jr., Foundation, 1976).

11. Edward Shorter, *The Health Century* (New York: Doubleday, 1987), 32ff.

12. James T. Patterson, *Grand Expectations: The United States, 1945–1974* New York: Oxford University Press, 1996), 10.

13. Ibid., 70–71.

14. Ibid., 72.

15. Ibid., 70.

5

Changing Social Attitudes

That a country built on a vision of human possibilities emerged from World War II examining itself in terms of the values it had been fighting for should surprise no one. After the war people on the home front, along with returning vets, felt proud that they had worked together to protect democratic ideals all over the world. As a photographer in one of Studs Terkel's interviews put it, "To see fascism defeated, nothing better could have happened to a human being. You felt you were doing something worthwhile."[1] Perhaps wartime propaganda persuaded Americans to take individual human rights as seriously as they had taken their civic responsibilities when the war was still on. Just after the war many sustained that sense of optimism in terms of a commitment to building a better life.

The popular Academy Award winning movie *The Best Years of Our Lives* (1946), in attempting to show the problems of readjustment to civilian life for three very different returning veterans, reflected the economic and emotional problems ex-soldiers were having all over the country. Its happy ending may have been more Hollywood than real— the handless vet discovers that his high school sweetheart still cherishes him; the mismated gunner gets a divorce from his hastily wed unfaithful war bride and finds a better woman to stand behind him as he restructures his career around skills picked up in the war; and the successful banker persuades the community that everyone will prosper if he makes loans to strong individuals based on faith in their character, not on evidence of their collateral. In this film the sense of trust—the belief in human integrity that grew out of the ideology of the New Deal—seemed able to inspire people to recreate their lives together after the fighting stopped.

Perhaps not entirely representative of most Americans because culled from only 600 women is a moving collection of letters, *Since You Went Away: World War II Letters from American Women on the Home Front,* edited by Judy Barrett Litoff and David C. Smith. The women who wrote these letters were inspired by faith in a better future. Their messages suggest the high spirits and loyalty of a large group of earnest American mothers, wives, and girlfriends—both in corresponding with their soldiers and in fulfilling the daily demands of the home front. The families that saved such correspondence as historical documents had reason to be proud. There are no "Dear John" letters designed to break soldiers' hearts among them. But the letters are often critical of the United States in terms of issues like the internment of Japanese Americans or the dropping of the atomic bomb on Hiroshima. Making the future better is a large part of the commitment to the war shown by these women.

The collection suggests once again the competence of American women. Some put up forty quarts of tomatoes and fifteen pints of corn in a day; others worked long hours in defense plants. Many had never thought of themselves as patriotic, and also ended up surprised at others who looked "soft and easy going" but nonetheless proved themselves in America's "hour of need." The women who wrote these letters had a clear sense of being part of history as well as keeping records of the integrity of their own families. The letters represent decent people responding to each other's doubts with hope and encouragement—proud for a chance to be part of an enterprise larger than their own domestic worlds. One woman wrote that she looked forward to a future where her children could learn "kindness, patience and honesty without the tragedy of war." Such home front philosophizing must often have strengthened the morale of soldiers who found it in their love letters. A woman in Pocatello, Idaho, urged her soldier lover on with quotes from Henry David Thoreau about looking forward to having other lives to live. The belief was common that the end of the war would bring new and better choices despite the disappearance of high-paying defense jobs and the need to accept relocations as "home." For a time society maintained what has been called an implicit social contract, a commitment urging all people to work together to share the new prosperity.[2]

Roosevelt had asked Americans to go to war to protect the Four Freedoms: freedom of speech and expression, freedom of worship, freedom from want, and freedom from fear. Many questions surrounded the idea of these freedoms. Could they be guaranteed in postwar America? What did human beings need at that moment to provide a good life? And what role would the government have to play in helping people find shelter, education, and work? Conditioned by the New Deal to accept government agencies as tools of social change and by the war to accept federal subsidies to private business as good for the society as a whole, Congress had no trouble passing the Servicemen's Readjustment Act of 1944, familiarly known as the G.I. Bill. This program of earned entitlements answered the needs of huge numbers of Americans and changed the general quality of American life. So many Americans—over 16 million—took advantage of this program to get housing, job training, and education that it would become hard for most of them ever to realize that there remained still another America untouched by the range of possibilities Congress offered veterans at the end of the war.

Decent housing was the most pressing need. In 1947, 6 million families were doubling up with relatives or friends; another 500,000 occupied wartime temporary housing or quonset huts. In Atlanta the city bought 100 trailers for **The Rise of Suburbia** veterans' homes; in Chicago, 250 trolley cars were sold as homes. Responding to desperation, the federal government underwrote a new construction program for 5 million homes, adding billions to Federal Housing Administration (FHA) funding, which, along with the G.I. Bill, minimized down payments and guaranteed mortgages. Such government insurance promoted new single-family homes on the edge of cities. Construction grew from 114,000 homes in 1944 to 1,692,000 by 1950, as down payments for prospective homeowners diminished and long-term mortgages made it easier for owners to keep their homes. The rate of mortgage foreclosures dropped from 250,000 nonfarm units in 1932 to only 18,000 by 1951. Reinforced by President Roosevelt's belief that "a nation of homeowners, of people who own a real share in their own land is unconquerable," Congress continued to approve government backing for the vast building operations that flourished right after the war.[3]

The most famous housing developments to appear in response to ongoing federal support were the result of the enterprise of Abraham Levitt and his sons, William and Alfred. Like Ford, the name Levitt would become identified with a mass-produced consumer need. Before the war the Levitts had built expensive houses, but government contracts for temporary shelters and work with the Navy Seabees had given them the skills of assembly line production associated with winning the war. Immediately after the fighting stopped, the Levitts bought up 4,000 acres of potato farms in Hempstead, Long Island, where they initiated the biggest private housing project in American history. At the height of their house production their assembly line technique created one home every sixteen minutes to become a unit in the first famous Levittown.

Trucks dropped off building materials on cellarless concrete slabs every 60 feet. The invention of new power tools added to the increased productivity when freight cars loaded with lumber went directly into a cutting yard where one man could cut parts for ten houses in only one day. Construction was divided into 27 efficient steps done by crews who did only one job. Not only did the Levitts own their own forests and make their own concrete, but they paid their workers above average wages to avoid unionization and flouted standard union rules—such as those against spray painting—to finish the homes faster. Yet their employees never worked more than a five-day week. At its building peak, onlookers at Levittown often saw more than 30 houses a day going up. In four years 17,447 houses appeared on the Long Island potato field.[4]

Originally designed for rental to veterans at $60 a month with an option to buy, the houses became a steal starting at $6,990 because long-term government mortgage guarantees made buying even cheaper than renting. People lined up to put $90 down payments on the original models the way they would for tickets to rock concerts or sporting events in the future. And although these homes were $1,500 cheaper than any comparable housing at the time, the Levitts still averaged a profit of $1,000 on each one. With the basic Cape Cod-style home—which soon developed into choices of four other models—the purchasers not only got homes with windows placed so that mothers could watch their children at play, they also got an array of built-in appliances. Washing machines and later even television sets came with the houses.

Levitt took care to provide a larger social environment as well, including "nine swimming pools, sixty playgrounds, ten baseball diamonds and seven village greens."[5] He also set aside land for churches, schools, and libraries. All over the country builders imitated the Levitts with differing community scales to take advantage of the government subsidies that made it possible for builders to risk little and gain much. In Park Forest, Illinois, the FHA insured 8,000 houses; in Henry J. Kaiser's Panorama City in California, 3,000. The entitlements extended to veterans by Congress continued to provide incentives to the entire building industry. Moreover, at a moment when the fear of Communism was once again rising, it was easy for everyone to agree with William Levitt that no man who owned his own house could be a Communist because he had too much to do. (Few at the time would have imagined a woman in the position to buy her own house.) Nor did anyone suggest how "Communistic" were the enormous government subsidies that enabled Americans to own these properties. Indeed, when Frank Magruder suggested in a classic 1940 text, *American Government*, that the postal system, power projects, public free education, and old age assistance were examples of Communism, many educators wanted his book censored. Harry Truman's astonishing reelection in 1948 also suggested to many historians a national enthusiasm for active government involvement in the private economy. He had campaigned vigorously against a do-nothing Republican Congress.

Sociologists at the end of the decade struggled to understand the meaning of living in such homogeneous communities. Architectural historians, admitting that the Levitt homes were good value, deplored the possible rise of acres of suburban slums of ticky-tacky. People wondered if being surrounded by conformity would lead to intellectual stultification or to dangerous mass thinking. But owning a house by putting just $90 down gave many G.I.s a stake in the society they had been defending, just as FDR predicted. At the beginning the people who lived in Levittown were more interested in preserving prewar family values than in any politics. They did put their energy and their extra money into their homes. Far from turning into shambles or diminishing in value, by 1996 the classiest Levittown models were selling for as much as $180,000.

It would take a while for Americans to notice that the impoverishment of such communities lay—as predicted—in their social and cultural homogeneity. The predominance of young families, the exclusion of people of color—not challengeable legally at the time—and the scarcity of elderly inhabitants seemed to more sophisticated critics to make for a dull society. Even as late as 1960, after the original restrictions had been removed, not one of Long Island's Levittown's 82,000 residents was African American. Levitt insisted that economic reality, not prejudice, determined his policies on race. He had wanted black leaders to guarantee resales after African American purchases. Nor was the paternalism of Levitt's policies forbidding clotheslines and fences questioned. Some people might have been glad to get monthly bills for having the agency do the mandatory lawn cutting they had ignored. Just out of the army, many ex-G.I.s may also have found such community restrictions a source of order rather than an impediment to freedom.

Among the many valuable sociology texts that appeared after the war to help Americans understand who they were and where they were going was *The Levittowners: Ways of Life and Politics in a New Suburban Community* by Herbert J. Gans. Like an anthropologist living among natives as a participant-observer, Gans himself lived in a second Levittown community in New Jersey during the first two years of its existence. Believing in sociology as a democratic method of inquiry, he wrote of the experience from the perspective of his neighbors, not from preconceived academic ideas. Gans asserted that people had the right to be what they are. He found much more cultural diversity among his neighbors than many housing experts predicted. When he conducted a poll asking if people considered the community "dull," only 20% responded "yes." A former Philadelphian replied, "If Levittown is compared to city living there are no taverns or teenage hangout places, then it is dull. . . . We are perfectly content here." Another wrote, "We like quiet things . . . visiting, sitting out front in summer, having people dropping by."[6] Gans found that they also took satisfaction in the over 100 voluntary organizations that soon sprang up; 73% of those polled belonged to at least one. Of course their children—unlike the parents, who had grown up during the Depression, found fewer satisfactions in a home-centered life, but such restlessness might have been found among adolescents in any community in America. Many young people identified with James Dean's notorious character in the film *Rebel without a Cause* (1955). Intellectual stimulation became more certain when a branch of New York State's university system also soon appeared on different potato fields at nearby Stonybrook, offering educational opportunities to many whose families had not had any college graduates in the past.

Using class to define American differences remains a problem for sociologists, but Gans did not hesitate to assert that the criterion for vitality in Levittown was "home centered and private"—characteristic of lower middle class values as opposed to the more visible demands of professional class visitors and critics—who like himself might live there only temporarily as they pursued upward social mobility. Yet he concluded without hesitation that Levittown was a good place to live.[7] Creating more such communities, he believed, was a way to offer the benefits of uncrowded suburban life without high prices to the many poor and non-whites trapped in growing urban ghettoes.

The government spending on housing focused on single-family homes on the fringes of cities instead of on urban development and the rehabilitation of good older housing produced great social inequity. Many families would have been glad to remain within city limits and have more access to public transportation, but federal funds were shaping a different America. Herbert Gans helped Americans see that social planning as well as physical planning would be essential to optimize both social compatibility and individual liberty in a realistic future. Just as the freedoms we fought for could be achieved only by community effort and federal controls, so the response to postwar needs continued to involve the government. No piece of legislation would ever have more impact on the entire texture of American life than the G.I. Bill, not simply in terms of the creation of housing but, even more significantly, in terms of the great new access to higher education reaching across America.

Access to Higher Education

Specific entitlements offered returning soldiers the choice of a year of monetary benefits while job hunting or—more important for fulfilling the dream of human potential—a chance for paid higher education or additional training in skills that postwar America needed. As the gross national product expanded from $91.1 billion in 1939 to $213.6 billion in 1945 to $300 billion in 1950, 17 million new jobs had been created. Between 1944 and 1946 also, the 6 million working women who had done so well during the war were pressured to give up their lucrative jobs; 4 million either were fired or left voluntarily, offering returning vets a vast array of work opportunities. But many vets still chose more education over the immediate possibility of earning a living.

Instead of going to work, almost 8 million veterans took advantage of the G.I. Bill to pursue the higher education they would not otherwise have been able to afford. The creation of a new educated class meant extending professional status to all sorts of ethnic newcomers in law and medicine and in the university. For the first time on a broad scale, colleges and universities became multicultural. Unfortunately, "elite" admissions policies continued to work against blacks and women. But there can be no doubt that the expansion of all higher education in terms of huge enrollments and new buildings and new kinds of community colleges also opened doors wider for everyone, preparing the way for a more meritocratic society. Many people going to college after the war would become that first person in the family to get a higher degree. The government gave each veteran $65 a month ($90 to those with families) and $500 a year to cover tuition and books—adequate at most colleges at the time. State institutions felt a special mandate to meet the great need, expanding at new campuses—like Stonybrook—and offering new courses of intellectual pursuits.

Conservative educators predicted the end of quality education in the great tides of mediocrity flowing into America's most famous institutions. They began to give attention to creating more complex entrance exams for the best universities. But after only a few years of experience with G.I.s in the classroom, many had to concede that maturity, motivation, and hard work often produced scholarship as competent as that of young people trained at prep schools. Instead of lowering standards, these older students forced educators to reassess their vision of America's potential. By the 1990s the State University of New York at Stonybrook, built only 40 years before, was ranked the third best public research university in the country.

The creation of more possibilities to get an education grew out of the great sense of need that was discovered during the war. A 1940 census revealed that only 2 out of 5 people in America had gone beyond the eighth grade; only 1 in 4 had graduated from high school; and only 1 in 20 went on to complete college. During World War II the government was so concerned about the low level of American education that it set up all sorts of additional training programs for soldiers: to help make illiterates literate, to teach foreign languages, and to train mechanics and builders in new electronic skills. The courses set up by the United States Armed Forces Institute enrolled over 6,000 students during its peak. Many poor young men joined the army as a way to achieve the upward mobility that education promised. Indeed, the United States government spent $321 billion on education between 1941 and 1945, twice as much as in the entire preceding 150 years of its existence.[8] Investing in education represented an ongoing belief in America's citizens—an affirmation of faith in the future.

When the army was officially integrated in 1948 such training was clearly extended also to African Americans. As early as 1944, Wendell Willkie, the Republican who ran against FDR in 1940, asserted that the war should make us conscious of the "contradiction between our treatment of the Negro minority and the ideals for which we are fighting."[9] With the Congressional establishment of the Women's Armed Services Act, also in 1948, the country acknowledged that women too were entitled to the same educational rewards offered men. Yet Americans learned slowly that legalization may be just the first step toward achieving broader social goals. Fewer than 3% of the women eligible took advantage of this opportunity to educate themselves, and too many African Americans coming out of segregated schools did not have adequate preparation for higher education. Nevertheless, the G.I. Bill provided education for 50% of all the people who served in the armed forces. By 1956, when it ended, 7.8 million vets had taken advantage of its entitlements: 2.2 million (97% men) had gone on to college, 3.5 million to technical schools, and 700,000 to agricultural programs. In the academic year 1949–1950, 497,000 Americans got university degrees—over twice as many as in 1940. No longer would higher education be seen simply as the proprietary right of the upper middle class. The quality of cultural experience had begun to change for everyone.[10]

Children's Education

"No other idea has seemed more typically American," wrote Diane Ravitch, a historian of education, "than the belief that schooling could cure society's ills." In *The Troubled Crusade: American Education, 1945–1980*, she made a list of all the problems—from crime rates to unemployment, to ethnic differences, to health standards, to traffic accidents, to general morality—that most Americans placed at the door of public education. In a society that continued to pay teachers low salaries and to reward athletes and media stars with much more money than scientists and scholars earned, the government began to take greater responsibility for better education. Between 1944 and 1965, the United States was willing to spend 14.5 billion to educate its people.[11]

The disparity between the elementary education offered the middle classes and that offered the poor emerged sharply during the war. Community differences in income meant sharp differences in the quality of education, determining whether or not children had books and paper to write on—or even chairs to sit on. When defense jobs offered new opportunities for better pay, many teachers in poverty-stricken communities simply quit. In the three years following Pearl Harbor, 11,000 out of 20,000 teachers in Alabama left their jobs. In Iowa 800 rural schools had no teachers at all. In 1947 the *New York Times* reported that 350,000 teachers had quit teaching for better jobs. Those who remained worked at salaries lower than those of garbage collectors.[12] Twelve major teacher strikes took place after 1946, calling attention to the fact that both Russia and Great Britain spent more on education than Americans did.

Federal aid to education began to be considered essential to bring about equality of opportunity for American children. By the mid-1940s even "Mr. Republican," Robert Taft, congressman from Ohio, would agree that "children were entitled not as a matter of privilege but as a matter of right to a decent roof, decent meals, decent medical care and a decent place in which to go to school." Astonishing to many was his conclusion—"Education is socialistic anyway."[13]

After the war a variety of new schools—with some experimental programs—grew up in the midst of all the freshly built communities. Although the relaxed ideas of John Dewey's "progressive education" extended in many directions, there were ongoing debates on the need for rote learning versus more imaginative programs. The same debates would continue into the 1990s—not only in Walt Disney's utopian town of Celebration, Florida, but in every community where parents became involved in what children need to be taught to be civilized and productive members of society.

Funding for religious education came under renewed discussion. Since the G.I. Bill was sending people to all sorts of religiously oriented schools, and since lunches at every elementary school were also subsidized in the mid-1940s, it was hard to argue then that the separation of church and state was clear-cut. A 1947 Supreme Court decision even allowed public funds to be used for transporting children to parochial schools. But a strong anti-Catholic movement arose to limit such funding. Fear of church influence was ongoing. A book by Paul Blanshard, attacking the intrusion of the Catholic hierarchy into public education, went into 26 printings and remained on the national bestseller list for six months. Even Eleanor Roosevelt wrote in her "My Day" column in June 1949, "I do not want to see public education connected with religious control of the schools which are paid for by taxpayers' money." The issue of federal funding for education relating to the separation of church and state remains alive. The only federal money freely given at the time would be for local schools near military installations because such bases contributed no real estate taxes to subsidize the education of youngsters on base.

The postwar commitment to educating all the children in a democracy used the vocabulary of John Dewey's progressive education movement to define its goals. Such education stressed training in problem solving more than memorizing historical facts and arithmetic. Modern pedagogy favored projects, field trips, life experiences, and group learning instead of rote and drill to acquire knowledge. Although high school attendance went up by over 50% by 1950, such education was broadly attacked for lowering standards. The progressive faith, as Lawrence Cremin, another historian of education described it, believed that "culture could be democratized without being vulgarized, and everyone could share not only in benefits of the new sciences but in pursuit of the arts as well."[14] Yet narrow professionalism and anti-intellectualism often impeded such ideal goals. One of the most unfortunate results was a shift to "life adjustment" courses which taught little of substance and kept many young people—especially women and working class students—in social grooves.

In 1947 the National Commission of Life Adjustment for Youth created state commissions to respond to a general demand for vocational or functional education. Simultaneously the study of foreign languages and the serious study of the history of past civilizations were considered less significant for everyone. Later decades would call this "dumbing-down" education. By the mid-1950s only 20.6% of American high school students would study a second language. And multiple-choice exam questions began to replace essay writing in tests that measured the critical thinking skills students had mastered. Conservatives began to blame progressive education for all that was vacuous and anti-intellectual in postwar America. Before the decade was over strong debates would take place all over the country about what students should be taught. It must be an ironic comment on Americans' refusal to study the details of their history that the same intellectual debates recur at different times and people continue to argue about what is essential for everyone to know.

Even *Time* magazine ridiculed the frenzy for "life adjustment education" that seemed to absolve teachers from teaching and students from learning. A famous elite educator, Robert Hutchins, president of the University of Chicago, tried to define the direction general education in America should take. "Our mission here on earth is to change our environment, not to adjust ourselves to it." More specifically, Hutchins questioned how minds were to be trained. "Perhaps the greatest idea that America has given the world is the idea of education for all," he wrote. "The world is entitled to know whether this idea means that everybody can be educated or only that everybody must go to school."[15]

After World War II, when liberal education—once available only to a privileged few—became available to everyone, educators had to consider attitude changes related to who was being educated, not just to what was being taught. The social texture of postwar America no longer resembled Thornton Wilder's small town, Grover's Corners. "Our Town" might be a trailer camp or a Levittown more often than a community of elm-lined streets.

Yet the growing prosperity was real, and people did not complain about the federal taxes that were also subsidizing so much. In 1939 only 3.9 million people paid federal income taxes; in 1949, 35.6 million paid personal income tax. Just as higher education **The Growth of a Prosperous Middle Class** shifted from being an upper class privilege, so taxation shifted from being the burden of the very rich. As the country prospered more workers contributed to the national coffers. In the late 1940s the United States, with only 7% of the world's population, accounted for half of the entire world's manufacturing output. At that time Americans possessed 42% of the world's income. Per capita income in the United States in 1949 was $1,450—much higher than that of other prosperous nations. In Canada, Great Britain, New Zealand, Switzerland, and Sweden, the average was between $700 and $900.[16] And in 1945 unemployment was only 1.9% in America; it remained under 4% from 1946 to 1948. Controlled immigration eliminated the fear of job loss from invasions of cheap workers, while the small cohort of young men born during the Depression contributed to making most American cities safe places. From the 1930s to 1945 the murder rate in the United States had been cut in half. Such statistics do indeed suggest a kind of momentary postwar utopia. Yet millions of people—not defined by the more formal poverty level—still did not share what would be defined by the middle class in the 1990s as the good life.

The material changes in America from World War II to the 21st century have been so overwhelming that students may find it hard to believe that in 1947, 40 million people (30% of all Americans) were poor—even by the standards of the time. One-third **The Poor** of American homes had no running water, two-fifths had no flush toilets, three-fifths lacked central heat, and four-fifths were heated by coal or wood. And in spite of the miracle of Levittowns, most people still lived in rented housing. Many workers continued to labor at demanding physical jobs on farms or in mines, in factories, or in construction.[17]

In 1945, 17.5% of the population still made its living from the soil, but by the late 1940s the exodus from the land represented one of the greatest demographic shifts in contemporary history. The number of family farms would fall from 5.9 million at the close of World War II to only 3 million 25 years later. The shift to agribusiness, the control of gigantic farms created from the consolidation of small farms—again with the help of government subsidies—did little to improve the quality of life for most farm workers, many of whom were black or Hispanic.

What was truly utopian was a general belief that the postwar society could continue to achieve incredible goals, both social and material. As Americans emptied their wartime savings accounts and borrowed or took whatever the gov- **The Baby Boom** ernment offered as entitlements, the people who had put up tomatoes, made their own clothes, given their children toys made from clothespins and spools, and never took vacations turned into a nation of big spenders and players. "Consumer" became synonymous with "American citizen."

The idea of personal sacrifice that characterized the world of the Great Depression and World War II might have disappeared altogether had it not been for the "baby boom" that suddenly anchored many young people to new and larger families. In 1946 an all-time record of 3.4 million babies were born—26% more than in 1945. Into the next decade babies poured onto the American scene in record numbers. Indeed, by 1964 two-fifths of America's population had been born since 1946. Having developed a strong sense of their capabilities during the war, women transferred many of their skills into raising large families. It was no longer just religious opponents to birth control or the poor who had large families. The greatest jump in fertility occurred among well-educated white women with medium to high incomes.[18] And just as the war created new jobs and prosperity, so did the baby boom. Diaper services, baby food, educational toys and playgrounds, and special furniture for children became big business. Dr. Spock's book on "common sense" child care became an all-time best-seller. For a brief period—for a vast middle class—the sense of prosperity and family solidarity was real. Before the next decade was over the divorce rate would continue to climb again—as it had before the war—and the family would begin to lose power as a source of community stability in American life.

The Beginning of the Cold War   "The Community as Victim" is the title of one chapter in Victor Navasky's book *Naming Names*, a history of the United States government's attacks on citizens who had shown sympathy for Communist ideas during the late 1940s and 1950s. As the Cold War developed after Winston Churchill's 1946 speech at Fulton, Missouri, describing the Iron Curtain that had dropped between the Soviet Union and the West, a terrible paranoia replaced the good sense of many Americans. In 1945—only a year before—80% of all the people polled approved of the newly created United Nations organization as a forum to deal with world problems. But the House Un-American Activities Committee was rejuvenated in 1947, and by the beginning of the 1950s the Cold War had already begun to shape a national mentality of suspicion. The freedom from fear that so many Americans had fought for in World War II no longer was a priority of our heritage. In spite of all the prosperity, as the 1950s arrived the postwar American dream of communities of diverse individuals with differing opinions living harmoniously side by side appeared to slip away.

NOTES

1. Quoted in Studs Terkel, *"The Good War": An Oral History of World War II* (New York: Ballantine Books, 1985), 382.

2. See Judy Barrett Litoff and David C. Smith, eds., *Since You Went Away: World War II Letters from American Women on the Home Front* Lawrence: University of Kansas Press, 1991), 271, 276, 279.

3. Quoted in Kenneth T. Jackson, *Crabgrass Frontier: The Suburbanization of the United States* (New York: Oxford University Press, 1985), 190.

4. Ibid., 234–238.

5. Ibid., 236.

6. Herbert J. Gans, *The Levittowners: Ways of Life and Politics in a New Suburban Community* (New York: Vintage, Random House, 1967), 200.

7. Ibid., 432.

8. Lawrence Cremin, *American Education, 1876–1980: The Metropolitan Experience* (New York: Harper and Row, 1988), 507.

9. Quoted in Diane Ravitch, *The Troubled Crusade: American Education, 1945–1980* (New York: Basic Books, 1983), 19.

10. James T. Patterson, *Grand Expectations: The United States, 1945–1974* (New York: Oxford University Press, 1996), 68.

11. Ravitch, *Troubled Crusade*, xii.

12. Ibid., 4, 6.

13. Quoted in ibid., 26.

14. Quoted in ibid., 46.

15. Quoted in ibid., 74, 75.

16. Patterson, *Grand Expectations*, 56, 61.

17. Ibid., 62, 63.

18. Ibid., 77.

Part II

The 1950s: The Postwar Years and the Atomic Age

6

1950: A Brand-New World

In 1997 the New England American Studies Association held
a conference in Salem, Massachusetts, a town associated with **Targets of**
the witch trials defining community turmoil in the 17th cen- **Suspicion**
tury. The 1990s meeting—appropriately entitled "Fear Itself:
Enemies Real and Imagined in American Culture"—reminded serious
students of American history that irrational behavior has often characterized the way we treat each other. Conference papers included discussions of World War II Japanese American internment camps, Cold War
repression in Erie, Pennsylvania, ongoing fear of both Freemasons and
Catholics, and anxiety about crime and atomic espionage. The discussion
of Cold War anti-Communism underlined the peculiar anxiety in a culture of affluence. A plenary session concentrated on homophobia; other
sessions included reports on fear of praying Indians, fear for women's
seduction with alcohol, and fear about miscegenation. Of course, discussion of the post-millennial constant—the end of the world—was included on the program, along with a look at how the media, specifically
radio and TV, contributed to all these underlying anxieties about who
we are and what we want to be. Such a banquet of fear and anxiety may
well be more characteristic of American culture than of more homogeneous societies.

Without one unified cultural heritage, Americans have had the burden
of defining norms that must include much eccentricity. It is easy to be
suspicious of people whose appearance and customs are alien. From the
very beginning of this country people have asked, "What is an Ameri-

can?" At certain times irrational fears have overwhelmed the common sense that ought to rule in a democracy, and the legal protection designed to shelter differing opinions seemed to fade. Such a time was the end of the decade of the 1940s. From 1947 until the censure of Senator Joseph McCarthy in 1954—a time of remarkable economic productivity and realizable social mobility—the country experienced a period of turmoil and fear as great as any in American history. This was a period of painful paradox. The same people who had accepted Russia as a wartime partner suddenly saw Soviet Communism as a terrible threat.

Few questioned U.S. intervention in Korea under United Nations auspices in 1950 to keep the Communists from taking over the country. The memory of capitulation to Hitler at Munich in 1938 made it seem right to intervene to stop a new imperialism. Under General Douglas MacArthur as head of the United Nations command, 1.8 million Americans served in Korea. By the time the Korean armistice was signed in 1953, 54,200 Americans had been killed there, 103,300 had been wounded, and 8,200 remained missing in action.[1] When Harry Truman relieved MacArthur of his command for wanting to extend this war into China, however, the mail in favor of MacArthur ran twenty to one. The Russians, who had their own hydrogen bomb by 1953, terrified some into believing we might be wise to begin an atomic war with a preemptive strike. When asked how the Third World War would be fought, Albert Einstein replied that he had no idea what weapons would be used, but he assured the questioner that after that war, the next one would be fought with stones. Yet it was not overseas confrontations that caused the tensions of the 1950s—it was fear of enemies on the home front.

Hollywood in the McCarthy Era
The House Un-American Activities Committee (HUAC), designed to ferret out Communists in labor unions in the 1930s, became an invigorated source of terror under the control of Congressman J. Parnell Thomas. In 1947 a group of Hollywood screenwriters and directors summoned before the committee to account for past Communist beliefs was considered especially dangerous because of their power to influence American opinion through the movies. Called "unfriendly witnesses" because they took the Fifth Amendment (see Appendix) to keep from having to name friends, "the Hollywood Ten" were all indicted for contempt of Congress. Although even film star Ronald Reagan testified at the time that he did not believe Communists had ever been able to use motion pictures to spread their ideology, the Supreme Court upheld the indictment. These people were fined a thousand dollars each and sent to jail for a year. Richard Nixon, who would become the most prominent committee member during the 1950 Alger Hiss trial, demanded that new movies be made to spell out "the methods and evils of totalitarian Communism." But the only examples J. Parnell Thomas could find of dan-

gerous old movies were those made during the war, like *Mission to Moscow* and *Song of Russia*—corny propaganda films created to help wartime allies appear sympathetic. Ironically, Chairman Thomas, accused of stealing from the government he had been protecting from Communists, would soon find himself in the same prison where he had sent one of the Hollywood Ten, Ring Lardner, Jr. As a result of this arrest Lardner, a particularly talented writer, would not see his name on any list of screen credits for seventeen years. But by 1970 his gifts would be valued again; he won an Oscar for work on *M*A*S*H*.

After this trial the atmosphere of fright was so great that a national blacklist was set up not only to deny future employment to the Hollywood Ten but also to keep anyone with questionable political allegiances from working in the media. Loyalty oaths became a part of the American scene, and many less talented and less influential people lost government and teaching jobs—also considered positions of influence. Fortunately for the history of freedom of speech, a panoramic array of gifted writers has recorded many versions of this period of anxiety, labeled "Scoundrel Time" by playwright Lillian Hellman in her book of the same name.[2] In the future when scholars and critics collect all such memoirs and compare them, careful research may reveal how much prejudice may have been involved in accusations against intellectuals and New Deal civil servants and whether, indeed, 1930s writers connected with the Communist party continued to support the Soviet Union.

Although a number of films tried to capture the mood of this decade, two remain classical comments on the emotions of the time. "Friendly witnesses" (the label for those who believed it a patriotic duty to name all the Communists they knew) Elia Kazan and Budd Schulberg collaborated on the 1954 prize-winning movie *On the Waterfront*. Awarded eight Oscars, it examined the dilemmas involved in becoming an informer. Kazan acknowledged using his own story in the film to justify his testimony before the House Un-American Activities Committee. In the movie the informer, whose moral choices are relatively simple, becomes a hero.[3]

A film offering a different viewpoint could be made only at a much later time. In 1976 once blacklisted artists Walter Bernstein and Martin Ritt wrote and directed the Woody Allen production *The Front*, recreating the lives of a writer and comedian barred from work during the 1950s. Although there is humor in the delicatessen cashier character who "fronts" for the talented writer denied his livelihood, the themes of humiliation and loss of self-esteem involved in being blacklisted dominate the film. The comedian, brilliantly played by Zero Mostel, who had himself been a victim of the blacklist, commits suicide. Such despair was real for artists at this moment because their survival demanded audiences. "The Great Fear," as British scholar David Caute termed the fear of Com-

munism in a long book on anti-Communist purges under Truman and
Eisenhower, touched almost every kind of contemporary activity.[4]

To be sure, by the 1990s, when Russian spy files were opened to reveal
the Venona documents of deciphered codes passed by the Russian Secret
Service, the KGB, to its American agents, there could be no doubt that
the American Communist Party had been controlled by the Kremlin.
And there was evidence for espionage where many believed none had
existed. But the number of actual subversives remained small. In an eloquent 1950 book, *The Loyalty of Free Men*, Alan Barth, a journalist for
the *Washington Post*, pointed out that the number of Communist Party
members equalled about 1/30th of 1% of the population—yet the general
hysteria of the late '40s and early '50s appeared extreme. In 1954 a famous critic of American civilization, Lewis Mumford, echoed the concerns of liberals: "In the name of freedom we are rapidly creating a police
state; and in the name of democracy we have succumbed not to creeping
socialism but to galloping Fascism."[5]

Attitudes of the Times

Statistics and anecdotes say much about the atmosphere.
For the single year 1949 the *New York Times Index* entry
for "U.S. Espionage, Sabotage, Treason, and Subversive
Activities" took up seventeen pages of small print. As
early as 1940 the Smith Act had been passed to prohibit "the teaching
and advocating of subversive doctrines," enabling the government to
arrest Communist leaders and to put several hundred others in jail, as
well as to deport many foreign-born Party members. During the next
decade the Civil Service Commission actually fired 2,611 "security risks"
and reported that 4,315 other government workers had resigned.[6] Neighbors and fellow workers were encouraged to report possible risks, creating
an atmosphere of suspicion and fear that seemed broader than the red-
hunts of earlier periods. Librarians and teachers, considered dangerous
influences on the general public, were singled out for special scrutiny.

Among the earliest protest publications was Dalton Trumbo's *The Time
of the Toad: A Study of Inquisition in America* (1949). Trumbo, a gifted
writer and one of the Hollywood Ten, had gone to jail rather than name
names. His strength of conviction was admired by many. Believing, with
Archibald MacLeish, poet and librarian of Congress, that a "nation of
beginners and begetters, changers and challengers, creators and accom-
plishers" was putting strategic advantage in the Cold War above our
long commitment "to exalt the dignity of man," Trumbo extended his
sense of injustice to other areas of American life.[7]

Education

Particularly shocking to Trumbo was the HUAC's desire to
inspect university curricula and expose Communist teachers.
During 1948 a great number of professors were interrogated
for "free thinking." Across the country, from Oregon to Vermont to Florida, from Rutgers University to Reed College to the University of Mich-

igan, sixteen lost their jobs as so-called subversives without tenure. "No university administration in its right senses would knowingly hire a Communist," declared Arthur Schlesinger, Jr., of Harvard.[8]

Harvard, like most great American academic institutions, was committed to the protection of freedom of speech. The Jeffersonian belief that we can tolerate error as long as reason is free to combat it has been essential to America's intellectual heritage. Yet Harvard too at one point refused to hire or retain a small group of radical nontenured teachers because they had been Communists. In another excellent memoir of this period, *Previous Convictions: A Journey Through the 1950s*, Nora Sayre documents the firing of a young Harvard sociologist/historian for refusing to name names to an FBI investigator. At the Law School, Zechariah Chafee asserted what may well have been true in most tenured cases—that Harvard would never dismiss a professor because of honestly held opinions whenever they were expressed. But by the 1950s there were few Communists teaching. Often those Marxists who were lecturing on physics or archaeology were tolerated more readily than those teaching history or philosophy. Yet Sayre also documents a painful incident in 1948 at Ohio State, where a distinguished archaeologist and museum curator was fired because his stepson was a Communist. To its credit the Harvard Corporation also made much of refusing to dismiss a famous physicist who had admitted a Communist past. Tenure—designed as protection in exactly such moments—is worth discussing in terms of ideas. Too many citizens regard tenure as a shelter for incompetence rather than as the guarantee of academic freedom it was meant to be. But in California, where the faculty senates at both U.C.L.A. and Berkeley had voted against loyalty oaths, tenure provided no protection at this moment in history. Six faculty members, "in gross violation" of the university's tenure policy, were dismissed for refusing to sign such oaths, imposed by the state in 1950.[9]

Many who lived through these times of suspicion speak of the peripheral damage that occurs. What kind of scholars would want to teach at any school unwilling to uphold the tradition of academic freedom? Self-censorship also often takes over the minds of the less assertive even when administrations appear open-minded. Trying to be "objective" inhibited the honest enthusiasm of many committed teachers. Innovative courses and new programs of study do not generally emerge at moments of anxiety. Scholars in the late '40s and early '50s became afraid even to teach about what Marxism stood for. As Senator McCarthy grew more hostile to the Ivy League and its New Deal connections and went after what he called "the Kremlin on the Charles," Harvard also extended its cooperation. Sayre notes that the FBI, the CIA, and the State Department all became involved in the shaping of the university's new Russian Research Center. Ellen Schrecker, a serious scholar of the McCarthy era, suggests that such internalized censorship may well have inhibited much necessary study on Vietnamese culture, making necessary experts less available at a later time.[10]

Every level of education became an arena of fear. The National Education Association and the American Association of School Administrators not only barred Communists from faculties but also pledged to create a new Cold War education program designed to stress loyalty. Twenty distinguished educators signed this administrators' report, causing Dalton Trumbo to despair. But he also cited a number of brave champions of FDR's belief that "the truth is found where men are free to pursue it."[11] Robert Hutchins of the University of Chicago and Dwight Dumond of the University of Michigan were among his outspoken heroes. In 1947 Hutchins chaired a Commission on Freedom of the Press. He also made a clear defense of a university club, insisting that the study of Communism is not a subversive activity. Another academic hero, Merle Curti, professor of history at the University of Wisconsin, did not hesitate to denounce loyalty oaths, anti-intellectualism, and McCarthyism in his 1954 presidential address to the American Historical Association.

It may seem peculiar to note that by the 1990s some academics would also review this period with nostalgia, remembering that huge amounts of government funding poured into universities to augment Cold War defense programs. Such money for military purposes often filtered into many parts of the research universities receiving them.

The facts remain. Between 1951 and 1957, 300 teachers were actually fired from New York City public schools for refusing to name other teachers "who may be or may have been" Communists. Most had been teachers since the Depression—their pedagogical skills were not questioned. No evidence appeared that they had ever taught any Communist ideology, but they were considered insubordinate. As Nora Sayre neatly puts it, "They were pronounced to be fine teachers—who were unfit to teach."[12] By 1973, 33 of this group were brave enough to sue for reinstatement. Their original dismissals were declared unconstitutional. But the money they won was far less than the back pay and pensions they deserved—and they had suffered the loss of respect.

One of the government's favorite anti-Communist witnesses boasted of providing "insubstantial evidence" against teachers. In his memoir *False Witness* (1955), Harvey Matusow made himself infamous for disclosing the range of phony identifications of "ex Communists" he had produced for $25 a day. Students discouraged with 1990s politics who tend to think sleaziness is new have only to look a short distance into the past to discover the history of corruption. The lives destroyed by Matusow's trumped up testimonies meant nothing to him.

Trumbo was equally disheartened by the government's intrusion into the world of art. George Dondero, a representative from **The** Michigan, insisted on inserting ten columns into the *Congressional* **Arts** *Record*, titled "Communism in the Heart of American Art—What to Do About It." Dondero was incensed by an exhibit put together to cheer men in veterans' hospitals. Any artist who had supported Henry Wallace, the Progressive candidate who ran against Dewey and Truman in 1948, was automatically suspect. "The art of the Communist and Marxist," Dondero declared, "is the art of perversion."[13] At a time when American artists felt free to awaken the world with their imaginative daring, and when Communist artists in Russia were producing heavy ideological work of social realism, it should have been clear to American buyers that identifying politics with creativity made little sense. Yet this congressman's attacks even attempted to persuade people to return paintings by suspect artists to their New York dealers. Art critics, Dondero insisted, were yet another dangerous group because they influenced taste; he recommended that they be censored by their publishers.

Trumbo was also concerned with the control the government was threatening to exercise over atomic scientists. Anyone in- **Science** volved with specialized military knowledge had always had to be scrutinized. In the decade after the war the case that embarrassed the entire country was that of J. Robert Oppenheimer, former director of the Manhattan Project to build the atomic bomb. After his success at Los Alamos, America valued Oppenheimer as the man whose energies created the bomb that ended the war. He became a national hero and in 1948 was on the cover of *Time*. And a new professional journal, *Physics Today*, also displayed his picture on its first issue—in spite of Oppenheimer's having put aside his career as a research physicist to build the bomb. As head of the Manhattan Project he experienced no doubts about his status, but the intellectual depth that made him question future atomic wars and oppose the development of the devastating hydrogen bomb turned Oppenheimer, in many eyes, into a security risk.

Edward Teller, a physicist enthusiastic about building the "Super"— as the new hydrogen bomb was called—blamed Oppenheimer for alienating the best scientists from working on the project. Because of the witch-hunting atmosphere the tensions among scientists and government officials in 1954 were extreme. When Oppenheimer had gone before the HUAC in 1949, the young Nixon had praised him for his candor. But in 1954, the government moved to strip Oppenheimer of his security clearance. Always naive about politics, the great physicist had confessed to past left-wing beliefs and Communist associates. But these had not been held against him as director of the Manhattan Project. Suddenly his opposition to the H-bomb made Oppenheimer a target for spy hunters who wanted to define all disagreement as treason. The trial of J. Robert Oppenheimer, a series of hearings before the Atomic Energy Commission, remains a scar on the history of America justice. With abundant personal detail David Halberstam captures its intensity in *The Fifties*: "There hadn't been a proceeding like this since the Spanish inquisition," declared David Lilienthal, former head of the Atomic Energy Commission.[14]

The hearings against him left Oppenheimer stunned. Although the most distinguished scientists in America testified on his behalf, the government's judges paid no heed. After a lifetime of eloquence, Oppenheimer wilted. He could no longer be "the powerful witness for freedom of scientific opinion" his friends had expected him to be. At this moment, as one journalist reported, the great scientist appeared sadly as a man "diminished by tiny misdeeds from the past."[15] Edward Teller's calculated praise of Oppenheimer's patriotism ended with implications that he was no longer fit to protect the vital interests of the country. In April 1954 the AEC voted two to one to deny security clearance to the man who had enabled the United States to build the atomic bomb.

Meanwhile Harry Truman had already gone ahead with the construction of the hydrogen bomb. He had never shared Oppenheimer's doubts about using the atom bomb. He knew he had done the right thing. Moreover, Truman listened to political advisors, not to scientists. In March 1954 the United States made a series of hydrogen bomb tests at Bikini Atoll, spreading radioactive ash over 7,000 square miles and incidentally harming a boatful of Japanese fishermen 80 miles away, who were labeled, in this era of paranoia, as possible Communist spies.

The Trial of Alger Hiss   Perhaps the most famous case during this epidemic of suspicion, dramatized by the patriotic intensity of Richard Nixon, was that involving Alger Hiss begun in 1948. At the time Hiss was president of the Carnegie Endowment for International Peace. Once law clerk to the great jurist Oliver Wendell Holmes, Hiss had been visible if not prominent in the State Department, an assistant to Roosevelt at the Yalta conference, and more recently one of the main planners of the United Nations. An elegant Ivy League type whose character references came from the highest levels of the government, Alger Hiss was accused of having given State Department documents to Communist connections by an unprepossessing writer at *Time* magazine, Whittaker Chambers. Chambers claimed to have been in a '30s Communist group with Hiss. The disparity in the backgrounds of the two men at first made Chambers' testimony seem ludicrous. Coming from a shady past full of aliases and shifts of ideology, slovenly in appearance, Chambers seemed in every sense an unworthy opponent for the impeccably credentialed Hiss. Even the House Committee on Un-American Activities scorned Chambers when Hiss promptly denied ever having known him. Alistair Cooke, a British journalist reporting the case, was so impressed by Hiss' gentle certitude of behavior that he described him as "an American gentleman, one of the incomparable human products"—like a noble character in a Henry James novel.[16] Under oath Alger Hiss denied ever having been a Communist or knowing Whittaker Chambers. Yet Richard Nixon, the youngest member of the committee, made a target of Hiss. He demanded a face to face confrontation between the two men, at which Hiss did acknowledge knowing Chambers by one of his aliases, George Crosley. Their confrontation included Hiss' inspection of Chambers' teeth as a means of identification. The very first televised Congressional hearing, the Hiss case opened a new world where Americans could see their political representatives in action.

In 1949, when the Soviets asserted oppressive power all over eastern Europe, Hiss became a symbol of the part of FDR's State Department that had been too soft on Russia. The drama accelerated when Chambers produced from a pumpkin on his farm a series of State Department documents typed in the 1930s on Hiss' typewriter—with handwritten notes as well. Chambers had hidden the documents as evidence when he left the Communist Party. Yet many details remained mysterious. Hiss continued to insist that the typewriting was forged and the notes stolen. Because the statute of limitations on espionage had expired and because the evidence was far from flawless, Hiss was indicted simply for perjury. After one hung jury trial, where the vote was eight to four against him, he was convicted of perjury at a second trial in 1950 and sent to prison for five years. Chambers went on to write a powerful confessional autobiography, *Witness*, convincingly authentic in its details. He knew incredible minutiae about the life Hiss led. Social analysts at the time wondered if Hiss had lied to protect his wife, the typist. They would also speculate on personal reasons for Chambers' vindictiveness. In 1957 Alger Hiss told his side of the story in *In the Court of Public Opinion*.

A scholarly exploration of the trial appeared in 1978, the 622-page *Perjury: The Hiss–Chambers Case* by Allen Weinstein, then a historian at Smith College. Weinstein used 40,000 pages of previously classified documents and interviewed Soviet agents who confirmed Chambers' testimony. Yet Weinstein concluded that there could still emerge a coherent body of material to undermine the evidence against Hiss.[17] Students might be challenged to pursue new discoveries on what has been called the most dramatic court case of the century.

What there can be no doubt about is that the Hiss conviction provided Senator Joseph McCarthy with fuel for **Government** his personal pursuit of Communists in government. The term "McCarthyism" now lives in the dictionary, defined as "the political practice of publicizing accusations of disloyalty or subversion with insufficient regard for evidence" (*American Heritage Dictionary of the English Language*, 1969). When the senator from Wisconsin sensed the mood of disillusionment after the Hiss trial he used it to further his political career. McCarthy shared Nixon's hostility to those who were running the State Department, which he claimed was infested with Communists. He boasted a list of 205 State Department spies, but when challenged to produce proof McCarthy changed his accusation to "bad risks" and lowered the number to 57.[18] Later Senator Millard Tydings of Maryland offered McCarthy $25,000 to convict just one actual employee of the State Department. He never collected the money.

The country was looking for scapegoats to compensate for Russia's Cold War aggression and for the "loss" of China to Communist ideology. McCarthy came up with Owen Lattimore, a Johns Hopkins professor and China scholar who would call his memoir *Ordeal by Slander*[19]; Lattimore retired to England after being accused of spying for Russia. John Stuart Service, a State Department China desk expert in the '40s who favored withdrawing U.S. support from Chiang Kai-shek, was fired in 1951 on trumped-up charges. The simple idea that ridding America of Communists at home would cure world tension and purify democracy appealed to many. By the end of 1950 Congress had also passed the Internal Security Act, also known as the McCarran Act, to register all Communists, strengthen espionage and immigration laws, and set up detention camps for spies and saboteurs in case of emergency. As early as 1947 the *American Legion* magazine boasted that the House Un-American Activities Committee had not summoned any farmer or workman or "common man." Without exception, the legionnaires pointed out, the suspect people examined were college graduates, Ph.Ds, summa cum laudes, and Phi Beta Kappas from Harvard, Yale, Princeton, or other great colleges. Such dominant populist sentiments made it easy for Eisenhower to defeat the "egghead" Adlai Stevenson, who ran a sophisticated campaign against him in 1952. A professor at the University of Utah commented on Stevenson's defeat, "A whole era is ended, is totally repudiated, a whole era of brains and literacy and exciting thinking."[20]

After the tremendous Eisenhower landslide in the presidential election of 1952, the Republican Senate made McCarthy head of his own committee on government operations. He himself had been elected by a margin of more than 140,000 votes. Immediately McCarthy sent two young assistants, Roy Cohn and G. David Schine, on a whirlwind tour of United States Information Services abroad that ended with the banning of "books, music, painting and the like" of any Communist or fellow traveler. Included were books by Henry David Thoreau and Foster Rhea Dulles, an anti-Communist professor who was a cousin of the secretary of state. Ordered to remove dangerous thinkers from libraries, some custodians actually burned books. Many librarians lost their jobs. Eisenhower openly criticized this outrage at a graduation speech in June 1952 at Dartmouth College. "We have got to fight Communism with something better," he declared, "not try to conceal the thinking of our own people." But the President did not countermand McCarthy's directive.

The Wisconsin senator was as out of control as a forest fire in a high wind. He made outrageous accusations and bullied innocent people to try to establish guilt by association or past connection. Such irresponsible behavior caused a fellow Republican, Margaret Chase Smith from Maine, to present to the Senate "A Declaration of Conscience," signed by six other brave Republicans. "I don't like the way the Senate has been made a rendezvous for vilification, for selfish political gain at the sacrifice of individual reputations and national unity," Smith proclaimed. "The American people are sick and tired of being afraid to speak their minds lest they be politically smeared as Communists." She concluded with a common sentiment: "I want to see our nation recapture the strength and unity it once had when we fought the enemy instead of ourselves."[21] In 1952 Smith's name had been put in nomination for vice president by approving Republicans, although she did not receive the nomination.

Yet McCarthy seemed unable to stop. He did not even hesitate to accuse General George Marshall, wartime chief of staff and later secretary of state, of being a longtime Communist sympathizer, although it was Marshall's economic plan for rebuilding Europe that kept much of the West out of Communist control. Perhaps for party solidarity Eisenhower tolerated many of McCarthy's antics, but he responded to the attack on Marshall by declaring the general a distinguished patriot—"a man of real selflessness." He went on to assert, "I have no patience with anyone who can find in Marshall's record of service to this country cause for criticism."[22] By 1951 many Americans began to agree with Harry Truman that Senator McCarthy was an asset to the Kremlin. Adlai Stevenson, twice the Democratic presidential nominee, commented that "perhaps this hysterical form of putrid slander . . . flourishes because it satisfies a deep craving to reduce the vast menace of world Communism to comprehensible and manageable proportions." Stevenson also noted the damage done to freedom: "We have all witnessed the stifling choking effect of McCarthyism, the paralysis of initiative, the discouragement and intimidation that follow in its wake and inhibit the bold, imaginative thought and discussion that is the anvil of policy."[23]

When McCarthy took on the rest of the army, people speculated it was because his protégé G. David Schine had been denied special status when drafted, bringing his flashy political career to an end. Not only did McCarthy once again come up with no proven Communists in leadership positions in the U.S. Army beyond one sympathizer dentist, but he also flaunted his bullying tactics on camera before the American people. The Army–McCarthy hearings provided 35 days in 1954 of riveting television performances demonstrating the new medium as a strong force for exposing truth. No doubt remained about McCarthy's cruel character as he browbeat witnesses and lawyers alike. A documentary film, *Point of Order*, released in 1964 by Emile De Antonio, remains to show how offensive McCarthy's performances were. After eight years of destructive misuse of senatorial authority McCarthy was condemned by the Senate for misconduct 67 to 22 in 1954. Through their representatives the American people made clear that they had enough of profitless ranting. Three years later McCarthy would be dead of acute hepatitis. Yet the anxiety about Communism lingered in underlying fears of what the Russians might be up to in the postwar world. As late as 1958, 300 subscriptions were canceled when *Esquire* magazine published an anti-McCarthy article.

The Trial of the Rosenbergs The final significant Communist trial of this period, that of Julius and Ethel Rosenberg, reached beyond America. The whole world commented on the capital punishment meted out to these "atomic spies," who were also parents of two small boys. Their execution seized the literary mythic imagination and continues to haunt the definition of American justice. Even many who believed in capital punishment were appalled at the lack of moderation in the justice system that sent the Rosenbergs to their deaths with so little concrete evidence against them.

The British atomic physicist Klaus Fuchs had acknowledged in 1950 that he stole atomic bomb plans from Los Alamos. He served but nine years of a fourteen-year sentence in a British prison. Yet in the United States anti-Communist fervor became so fierce that the Rosenbergs—whose messenger roles for an allegedly similar theft were much less certain—were executed. Later evidence made it clear that Ethel knew almost nothing about her husband's role. The government had arrested her as a bargaining chip to get more information from him. But the Rosenbergs' refusal to cooperate with the justice system they trusted was their undoing.

Years later, in March 1997 Alexander Feklisov, a retired KGB agent who had had frequent direct contact with the Rosenbergs, told the *New York Times* that the couple had given Russia no useful information at all about the atom bomb. Although Julius had given away some military secrets during 50 or so meetings between 1943 and 1946—when Russia was also our military ally—Feklisov claimed that Ethel was completely innocent. He thought she probably knew of her husband's activities, but added, "You don't kill people for that."[24]

Convicted mainly on the testimony of Ethel's brother, David Greenglass, who had worked on the bomb, the Rosenbergs appeared to be an affront to the American myth of family solidarity. The press, instead of revealing the couple's affection for each other and their concern for their little boys, dehumanized them as robotlike Soviet ideologues. This practice continued even after the Rosenbergs' executions when their collected letters were edited to exclude homey details like their passion for baseball and music and the sustenance they found in their Judaism. To be sure, the Rosenbergs were unrealistically committed to Communism as a means to making a better world, but in 1942, a freer time, a *Fortune* magazine poll revealed that as many as 25% of all Americans considered themselves "socialists" and another 35% were open-minded about socialism.[25] Just a few years earlier the dogmas the Rosenbergs accepted would never have brought about such extreme punishment. Yet the dogmas of the man who passed judgment upon them seemed equally distorted. Judge Irving R. Kaufman, perhaps afraid of being labeled soft toward fellow Jews, accused the couple of "a crime worse than murder" in putting the A-bomb into the hands of the Russians.[26] When Eisenhower denied the Rosenbergs clemency, it was because he too believed they had increased the chances of atomic war and "exposed to danger literally millions of our citizens."[27] He ignored the pleas of Pope Pius XII and the 40 members of the British Parliament who had joined the pope in urging leniency. Jean-Paul Sartre, a powerful French philosophic voice, called the executions "a legal lynching that covered a whole nation with blood."[28]

Whether the Rosenbergs' deaths made Americans feel more secure or merely heightened their anxiety is worth debating. What is certain is the role that the Rosenbergs began—almost at once—to play in the literary imagination. They joined abolitionist John Brown, slave rebel Nat Turner, and anarchists Sacco and Vanzetti as characters in the mythology of American martyrs. As scapegoats, as government pawns, as intellectual outsiders, the Rosenbergs would find literary definition in such works as E. L. Doctorow's novel *The Book of Daniel* (1971) and Robert Coover's *The Public Burning* (1977) and in the poetry of Adrienne Rich and Sylvia Plath. The 1990s drama by Tony Kushner, *Angels in America*, would present a confrontation between Ethel Rosenberg and Roy Cohn, Senator McCarthy's aide, who boasted of getting her executed. "You could kill me," Ethel tells him, "but you couldn't ever defeat me."[29]

Prominent liberal culture critics Leslie Fiedler and Robert Warshow reflected the general public's hostile approach to the doomed couple. Falling in with the consensus of Cold War intellectuals, they made it clear that there could be little humanity in people who pursued the rigidity of Communist ideology.

In 1990, *Ethel: The Fictional Autobiography* by Tema Nason created a brave characterization. And a movie version of *The Book of Daniel* (1983) attempted to make her sympathetic—unfortunately, not by remembering Ethel as she was but by turning her into a compliant blonde. Tony Kushner's Ethel may well have captured her most essential traits. Students trying to evaluate this trial and what it meant for America must look into *Invitation to an Inquest: A New Look at the Rosenberg and Sobell Case* (1968) by Miriam and Walter Schneir.

Other Writing about the McCarthy Era
Peculiar strengths and remarkable literary talents emerged from this period of fear and persecution. By the time of McCarthy's death in 1957, blacklisted writers were working again using their own names. In 1996 the Brooklyn Museum produced its own film to honor the blacklisted, *Hollywood on Trial: Films from the Blacklisted Era*. The museum also screened a long series of such films, introduced by critics, scholars, and individuals whose lives had been affected by the blacklist. By then 50 years had passed since the original indictments of the Hollywood Ten and the more general discrimination against so many in the entertainment world.

When Arthur Miller's play *The Crucible* appeared on stage in 1953, audiences recognized at once that Miller was using the hysteria of the Salem witch hunts to represent the irrationalities of his own time. Yet the anxieties of the past seemed just as complicated as those of the present. The State Department denied Miller a passport to see the Brussels production of his play in 1954.

How much ordinary people were damaged by such excessive fear and unreasonable persecution is worth attention. In other societies hundreds of suspect individuals might have been executed for treason. Here the "great trials" were the exceptions. Yet the 2,611 "security risks" who were fired and the 4,315 other government workers who resigned continue to pose a problem for civil liberties in the United States. Fortunately, by the 1990s Americans would be able to examine the range of historical material describing the tensions of this period, much as they study the records of the Salem witch trials to document the hysteria of an earlier anxious time.

NOTES

1. William T. Patterson, *Grand Expectations: The United States, 1945–1974* (New York: Oxford University Press, 1996), 207–208.

2. Lillian Hellman, *Scoundrel Time* (Boston: Little, Brown, 1976); also *An Unfinished Woman: A Memoir* (Boston: Little, Brown, 1969).

3. See Stephen J. Whitfield, *The Culture of the Cold War* (Baltimore: Johns Hopkins University Press, 1991), 110–113.

4. David Caute, *The Great Fear: The Anti-Communist Purges under Truman and Eisenhower* (New York: Simon and Schuster, 1978).

5. Lewis Mumford, *In the Name of Sanity* (New York: Harcourt, Brace, 1954), 155.

6. Stephen E. Ambrose, "The Ike Age," *New Republic*, May 9, 1981, 33.

7. Quoted in Dalton Trumbo, *The Time of the Toad: A Study of Inquisition in America* (New York: Perennial/Harper and Row, 1949), 40.

8. Quoted in Ibid., 43.

9. See Nora Sayre, *Previous Convictions: A Journey Through the 1950s* (New Brunswick, NJ: Rutgers University Press, 1995), 114–126. Also Sigmund Diamond, *Compromised Campus: The Collaboration of Universities with the Intelligence Community, 1945–1955* (New York: Oxford University Press, 1992).

10. See Ellen Schrecker, *Many Are the Crimes: McCarthyism in America* (Boston: Little, Brown, 1998).

11. Quoted in Trumbo, *Time of the Toad*, 55.

12. Sayre, *Previous Convictions*, 290.

13. Quoted in Trumbo, *Time of the Toad*, 51.

14. Quoted in David Halberstam, *The Fifties* (New York: Fawcett Columbine, 1993), 350; see also 349–353.

15. Ibid.

16. Quoted in ibid., 12.

17. Allen Weinstein, *Perjury: The Hiss–Chambers Case* (New York: Random House, 1978; updated 1997).

18. Quoted in Eric Goldman, *The Crucial Decade—And After: America, 1945–1960* (New York: Vintage Books, 1956; updated 1960), 142.

19. Ibid., 144.

20. Ibid., 235.

21. Jack Anderson and Ronald W. May, *McCarthy: The Man, the Senator, the Ism* (Boston: Beacon Press, 1952), 408–409.

22. Ibid., 357.

23. Ibid., 410.

24. *New York Times*, March 16, 1997.

25. *Boston Globe*, February 6, 1997.

26. Quoted in Stanley Goldberg, "The Secret About Secrets," in *Secret Agents: The Rosenberg Case, McCarthyism and Fifties America*, ed. Marjorie Garber and Rebecca L. Walkowitz (New York: Routledge, 1995), 48.

27. Blanche Wiesen Cooke, "The Rosenbergs and the Crimes of the Century," in Garber and Walkowitz, *Secret Agents*, 26.

28. Quoted in Caute, *Great Fear*, 68.

29. For a valuable discussion of Kushner, see Michael Cadden, "Strange Angel: The Pinklisting of Roy Cohn," in Garber and Walkowitz, *Secret Agents*, 97–104.

7

Changing Institutions

Life in the United States during the 1950s has inspired more
than one historian to quote Charles Dickens' description of
the French Revolution: "It was the best of times, it was the
worst of times." It was also an "epoch of belief" as well as
an "epoch of incredulity."[1] Although a 20th century American backyard
may seem far from the bloodied cobblestones of 18th century Paris, one
element clearly defined both moments in history. Social upheaval was
real. Never again would habits and traditions and practiced conventions
be as they had been. Such moments—perhaps with good reason—terrify
many people even as they exhilarate others. The anxiety of the Cold War
was just as real as the grand expectations created by affluence. But just
as after the French Revolution, new definitions of human rights began
to expand. In post–World War II America a more complex vision of
moral progress began to take hold.

World War II had been fought against fascist dictatorships to maintain
democratic values. After the fighting stopped though, many nonwhite
Americans realized that they had not yet acquired full citizenship on the
terms offered their fellow soldiers. African Americans who had risked
their lives all over the globe for the Allied powers and women who had
contributed to the high production of armament factories could not easily go back to defining themselves as second class citizens. If we continue
to believe in the United States as a country of ever-expanding opportunity, we can readily understand the social unrest that began to take shape
during the 1950s. Every class had great expectations after the war, yet

when reality failed to match the dreams of black Americans, whose median incomes dropped to only 43% of what whites earned in the years from 1952 to 1963, social action seemed necessary.

Because the G.I. Bill during these years was creating a new group of upwardly mobile Americans, many the first in their families to get a college degree and own a house, most white people did not notice the vast racial discrepancies. Many vital young people went on to become part of a new establishment of educated leaders: doctors, professors, lawyers, and managers who would use their sophisticated training to shape the country. All over America the best and brightest—the social achievers—were moving up and away from the new communities they were the first to settle. Few young couples put down roots as their parents had done. As soon as many suburbanites learned to make allowances for diverse and quirky neighbors, the neighbors frequently moved away. *On the Road* (1957), Jack Kerouac's astonishingly successful novel about the vagabond Beats, could have spoken in some degree for the totally different "organization men" moving ever upward. The archaic idea of a stable community where neighbors knew each other and grew old together became a television dream.

How did places like Levittown fulfill the social designs that stimulated their growth? The original Levittown probably changed more slowly than most planned towns because of William Levitt's social control. The "whites only" clause Levitt included in the original contracts for his mass-produced houses took many years to eradicate. Indeed, a sense of racial hostility had been built into the community. By 1990, of 53,286 residents, the majority, 51,883, were whites. Although 2,184 Hispanic people and 950 Asians and Pacific Islanders had settled in Levittown, there were only 137 blacks (.26%) and 31 Native Americans; 1,285 people were listed as "others." But one sign of change was that by the 1990s the editor of the *Levittown Tribune*, an important local voice, was black.[2] Columbia historian Kenneth T. Jackson speculated that if William Levitt had attempted to integrate his project at the beginning when the demand for housing was overwhelming, Levittown might indeed have become a great social experiment as well as a great economic success. By 1958, when the Supreme Court dismissed the builder's Caucasian clause as unenforceable and contrary to public policy, a few black families trickled in. Housing has often been the slowest area of social change. A Hofstra College political science professor who lived in Levittown from 1953 to 1965 remarked that in the early days even liberals simply took residential segregation for granted without approving of it. Many of the people who bought houses in Levittown had not even read the fine print on the housing documents they signed. The prize-winning black playwright Lorraine Hansberry, in her 1959 play *A Raisin in the Sun*, helped many unaware whites to understand what the experience of buying a decent house was like for African Americans, even as Ann Petry had helped others experience black ghetto life in her 1946 novel, *The Street*. Yet many people kept acting as if serious discrimination did not exist.

Because Jackie Robinson had broken the color line in major league baseball in 1947 and Harry Truman had desegregated the army in 1948, most Americans could see that moral progress toward equal oppor- **The Beginning of the Civil Rights Movement** tunity was real. Few people noticed the tremendous number of African Americans, denied work in the South by new agricultural machines, who had flooded into most large cities. When the New Deal sought to help the one-third of the nation that was ill fed, ill housed, and ill clothed in the 1930s, Congress supported the president because so many Americans recognized these people as their neighbors. But a third of those excluded from postwar economic gains were black. Most white Americans ignored these African Americans. John Kenneth Galbraith's defining book on the 1950s, *The Affluent Society*, mentions race only once. Although *Black Metropolis* by St. Clair Drake and Horace Clayton described Chicago in 1945, it would not be until 1992, with Nicholas Lemann's broader national treatment, *The Promised Land: The Great Black Migration and How It Changed America*, that serious attention was given the greatest postwar social need.

That the best book written by a black intellectual during the 1950s should be called *Invisible Man* (1952) was entirely appropriate. Ralph Ellison's hero made it clear that he was invisible because people simply refused to see him. His story dramatized a number of American situations the black man found himself in: rural poverty, Negro colleges, Communist groups, religious fellowships, and race riots. The hero hiding in the sewer at the end of the novel was drawn to conclude that his invisibility had to be "covert preparation for a more overt action."[3]

When in 1954 the Supreme Court, with the *Brown v. Board of Education of Topeka* decision, established that separate was not equal, the overt action began. During the second half of the 1950s black rights were tested in many ways. The period brought forth a number of dignified and courageous civil rights leaders and lawyers as well as many brave black individuals willing to put their lives on the line for justice. Some whites also worked behind the scenes with African Americans to help bring about successful school integration, to begin voter registration, and to extend the privileges of using facilities then denied blacks. Imagine that Jackie Robinson could not get a cup of coffee at a drugstore lunch counter or sleep in the same hotel with his teammates.

The event, modest though it seemed, that first turned everything upside down in the South was the 1955 refusal of Rosa Parks, a department store seamstress too tired after a long day's work, to give up her seat on an overcrowded bus in Montgomery, Alabama, so that a white man could sit down. After her arrest Parks urged fellow bus travelers to join her in a boycott aimed at getting fair treatment for blacks on all local buses. Parks was not the first person to protest the segregation of public transportation, but she was perfectly trained to make a trial case. Educated in the North and a former secretary of the National Association for the Advancement of Colored People (NAACP), Rosa Parks became a national heroine. Yet the store where she worked closed its alterations department putting her out of work; and her husband was also fired from his job as a barber. Menacing telephone calls made their lives so miserable they eventually had to move away from Montgomery. But the boycott, inspired by the eloquence of a young Martin Luther King and the know-how of Bayard Rustin, an experienced lawyer, was a success. After 381 days during which many white women picked up their domestic help, and many blacks walked for miles, the bus company acknowledged defeat. A national sense of fairness shaped attitudes—the entire country had begun to support the boycott. The United Auto Workers sent $35,000 to help run the carpool set up to drive black workers to faraway jobs. In 1991 actress Sissy Spacek helped dramatize the interracial nature of the protest on film in *The Long Walk Home*. Rosa Parks' defiance remains among the most productive acts of civil disobedience in American history.[4]

When this moment pushed Martin Luther King onto the broad public screen as the head of the nonviolent Montgomery Improvement Association, people recognized a remarkable new leader. In the 1950s, as Taylor Branch's detailed book on the civil rights movement, *Parting the Waters: America in the King Years, 1954–1963*, reveals, there were a number of brave African American leaders such as Bayard Rustin, E. D. Nixon, Ralph Abernathy, and James Lawson equal to the moment. King saw the black people at this time injecting new meaning into the veins of civilization with protest, not with guns. He was right. His eloquence was special; he made everyone feel that the great glory of American democracy is the right to protest for right, underlining the patriotism of his followers: "If we are wrong, the Constitution of the United States is wrong. . . . If we are wrong, justice is a lie."[5] Under the guidance of King and the talented black lawyers Thurgood Marshall and Constance Baker Motley, the African American community asserted its demands for equal rights with considered dignity—in welcome contrast to the hysteria that had spread during the McCarthy period. The blacks' behavior in the civil rights struggles of the 1950s represented great courage, even as Martin Luther King's rhetorical skills seemed perfectly matched to every occasion. Aware of the risk to his life, King famously promised "to work and fight until justice runs down like water and righteousness like a mighty stream!"[6]

The many photographs of people enjoying backyard barbecues and drive-in movies in 1958 belied the social complexity of the period. There were always some white people volunteering behind the scenes to make the society fairer—to demonstrate their commitment to making the new decision against segregation work. In 1957 as many as 10,000 students took part in a youth march for integration. Most Americans outside of the South believed integration would improve racial understanding.

But an unfortunate incident at Arkansas's Little Rock Central High School in 1957–58 may remain the most important historic measure of the integration mandate. When Orval Faubus, the governor of Arkansas, approved of local segregationists preventing nine black students from attending the all-white high school by using the state national guard to keep them out, President Eisenhower called in federal troops to protect the students and to enforce the law. In 1997 President Clinton returning to Little Rock to welcome back the then middle-aged students, noted that what happened in Little Rock changed the course of our country forever. Television news cameras in the '50s caught the hatred of the menacing whites as well as the bravery of the well-starched blacks (eight were girls). Daisy Bates, the courageous president of the Arkansas NAACP, made herself the protector and counselor of the young people. It was she who demanded that Eisenhower call in the army. In spite of many threatening phone calls she did not lose her life, but, like Rosa Parks, Daisy Bates lost her livelihood when her fellow townspeople took all the advertising out of the newspaper she and her husband had run for eighteen years. Later Daisy Bates wrote a painful memoir of the crisis, *The Long Shadow of Little Rock.*

In 1997 President Clinton had to acknowledge that the law that reshaped Little Rock had failed to bring about equal educational achievement and the kind of social change that might enable blacks and whites to be close friends. By refusing to attend Clinton's 40th anniversary celebration of the Little Rock Nine, the NAACP underlined how much work remained to be done. Yet the years between 1957 and 1997 saw Central High become 60% black, and African Americans managed to get training for professional jobs as librarians, counselors, and information specialists. If too few blacks managed to fulfill their potential in terms of what was available to them, at least after 1957 a sense of possibility had replaced a sense of hopelessness. The black president of the Central High School Student Council in 1997 valued the motivation the students retained, saying that today's scholars had taken the torch from the Little Rock Nine and passed it from class to class.[7]

During the 1950s, in a final effort to outwit the federal government, Orval Faubus temporarily closed all the public high schools. The remaining black students then had to get their diplomas through correspondence courses from the university (while whites created private academies so that they would not have to integrate their local schools).

These extreme measures contented many older whites, who persuaded themselves that the pursuit of American justice for blacks was simply another Communist plot.

Such sentiment was displayed in the hardships faced by Autherine Lucy, a 26-year-old black woman who applied to the University of Alabama in 1956 to study library science. The first black student in 125 years, Lucy was labeled "too old." Mobs tried to kill her. Many suspected she was a Communist tool. For the Voice of America, Lucy bravely broadcast an honest statement of her position: "I know very little about Communism," she declared. "I am an American. . . . In my struggle for recognition as an American student, I have approached it in the American spirit and without the help of any enemies of our country."[8] Suspended from the school for her own safety and called before the Alabama House of Representatives for an investigation of Communist affiliations, Lucy continued to maintain her Christianity and her faith in democratic principles. The inspirational words of Martin Luther King helped many blacks to stand up for their beliefs in nonviolent confrontation: "Don't ever let anyone pull you so low as to hate them," he urged. "This is not a war between the white and the Negro but a conflict between justice and injustice."[9]

Yet the roots of American racism run deep. In the 1950s television became a strong force in exposing many problems that the most idealistic Americans wanted to ignore. In 1956, when Emmett Till, a 14-year-old African American from Chicago, was brutally murdered in Mississippi for allegedly flirting with a white woman, the entire press corps was on the scene. His murderers were acquitted after the defense attorney, appealing to prejudice, asked that every Anglo-Saxon member of the jury have the "courage to free" the defendants—who then arrogantly sold the story of their crime. Thousands of people showed sympathy by visiting the black funeral home in Chicago where the young victim's mutilated body was on display. A sense of general outrage did not subside quickly.

David Halberstam, an important voice of '50s journalism, speaking about the responsibility of the American press corps, noted that the *Brown v. Board of Education* decision had made a critical moral and social difference in the way the entire country viewed civil rights. When the Till case arrived there was a national agenda on civil rights in place, defining a crucial moment for the national media. Over the next decade, the *New York Times*, the American newspaper of historical record, would lead the way in making sure the nation as a whole became aware of the need to end the racial discrimination that prevented the fulfillment of American ideals among black citizens. Many responsible journalists helped make what was invisible become visible.[10]

Still, in 1956, 19 Southern senators and 82 representatives formulated a "Southern Manifesto" declaring that the Supreme Court had abused its judicial power in the *Brown* decision. All sorts of ruses, such as "pupil placement scores" and "private" public education, were inaugurated to make sure that opportunities for blacks remained unequal. Deeply institutionalized discrimination defined the civil rights struggle. When the Civil Rights Act of 1957 was so weakened by Congress as to be useless, Martin Luther King helped create the Southern Christian Leadership Conference (SCLC) to bring about political change. Thirty-five years after the *Brown* decision it must be noted, 30% of all black children in the United States still went to public schools that were 90% nonwhite.

After World War II white middle income Americans became more aware of their own prejudices. The movie *Crossfire* (1947) confronted antisemitism head-on, while *Gentleman's Agreement* (1947), based on a popular novel, made people realize that Americans also sanctioned unofficial quotas and subtle discrimination systems to keep Jews out of establishment schools as well as clubs and resorts. Although often reluctantly, American movies turned from wartime propaganda to becoming a source of education about social problems. *Pinky* (1949) was an extraordinary film about a black woman's "passing" as white. *The Defiant Ones* (1958) used the metaphor of the chain gang to show black and white linked together, while John Ford's 1956 classic Western *The Searchers* looked at racist attitudes toward Native Americans with new complexity. Edna Ferber's huge novel about Texas, *Giant* (converted into a box office success in 1956) also dealt with prejudice against Mexicans in its Texas panorama. A distinguished drama, Carson McCullers' prize-winning *Member of the Wedding*, turned into a movie in 1953, made audiences consider how deeply black and white lives were intertwined. Such films also offered young people a chance to see themselves involved in social conflicts.

In May 1959, Irene Dobbs Jackson, sister to the distinguished Metropolitan Opera diva Mattiwilda Dobbs, offered to make herself a test case for getting blacks into the Carnegie Library in Atlanta. The trustees agreed at once to give this remarkable woman, who had six children and a doctorate from the University of Toulouse, a library card. From that moment on all the libraries in Atlanta were open to African Americans. An embarrassed white Atlantan wrote the local paper to acknowledge that he had never even realized that the libraries were segregated.

During the 1960s, labeled the civil rights decade, when many whites entered the South to help register black voters, some of the weaknesses of passive resistance would be revealed. But during the 1950s there was good reason to accept historian Howard Zinn's conclusion to Irene Dobbs Jackson's story: "The twentieth century may, eons from now, be viewed as the time when peaceful social change came into its own."[11] The dignity of the civil rights movement, strongly begun in the 1950s, should remain a source of American pride.

Human Rights   Although progress was slow, the 1950s was clearly a time of emerging awareness of human rights. There were nine race riots in Chicago between 1945 and 1954, but there were also moments of important social progress, like Thurgood Marshall's 1950 success in getting the Supreme Court to sanction the admission of Heman Sweatt, an African American, to the all-white University of Texas law school—where hostility finally drove him out. Balancing the scales of justice has to become a skill of the good historian as well as the good lawyer.

New Americans. Even as Americans became more involved in the "war of containment" in Korea, small changes occurred that improved the status of Asian immigrants. In 1952 the McCarran-Walter Act, designed to restrict immigration by East European Communists, finally ended the total exclusion of Asians by permitting small quotas of immigrants from East Asian countries. After World War II we reopened the gates to our allies: Chinese, Filipinos, and Asian Indians. By then it became easier to accept the 1953 Refugee Relief Act, which had a war bride section admitting wives and children outside quotas. Between 1946 and 1953, 7,000 Chinese war brides came in as American citizens, and between 1950 and 1965, 17,000 Korean spouses entered the United States. The idea of equality in education, shaped by the *Brown* decision, also had an impact on immigration policy. By 1965 the strict definition of national quotas was ended.[12]

When Hawaii and Alaska became part of the United States in 1959 celebrations burst forth. At the time few people would have considered the impact of statehood on the native races of Hawaii or on the ethnic groups of Eskimo communities in the North. Assimilation into mainstream American life was then considered a positive value.

Mexicans were crowding into the Southwest. In the two decades following World War II more Mexicans settled in the United States than in the previous 100 years. New York City began to have more Puerto Ricans than San Juan. But during this decade Hispanics were also treated with contempt. In 1953, the independent journalist I. F. Stone reported the deportation of 483,000 migrant workers, including many who were American born, in a terrible and lawness manner. Such outrages were meant to intimidate workers demanding higher wages and better conditions. Big unions seemed unconcerned. Stone—continuing the tradition of the outspoken journalist George Seldes who gave up publishing his protest pamphlet "In Fact" in 1950—had only a modest audience for the new *Weekly*, a one-man crusade for social justice.[13] But Stone's uncompromising defense of the Bill of Rights continued to stress the importance of freedom of the press in a mental climate of hostile indifference. He was fearless in reinforcing the power of dissident culture. In future decades more whites would get involved with the problems of Hispanic agricultural workers in the West. And more Latinos would become engaged in politics.

Native Americans. Native Americans, proud to have fought bravely during World War II, were in the public eye on TV during the 1950s in simple stereotyped cowboy and Indian shoot-outs. A complex classic like John Ford's *The Searchers* (1956) managed to reinforce the myth of Indian barbarism as it also exposed different levels of hostility in the obsessive hero John Wayne. Although during the Korean War Harry Truman ordered John Rice, a Winnebago soldier who had been killed in Korea, buried in Arlington Cemetery after the people of Sioux City denied his non-Caucasian body access to the local burial ground, few could point out much good about the treatment of Native Americans during this decade. Efforts to get natural resources away from Native American lands—called an "Indian takeaway" by John Collier, New Deal head of the Bureau of Indian Affairs—plagued many. As tribal holdings were terminated and divided among different groups and individuals too poor to hold onto their property, many Indians were forced to sell land. Relocated to cities, they were meant to become assimilated but often ended up beside the African Americans as poorly paid unskilled urban workers—except for the Mohawk builders of skyscrapers. Dillon S. Myers, who had been director of the internment camps for over 100,000 Japanese during the war, was made Indian Commissioner in 1950, suggesting the kind of control Eisenhower may have wanted. John Collier openly accused the Eisenhower administration of trying to "atomize and suffocate the group life of the tribes—that group life which is their vitality, motivation, and hope."[14]

Women. Although "race" had emerged from the war as a clear category, "gender" was not used in the 1950s to help women define their rights. But the experiences of American women from the end of World War II through the 1960s also reflected the underlying social upheaval. The high marriage and birth rates and the low divorce rate intertwined naturally with the "feminine mystique"—the idea that woman's fulfillment was in the home and nowhere else. Yet women were already questioning domesticity as a consuming and permanent role. Like many blacks they needed to make invisible selves visible and valued. They came slowly to realize that sex discrimination could be subtle as well as overt—even as they played the roles of wife and mother that society demanded. Most women were content for a time to make the most of these old-fashioned roles. Yet although many middle class 1950s women are identified in women's magazines with suburban homes and large families, the truth is that many others kept working after the war—not just to help pay the mortgage, but because work outside the home was satisfying. In 1955 that stalwart feminist, Eleanor Roosevelt, published an article entitled "What Are the Motives for a Woman Working When

She Does Not Have to for Income?" Self-esteem was Roosevelt's con-clusion. She made readers recognize women's right to fulfill all their potential.

In *Personal Politics: The Roots of Women's Liberation in the Civil Rights Movement and the New Left*, a documentary book on radicalism, Sara Evans asserts that throughout the 1950s "women from middle income families entered the labor force faster than any other group in the pop-ulation."[15] By 1956, 70% of all families in the $7,000–$15,000 annual in-come range had two wage earners. Although women usually took the duller jobs offered them and suppressed the higher aspirations provided by better educations, they often saw such jobs as temporary. Instead of regarding themselves as "victims"—as later feminists often saw them—they just put their lives on hold while their children were very young. By no means did they accept domesticity, as their mothers might have, as their only choice—any more than they believed the television com-mercials that made the dirt "ring around the collar" the reason for their husbands' failures. American women have never been as gullible as Madison Avenue advertising writers—or historians—see them. Tupper-ware may have made life in the kitchen easier for some women, but it also made jobs for the many who sold it.

Nor were women obsessed with the appliances that Ronald Reagan and Miss America displayed on television. Large refrigerators with freez-ers allowed people to shop less often. And middle class women with families made good use of washing machines without wringers and dry-ers that did away with clotheslines. Some still liked the smell of clothes dried in the wind, and others enjoyed baking as a kind of escape therapy. Prepared foods like soup mixes and cake mixes—and even instant cof-fee—entered the kitchen slowly. Whether most housewives felt guilty—as supposed—for making their chores simpler is worth examining in oral history interviews. When labor-saving devices like dishwashers ap-peared, homemakers of childbearing age often took advantage of freed time to explore new opportunities to do volunteer work.

In the 1950s, to be sure, women were denied access, as blacks were, to equal professional education and equal salaries. They were not readily welcomed back into competition with men. Betty Friedan, a Smith Col-lege summa cum laude graduate, with her famous book on domesticity, *The Feminine Mystique* in press, was labeled "too old" at age 42 to master statistics for a Ph.D. at Columbia. Most medical schools at the time had quotas to admit fewer than 5% women. And a number of prestigious law schools, and some graduate schools, often denied all women admis-sion, asserting that they would be taking places away from more serious men. Too many women grew depressed at being locked out of profes-sions and high paying jobs. Psychotherapy flourished. But other women found ways to escape confinement. As Friedan discovered even as she decried "the feminine mystique," the glorification of homemaking in the three million copy book based on 1957 questionnaires sent to Smith College graduates, American women often became ingenious at creating lives that enabled them to be useful citizens outside the home. In the '50s, however, women put family needs first. Although women's struggles to redefine their roles were far from easy, they came through the 1950s with the same egalitarian sense of possibilities African Americans experienced.

A belief in Cold War victimization that shed light on some women's lives at this time by no means captured the energies of vast numbers who defined themselves beyond the narrow confines of one decade. Historians need to adapt interpretive time frames to women's biological roles in order to value women's achievements more precisely as opposed to those of men. The magazine articles usually cited to describe women's lives during the 1950s suggest little about their vision of society in any depth, or about their future goals for themselves. And such articles do little to assert the significance of the many important older women on the scene. The same magazines that celebrated domesticity offered lively journalism by Martha Gellhorn, Dorothy Thompson, Marguerite Higgins, and others. Betty Friedan suggested at one point that mothers be given the G.I. Bill to compensate for childrearing years, as men were rewarded for a different kind of social service. Of those women who had been in the armed forces, fewer than 3% were able to take advantage of the G.I. Bill.

A good number of women did not envy the lives of middle income "organization men," advertising executives in gray flannel suits, or even well-paid factory workers creating appliances for the new world of consumers. At a time when there was no organized child care, few families had relatives nearby to help with babysitting, and the jobs offered women—still advertised in separate sections of the newspapers—were dull and ill-paid, many women willingly stayed home with their children if they could afford to. At that time it was still possible for many families to live on just one income. People seemed to have fewer needs.

Even if they did not see themselves fighting the Cold War in the kitchen, many middle class college grads seemed to take Adlai Stevenson seriously when he urged the young women at Smith College's 1955 graduation to value the role of nurturing the "uniqueness of each individual human being."[16] Yet new patterns of domesticity were emerging more deeply connected with the human rights of the nurturers. When Dr. Benjamin Spock rewrote his bestseller *Baby and Child Care* (originally published in 1945) for the third time, it was to eliminate sexist biases that perpetuate discrimination against girls and women. Spock acknowledged that his use of the male pronoun and his early childhood gender differentiation might well begin "the discriminatory sex stereotyping that ends in women so often getting the humdrum, subordinate, poorly paid jobs in most industries and professions; and being treated as the second-class sex."[17]

In 1957, when Betty Friedan read the responses to questionnaires sent to her college classmates as the basis of her research on what was happening to women, she discovered a deep restlessness among the respondents. But she also found an attitude different from earlier decades that saw having children as limiting access to other roles. The "either/or"—children or career—dilemma that had characterized women's lot before the war was changing. Although Friedan herself acknowledged never having known a woman who had both a good job and children, the 1950s brought about a decided change. All the women she interviewed were planning ahead for freedom to be themselves. Postwar actuarial statistics revealed that women lived longer than men and would often have as many as 40 years ahead to lead creative lives after their children left the nest. Most women entering the work force in the 1950s were older. The number of women over age 35 in the labor force had jumped from from 8.5 million in 1947 to almost 13 million by 1956. As the median age of women workers rose to 41, the proportion of married women who worked outside the home also doubled between 1940 and 1960.[18]

Powerful older women—often shaped in other decades but nevertheless still strong in the 1950s—helped women recognize the variety of things they could do. Foremost among them of course, was Eleanor Roosevelt, who wrote her newspaper column three times a week and wrote a monthly query page for the *Ladies' Home Journal* during the '50s. She also worked tirelessly for the American acceptance of the United Nations and then for the ratification of the Universal Declaration of Human Rights. Roosevelt felt her own power when Harry Truman made her U.S. Ambassador to the UN. Other older women frequently appeared in the news demonstrating a vitality rarely noticed in the past. The anthropologist Margaret Mead wrote in women's magazines to popularize her knowledge of how different cultures dealt with the problems of child-rearing, marriage, and work. Mead believed that parenting could be shared, and she was also an early celebrant of the vigor of postmenopausal women. Margaret Chase Smith, the Republican senator from Maine who had had the courage to challenge Joseph McCarthy, was the first woman put in nomination for the Republican vice-presidency in 1952. Grandma Moses astonished everyone with the vast quantity of skillful paintings she produced after taking up genre painting at the age of 67. Gifted photographers and artists associated with the 1920s and 1930, among them Berenice Abbott, Dorothea Lange, and Georgia O'Keeffe, were still on the scene creating remarkable work that had nothing to do with age or gender, even as Martha Graham continued to choreograph and dance in her own productions. Writers like Edna Ferber and Katherine Anne Porter, and Elizabeth Bishop, associated with earlier periods, were still publishing distinguished work. Movie stars like Katharine Hepburn, Bette Davis, and even Gloria Swanson would make some of the best films of the 1950s, suggesting what the movie critic Molly Haskell wisely labeled "the freedom to start over"—the woman's version of the American Dream.[19]

American society has been slow to celebrate the achievements of older women. Historians of the 1950s also contributed to their invisibility by simply ignoring the astonishing range of their accomplishments. Listing the women over age 40 who contributed to the social, intellectual, political, and artistic richness of the 1950s would fill a book or more than one web page. Historians, trained to evaluate women only in terms of their childbearing years, often did not recognize that older women remained strong individualists during this age of conformity. And older women continued to provide inspiration for the many young women locked into domesticity at the time. Grandma Moses produced 25 paintings after her 100th birthday. The California photographer Imogen Cunningham published a volume of tributes to people who, like her, lived and worked beyond the age of 90.[20]

"Never Underestimate the Power of a Woman" was the slogan of the *Ladies' Home Journal* at a time when women had almost no power in the formal institutions that shaped American life. Yet the over 5 million women who subscribed to the *Journal* in 1955 would surely not have considered the idea ironic. They struggled to define exactly what their power could be.

When Betty Friedan's research revealed the uneasiness many women felt as "invisible servants," she also discovered ways many managed to assert themselves in volunteer activities. The 1950s was labeled a great period of voluntarism. The dean of the New York School of Social Work remarked in 1951 that if all the volunteers were to go on strike, the country would degenerate into bureaucratic dictatorships.[21] Friedan herself was surprised to record the activities of the homebound:

> They set up cooperative nursery schools, teenage canteens, and libraries; . . . they innovated new educational programs that finally became part of the curriculum. One was personally instrumental in getting 13,000 signatures for a popular referendum to get politics out of the school system . . . one got white children to attend a *de facto* segregated school in the North. One pushed an appropriation for mental health clinics through a state legislature. One set up museum art programs for school children, etc., etc., etc.[22]

Such activities did much to improve the quality of American life. Women were proud at the time to bring more complex values to the world of

Cold War suspicion and military-industrial goals Eisenhower would warn about. The women who returned Friedan's questionnaires also read a great deal, kept up with current affairs, and took the trouble to vote. They did not regard their childrearing years as useless.

During the 1950s the League of Women Voters, a nonpartisan political study group, gave much attention to making government more efficient. Membership in the League expanded by 44%. Extending over 48 states in 1,050 local groups, at the time the League had 128,000 members committed to advancing human life and thought. The next generation of feminists would find their caution too genteel, but there can be little doubt that the League provided valuable training for women who wanted to enter the real political world. Ella Grasso (elected Democratic governor of Connecticut in 1978) was a member of the League, and so was Shirley Chisholm, an African American from Brooklyn who was elected to Congress and later also ran for president. A League member who later became the director of the Boston YWCA praised the organization for its humanistic goals and concern for freedom. "Society must somehow be affected," Lucia Bequaert declared.[23]

Many women gave huge quantities of time to causes that influenced the lives of others for the better. Dorothy Day's Catholic Worker Mission in New York's Bowery fed hundreds of homeless as she preached the "love that comes from community" and made an example of herself as a pacifist in the world of Cold War hostility.

Helping the brave black women and men risking their lives to integrate facilities and register voters in the South were also brave white women like Dorothy Rogers Tilly and Emily Foster Durr. The Fellowship of the Concerned, a network of volunteers from twelve Southern religious groups, worked tirelessly for "equal justice under law." Bombing threats from the Ku Klux Klan—another vicious reality of this decade—did not prevent the group from gaining an additional 4,000 members. History texts neglect these modest women who worked efficiently behind the scenes for social change. But their volunteer work was neither insignificant nor trivial. Indeed, they added a moral dimension to American life many believed to be missing.

One woman historians usually mention—emblematic of male power—was Oveta Culp Hobby, former head of the Women's Army Corps, made the first Secretary of Health, Education and Welfare by Eisenhower. Hobby performed a service for women by allowing the pregnant to be "released" from the army, rather than discharged, in order to protect their future careers. But she had no commitment to programs for women and children and even wanted to charge the poor for the newly discovered polio vaccine.

By way of contrast, during the New Deal and the postwar years Eleanor Roosevelt stood out as an extraordinary political figure because of her ability to understand and identify the needs and feelings of people on the margins of society. At this time, when so many Americans were truly afraid of Communism, Eleanor Roosevelt extended the range of her compassion to women and children all over the world. She seemed to embody what historian Mary Beard had called "Woman as Force in History" in her 1946 book of that name. Beard argued that women's socialization allowed them to prioritize human concerns with an influence that represented a different kind of power. The establishment of the United Nations Organization provided Roosevelt with a broader forum for the egalitarian values she had championed throughout her life.

In a radio interview with Malcolm Muggeridge in 1955 Eleanor Roosevelt declared she had come to believe that the women's vote had made a difference in the interests of men. Before women got the vote (1920), she insisted, "far fewer men . . . were concerned about social reforms."[24] She believed that improved working conditions and benefits to children resulted from women's political potential. Yet American women have often imitated Eleanor Roosevelt by playing behind-the-scenes roles rather than by competing with men for direct political power.

During the 1950s, when there was no official commitment to expanding women's rights, there were still a few powerful New Deal women on the scene.[25] And Eisenhower actually provided 26 high level positions in his government as a gesture of gratitude for the women who helped elect him. The *Ladies' Home Journal* kept urging its readers to play a bigger role in local politics in spite of all the difficulties involved in balancing child care with other activities. People made much of Mayor Dorothy Davis of Washington, Virginia, a mother of three who organized an all-female city council in 1955. But in this decade, politics seemed better suited to older, more experienced women. Frances Bolton of New Jersey ran for Congress at age 55 and went on to serve 28 years. Millicent Fenwick—inspiration for the comic strip *Doonesbury*'s Lacey—was elected to the board of education in New Jersey in 1950 and would go on to be elected to Congress from New Jersey at the age of 64.

Once experienced as a labor writer, Betty Friedan became allied with voluntarism when she limited her freelance journalism and her dreams about getting a Ph.D. in sociology to work on analyzing the collection of questionnaires she had gathered for Smith College. She clearly realized that women needed more institutional support to achieve practical goals. A few of the women she interviewed for her expanded book were deeply committed to long-range goals: some worked part-time in fields they wanted to enter; others found secretarial jobs that could lead to promotion; and some ran businesses out of their homes. Friedan called them women of the Fourth Dimension, seeing their lives shaped by time. They were all basically working alone, planning for the future as they confronted a culture that did not encourage women to make commitment to work as important as family. By the 1960s, like many other women, Friedan would realize that it was essential to foster solidarity to bring about social change. To make invisible women visible required political organization and numbers.

When she later became a founding member of the National Organization for Women (NOW), Betty Friedan spoke to the needs she had discovered in the lives of 1950s women. The statement of purpose of NOW proclaimed, "Above all, we reject the assumption that women's problems are the unique responsibility of each individual woman rather than a basic social dilemma which society must solve."[26]

Bringing about social change is never fast or easy. The self-consciousness of the 1950s became essential preparation for the decades of action ahead. Consensus and containment describe much of the post-war era, but history demands that more serious attention be given those—like Betty Friedan—who also worked hard to define and improve the moral quality of American life.

Education   Although larger numbers of women had begun to go to college in the 1950s, only 37% stayed to graduate, and the number going on for higher degrees was smaller than in the 1920s and 1930s. Yet women glad to sacrifice careers for family at the beginning of the decade were eager to get back to school by its end, even though most institutions would not let women with families attend college part-time. One brilliant Wellesley dropout, divorced with four children, was told that to return to college she would have to attend full time and take gym.

Betty Friedan praised the few enlightened institutions that modified their degree programs to accommodate women with children. In 1955 the New School for Social Research set up a human relations workshop to help the homebound pursue broader goals. In 1959 the University of Minnesota set up a revolutionary program to encourage older women to get degrees. By 1962, when Sarah Lawrence College announced a grant to help mature women finish their education or get graduate degrees, the number of eager inquirers put their switchboards out of commission. Most adult education programs during this decade gave no credits and led nowhere—except in fields like nursing and teaching, where there were labor shortages. In these fields a few programs also met women's needs by having classes during the daytime when children were in school. And some schools tried to make good use of women who already had bachelor's degrees by setting up masters of arts in teaching programs.

"Unless we get more women equal education we can't get them equal pay and opportunity," declared the president of the Federation of Business and Professional Women in the *New York Times* in 1952, anticipating the idea of equal rights embodied in the *Brown* decision in 1954.[27] Keeping women undereducated in the '50s by maintaining quotas for the young and denying older women—often in their early 30's—admission to professional schools was also a way to keep establishment power in the hands of white men. When the Educational Testing Service at Princeton went on to design college level equivalency exams to enable women students who had followed their husbands' jobs to write off credits such exams were often not accepted by schools that relied heavily on Scholastic Aptitude Tests—produced by the same company—to evaluate the young. No one wanted to make it easy for women who were also mothers to do anything more with their lives. In 1956 the *New York Times* described a mother and daughter who were both getting degrees at Rutgers. The mother—also still taking care of her house and family and commuting—was "permitted" to take six courses to catch up. Another mother commuting from New Jersey to Brooklyn College three nights a week so she would not have to leave her children alone managed to graduate Phi Beta Kappa. The *Times'* tone of amazement completed this story with her future plans for law school. Such "superwomen" stories made people pay attention to general concerns about what was happening to other bright women with complicated lives.

Perhaps just as embarrassing as the quota systems of the 1950s that kept women out of competition with men for professional jobs was what was called "sex-directed," gender-focused education. Mills College in California, trying to compensate for the indifference of Eastern establishment schools to talented women faculty, defined gender education that would cater to women's needs. Unfortunately, like the high schools that fostered functional education, these colleges often ended up emphasizing "life adjustment" rather than intellectual achievement. Categories of experts—sociologists, psychologists, and psychoanalysts—banded together to persuade women to believe they were better off in the role of housewife. As noted sociologist Talcott Parsons described the American woman, her life was as "her husband's wife, the mother of his children."[28] At a time when the Cold War made Americans critical of the "progressive" education designed to foster good judgment and problem solving skills rather than rote learning, women were urged back into functional feminine molds, not developed as critical thinkers.

Although progressive education, expressing the ideas of the great pragmatic philosopher John Dewey, reached back to the 1930s, it became another target for the paranoia of the 1950s. All sorts of local groups thought such education responsible for Marxist ideas and juvenile delinquency. In 1951 in Pasadena Willard E. Goslin, a creative progressive educator and president of the American Association of School Administrators, was pressured by organized right-wing groups to resign. In the same year the American Association of School Administrators chose to devote its entire annual meeting to examining widespread assaults on public education. Anxiety produced bestsellers like *Educational Wastelands* (1953) and *Why Johnny Can't Read and What You Can Do About It* (1955). But few new programs emerged. Successful schools long influenced by progressive ideas continued to produce well-trained, creative students. And Dr. Spock, whose childrearing classic was in almost every home with children during this era, did not hesitate to label his book a "common sense" guide to child care. "Trust yourself," he urged new mothers.

In 1957, when the Russians sent two *Sputnik* satellites to circle the globe, a huge outcry went up for more serious education that would improve standards for everyone. Americans confronted the reality that in Russia 69% of the medical students and 39% of the engineers were women, while in the United States in 1956 three out of five women in coeducational colleges took secretarial, home economics, nursing, or education courses. Only 20% of all science and math majors in American colleges were women. A 1957 book, *Signs for the Future*, prepared by a varied group of educators, urged greater flexibility in admissions and scheduling, and use of educational television, adult education, and refresher courses to enable more women with children to come back into a more high powered career stream. The Cold War concern that we had fallen behind the Russians inspired Congress to pass the National Defense Education Act in 1958, allotting over $900 million for scholarships and loans to encourage the study of science, math, and foreign languages. This act also provided 12,000 counselors for secondary schools. Although the pendulum seemed to be swinging back to conservative education, with the subsequent creation of a huge number of community colleges (one every two weeks by the mid-1960s), many child-free women as well as young men were given the chance to begin entirely different lives. The flexibility of our institutions was helping us turn away from what Betty Friedan had labeled a culture that educates its most capable women to make careers out of raising their families. Again the government was helping the individual find human fulfillment.

The importance of the G.I. Bill in enriching institutions and changing old-fashioned educational environments cannot be overestimated. Not only did the army of new learners not diminish academic standards, as feared, but the presence on campus of older students able to make mature judgments also worked to erode sophomoric customs like fraternity hazings and wearing freshman beanies. Older students were presumed to be wiser. The idea that college discipline replaced the parent—strong before World War II—began to erode by the '60s, when parietal rules and dress codes became quaint memories. Who could even imagine that women at Radcliffe College, going to classes at Harvard, were not permitted to wear pants on the streets of Cambridge, Massachusetts? Wellesley students had to leave their dormitory doors open while entertaining men. Because so many men everywhere also returned to college with wives, married women were slowly tolerated as part of the learning environment.

No greater revolution took place during the 1950s than the shift in attitudes toward sex. By the end of the decade all institutional **Sex** control over individual sexual behavior seemed to melt away. Beginning with the two gigantic Kinsey reports describing *Sexual Behavior in the Human Male* in 1948 and *Sexual Behavior in the Human Female* in 1953, and ending with the government's approval of the birth control pill in 1960, the nation's mores were turned upside-down within two decades. But it was still not possible to get a legal abortion during the '50s, when Massachusetts and Connecticut even made prescriptions mandatory for birth control devices.

Alfred Kinsey, a distinguished entomologist from the University of Indiana, identified his sudden interest in sexuality with his discovery of playwright Tennessee Williams' fascination with façades. Kinsey had come to appreciate the contrasts Williams presented between "social front and reality." His research into sex patterns, funded by the Rockefeller Foundation, his books marketed by Saunders, a respected publisher of medical texts, Kinsey represented himself as a crew-cut, bow-tied, middle-American square. He saw himself as a serious if somewhat quirky professor who remained stunned when his scientific sexual surveys became bestsellers.

What Kinsey revealed, as David Halberstam neatly summarized in his survey of the 1950s, was that "there was more extramarital sex on the part of both men and women than Americans wanted to admit," and that "premarital sex tended to produce better marriages."[29] Kinsey documented that masturbation also was a normal part of sexual development. Perhaps his most controversial discovery was that more homosexuality existed in the United States than Americans wanted to acknowledge. Scholars continued to question the sources of his homosexual statistics because he interviewed prison populations.

People were outraged at Kinsey's refusal to make moral judgments. His materials were delivered as pure statistics without emotional or moral contexts. Yet few scientists were willing to come forward to support his work. And although he poured his book royalties back into the Institute for Sex Research of Indiana University, his funding grew insufficient when the Rockefeller Foundation withdrew support after the book on female sexuality received hostile reviews. Following the spirit of the times, the Rockefellers shifted their money to Union Theological Seminary. On the defensive from then on, Kinsey saw his health deteriorate. In 1956, at the relatively young age of 62, he died.[30]

Even if the age of the "feminine mystique" was not any more eager to sanction women's sexuality than their need for serious education, all such social debate was liberating for women. Institutions began to change. By the end of the decade *Playboy* magazine was thriving, and the mail censorship of classics like Henry Miller's *Tropic of Cancer* and *Tropic of Capricorn* and D. H. Lawrence's *Lady Chatterley's Lover*, which contained sexually explicit material, would be a memory. Admitted to the United States after protests, Vladimir Nabokov's distinguished novel *Lolita* about an adolescent and her older lover, published in 1958, sold more than 3 million copies. And the big-time bestseller of the '50s, Grace Metalious' *Peyton Place*, about secret lives in a quaint New Hampshire town—far from Thornton Wilder's Grover's Corners—sold 6 million copies in 1958. It would go on to become the bestselling novel ever, surpassing 10 million copies.[31]

Even Hollywood modified its restrictive sexual codes by the end of the decade in which *Baby Doll*, a 1956 Tennessee Williams story about a child bride, had been condemned by the Legion of Decency as an evil film. Compassion for alienated, vulnerable heroes like the young men James Dean and Sal Mineo played in *Rebel Without a Cause* was as real as the ongoing cult of the cowboy John Wayne. The Mattachine Society appeared in California in 1951 to promote better understanding of homosexuality as well as to prevent individual harassment. One of the most popular films of the decade, *Some Like It Hot* (1959), featured Jack Lemmon and Tony Curtis in drag.

With the Food and Drug Administration's marketing approval of the birth control pill in 1960, Claire Boothe Luce declared modern woman became as "free as a man is free to dispose of her own body."[32]

Family Until the mid-1960s the early marriage boom and the baby boom continued to define preferences in American life. As long as women were willing to subordinate their ambitions to their husbands', marriages remained stable. But the family did not fully absorb most women's energies for long. The proportion of married women in the work force rose from 36% in 1940 to 52% in 1950. At the same time, the divorce rate went back to its steady rise. By the mid-1960s the American family—always more complex than portrayed by media myths like *Leave It to Beaver* or *Ozzie and Harriet*—found different representations in movies. *East of Eden* (1955) became James Dean's best performance as a misunderstood son, and *All that Heaven Allows* (1956) described an older woman who shocked people by loving her gardener. American women, who were now living longer, imagined richer lives outside their families. A useful book on changing images of women in the movies during the 1950s, *On the Verge of Revolt*, suggested that even in the world of media myths a new awareness was taking shape.[33] The seed of rebellion described in Molly Haskell's critical classic *From Reverence to Rape: The Treatment of Women in the Movies* (1973) germinated in the kitchen.

Other notable institutional changes took place within the religious establishments of the decade. Americans felt the need to protect their children from "Godless Communism." It **Religion** was a time when atheists and agnostics were fired from jobs with the same gusto that earlier inspired anti-Communists to take work away from liberals. An American skeptic, Elinor Goulding Smith, published an article in *Harper's* magazine in 1956 titled "Won't Somebody Tolerate Me?" Smith could not believe the extent of hostility she experienced as an agnostic in the Cold War. She felt it her duty to champion respect for diversity of opinion.

The rise in church membership during the '50s astonished those who identified America with the Enlightenment spirit that defined the founding fathers. During his administration Eisenhower even had himself baptized in the White House. In 1954, inspired by Eisenhower's minister, Congress added the words "under God" to the Pledge of Allegiance to the United States. And, beginning in 1955, "In God We Trust" was engraved on all U.S. currency. Statistics revealed that while only 49% of Americans were church members in 1940, just before the war, membership rose to 55% in 1950. And by 1959 an all-time high of 69% of polled Americans acknowledged church membership. The generalized breakdown was 66% Protestant, 26% Catholic, and 3% Jewish.[34] No other Western culture was so religious.

In 1952 the Revised Standard Version of the Bible sold 26.5 million copies in its first year of publication. For two years in a row—1953 and 1954—it was on the bestseller list. Unlike other periods in American history, the religious enthusiasm of the 1950s involved every class and economic division. A 1954 survey revealed that four out of five people would not vote for an atheist for president, and 60% would not permit a book by an atheist to remain in a public library.[35]

Will Herberg's popular book *Protestant—Catholic—Jew: An Essay in American Religious Sociology (1955–1960)* characterized the spiritual mood as "religiousness without religion."[36] He saw the new affiliations not as a way of reorienting life to God but as a way to sociability. Churches provided social communities for a nation of uprooted individuals. What might be more disillusioning about the 1950s was the degree to which American religion—committed to fighting the materialism of Communism—was also involved with marketing itself. In 1957 Billy Graham, an enormously popular evangelical preacher, reported a $1.3 million budget, a tremendous amount for the time.

Television provided a new arena for evangelism. Billy Graham, Fulton J. Sheen, and Oral Roberts became important leaders in the religious Cold War. Norman Vincent Peale sold over 2 million copies of *The Power of Positive Thinking* by 1955; Joshua Loth Liebman's *Peace of Mind* found thousands of readers beyond his own Jewish community. In California a drive-in church—"pews from Detroit"—matched the excitement of drive-in movies and fast foods. A dial-a-prayer service offered solace for those who could not get out. Religious movies like *The Robe* (1953), *The Silver Chalice* (1954), and *The Ten Commandments* (1956) dramatized Christian struggles in terms easily translated into Cold War images. Spiritual biographies like Catherine Marshall's *A Man Called Peter* (1952) and Jim Bishop's *The Day Christ Died* (1957) provided personal inspiration.

J. Edgar Hoover's minister preached that Communism was really just secularism on the march. Detective fiction writer Mickey Spillane quit writing corpse-strewn bestsellers to become a Jehovah's Witness. The well-endowed actress Jane Russell called the Lord a "livin' doll," Elvis Presley offered up a special Christmas record, and the notorious gangster Mickey Cohen joined Billy Graham's crusade for Christ. Commitment did not have to be associated with any special religion. Nor did religious choice necessarily involve social action. The focus, as in all else during the decade, was on the individual family—the personal, not the civic. A popular slogan claimed that "the family that prays together stays together." Both Billy Graham and Norman Vincent Peale discouraged social activism, too readily identified with socialism.

Socially committed groups like the Catholic Worker people and the Quakers called attention to the needy. And the black civil rights workers depended on African American churches and ministers as much as on lawyers to back their efforts toward change. For many, peace of soul and mind still centered around ideas of patriotism and community.

In the Levittown Herbert Gans described (see Chapter 4), thirteen houses of worship—including two synagogues—sprang up during the first two years. Controlled by outside organizations, these religious establishments met local social needs by providing nursery schools and couples' clubs and associations to bring about political changes. Gans saw no social hierarchies among churches. A Levittowner described the most common attitude: "Religious differences aren't important as long as everyone practices what he preaches."[37]

Memories of the Depression and World War II, nightmares of the Holocaust and of the H-bomb made the turn to religion often more than just social or material. The great power of the African American churches during this decade demands ongoing respect and study. In his recent detailed work on the civil rights movement, *The Children*, David Halberstam pays special homage to James Lawson, admitted to Vanderbilt Divinity School in 1959 in a token gesture. Along with John Lewis and James Bevel, Lawson helped connect religious faith—as Martin Luther King had—with social justice. He taught his followers to move beyond the passivity of their elders, yet to remain nonviolent as they became the next decade's "freedom riders." These black preachers spread their deep religion among people risking their lives for a better society, not for easy salvation. But they too were often invisible at the time.

Women denied access to power through careers and institutions also began to play a greater policy-making role in organized religion. Their great enrollment as church members demanded attention on other levels. As early as 1951 the first woman Methodist minister was ordained. And women deacons were encouraged by Southern Presbyterians to help in the fight against Communism. Mary Lyman, ordained a Congregational minister in 1950, became the first woman to hold a faculty chair at Union Theological Seminary. Before her retirement as dean of women students in 1955 she played a vigorous advocacy role for other women in the ministry. She also wrote about women's concerns for international accords through the World Council of Churches in a 1956 book, *Into All the World*. In 1957 New York City boasted its first woman Presbyterian minister, and also its first Episcopalian "vestry person."

On the West Coast, Georgia Harkness of the Pacific School of Religion published three books during the 1950s emphasizing Christianity's need to create greater meaning for the people in the pews, a belief designed to make better use of women's social gifts. Edith Lowry—an example of such outreach as a Protestant minister to migrant workers—in 1950 took over the directorship of the Home Mission for the National Council of Churches. "Golden Rule Christians" emerged in many church organizations to guide members toward ethics—lived religion—in everyday life.[38]

If Billy Graham did not suggest that his converts get involved in social action, a survey of the times would nevertheless reveal that many people of conscience continued to involve themselves in activities guided toward social change. Both the National Committee for a Sane Nuclear Policy and Women Strike for Peace were social action groups founded in the 1950s, the Age of Voluntarism. The "good life" for many had to be more than the turn away from acquisition that Helen and Scott Nearing described in the 1954 how-to-do-it book *Living the Good Life*. Having survived the 1930s as self-sufficient farmers and intellectuals, the Nearings became celebrated examples of back-to-earth simplicity in the age of affluence. The next decade would carry over many of their basic ideas to communal living.

Ethical Life

Perhaps the most philosophical theologian of the period, Reinhold Niebuhr, kept trying to help Americans examine their conventionally respectable lives. Niebuhr showed, as Stephen Whitfield asserts, "how to be a political progressive without shallowness, an anti-Communist moralist without fanaticism, and a religious believer without delusion."[39] That the '50s valued Niebuhr's voice in the midst of the shouts of demagogues remains a tribute to the basic common sense of the good people who survived this decade of extremes with dignity.

NOTES

1. Charles Dickens, *A Tale of Two Cities* (1893), available in many editions.
2. See *New York Times,* December 28, 1997.
3. Ralph Ellison, *Invisible Man* (New York: Random House, 1952), 508.
4. See Taylor Branch, *Parting the Waters: America in the King Years, 1953–63* (New York: Simon and Schuster, 1988), 128–159.
5. Quoted in William Leuchtenburg, *A Troubled Feast: American Society since 1945* (Boston, Little, Brown; updated edition, 1983), 98.
6. Quoted in David Halberstam, *The Fifties* (New York: Fawcett Columbine, 1993), 548.
7. Quoted in *New York Times,* September 21, 1997.
8. Quoted in *New York Times,* March 8, 1956.
9. Quoted in *New York Times,* February 25, 1956.
10. See Halberstam, *The Fifties,* 430–455.
11. Howard Zinn, "A Case of Quiet Social Change," *Crisis,* October 1959, 475.
12. See Ronald Takaki, *Strangers from a Different Shore: A History of Asian Americans* (Boston: Little, Brown, 1989), chap. 10.
13. Douglas T. Miller and Marion Nowak, *The Fifties: The Way We Really Were* (Garden City, NY: Doubleday, 1975), 203.
14. Quoted in ibid., 206.
15. Sara Evans, *Personal Politics: The Roots of Women's Liberation in the Civil Rights Movement and the New Left* (New York: Vintage Books, 1980), 8.
16. Adlai Stevenson, "Commencement Address," Smith College, June 1955.
17. Benjamin Spock, *Baby and Child Care* (New York: Pocket Books, 1976), xix.
18. See Eugenia Kaledin, *Mothers and More: American Women in the 1950s* (Boston: Twayne, 1984), 64–65.
19. Molly Haskell, *From Reverence to Rape: The Treatment of Women in the Movies* (Baltimore: Penguin, 1973), 276.
20. See Kaledin, *Mothers and More,* index entry "New Old Women," 260.
21. Ibid., 32.
22. Betty Friedan, *The Feminine Mystique* (1963; reprint, New York: Dell, 1974), 346.
23. Quoted in Kaledin, *Mothers and More,* 33–34.
24. Quoted in ibid., 89.
25. See Susan Ware, *Beyond Suffrage: Women in the New Deal* (Cambridge, MA: Harvard University Press, 1981).
26. Quoted in Betty Friedan, *It Changed My Life: Writings on the Women's Movement* (New York: Dell, 1977), 128.
27. Quoted in *New York Times,* June 26, 1952.
28. Talcott Parsons, "Age and Sex in the Social Structure of the United States," in *Essays in Sociological Theory* (Glencoe, IL: Free Press, 1949), 223.
29. Halberstam, *The Fifties,* 277, 281.
30. Ibid., 281.
31. James T. Patterson, *Grand Expectations: The United States, 1945–1974* (New York: Oxford University Press, 1996), 359–360.
32. Quoted in ibid., 360.

33. Brandon French, *On the Verge of Revolt: Women in American Films of the Fifties* (New York: Frederick Unger, 1978).

34. Patterson, *Grand Expectations*, 328–329.

35. Stephen J. Whitfield, *The Culture of the Cold War* (Baltimore: Johns Hopkins University Press, 1991), 84; chap. 4, passim.

36. Quoted in Kaledin, *Mothers and More*, 13.

37. Herbert J. Gans, *The Levittowners: Ways of Life and Politics in a New Suburban Community* (New York: Vintage, 1967), 84.

38. See Nancy T. Ammerman, "Golden Rule Christianity, Lived Religion in the American Mainstream," in David D. Hall, ed., *Lived Religion in America: Toward a History of Practice* (Princeton, NJ: Princeton University Press, 1997).

39. Whitfield, *Culture of the Cold War*, 99.

8

The Cold War and the Consumer

During the 1950s school children seeking safety from an atom bomb attack learned to dive under desks at the sound of sirens. The government at that time also published pamphlets on the necessary items citizens should

Shelter from "the Bomb"

include in home fallout shelters. Some public buildings with black and yellow markers were identified as shelters for everyone. Such shelters, based more on the memory of bombing during World War II than on the reality of what an atomic bomb experience would be like, took up a fair amount of space in the daily press. Americans behaved like ostriches, debating whether to hide their heads in sand or in pebbles. One couple made a magazine drama out of spending their honeymoon in a fallout shelter; another man took pictures of the gun he was mounting at his shelter's door to keep out desperate neighbors. The Russians' possession of the H-bomb created fear all over America. People put much money and energy into saving the middle class suburban nuclear family. In California, shelters were sold at prices ranging from $13.50 for a foxhole version to $3,500 for a luxury model with phone and Geiger counter. The government led individuals to believe that they might be among the survivors if they followed simple instructions for civil defense—again modeled on obsolete World War II patterns. As late as 1961, the head of the Atomic Energy Commission, Dr. Willard Libby, insisted that in the event of nuclear war 90–95% of the population could be saved by such shelters.[1]

To imagine sharing a family shelter with others was often intolerable, as the man with the mounted gun suggested, yet the myth of community loyalty remained. One woman in California built a shelter large enough for 100 to 150 neighbors, but hers was the exception.[2] And what would the 151st person do? Although the government had designated less vulnerable public buildings as shelters, no money was set aside for loans for building new shelters. In Beaumont, California, people resolved to arm themselves against the fleeing population from a bombed-out Los Angeles area. How successful such flight would have been on the new highway escape system might be imagined in terms of traffic to the beach on any sultry day.

All these efforts amounted to meaningless gestures to deal with unconscious fears. But because the burden for financing shelters fell on individual home owners and because renters and homeless citizens would have only makeshift protection, by the end of the decade people began to realize the limits of such "protection." In fact, Willard Libby's own family shelter caved in during a brush fire. In contrast to the period immediately after Hiroshima when many scientists tried to shape a realistic public policy, this later period produced few dissenting policy makers. More imaginative minds directed their thoughts to what the world would be like after thermonuclear war. A RAND think-tank study released in the early 1960s insisted that a 3,000 megaton attack on the United States would kill 80% of the population—hardly consistent with Libby's statement, and also questionable.[3]

The Effect of the Bomb on Popular Culture

The issue of subsequent fallout once again became threatening. Such movies as *On the Beach* (1957), based on Neville Shute's novel about radioactivity in Australia after an atomic war, and *Them* (1954), a science fiction classic about giant ants coming out of a bombsite, remain among the best examples of popular culture expressing the anxiety of the moment. Science fiction flourished. Books like Walter Miller's *A Canticle for Leibowitz* (1959) and Harvey Wheeler's *Fail-Safe* (1962) and even Kurt Vonnegut's *Cat's Cradle* (1962) also demonstrated the terrors of a world going up in flames. One unusual story, *Ladybug, Ladybug* (1963) by Frank and Eleanor Perry, described the fears of a child sent home in an air raid drill. Terrified, the little girl hides in an abandoned refrigerator and suffocates during the imaginary drill.

But by 1964 some Americans were also able to bring necessary humor to their anxieties. Stanley Kubrick's *Dr. Strangelove: Or How I learned to Stop Worrying and Love the Bomb* filled the need for laughter at the time and still remains a hilarious satire on bureaucracy. Tom Lehrer, mathematician and satirical songwriter, sang about a nuclear cowboy roaming Southwest test sites in lead BVDs. *Mad* magazine made fun of future generations with many sets of arms. Although by 1953 the New American Library had sold 17 million copies of Mickey Spillane's first six novels, in which heroes got their kicks from killing "Commies," the growing field of science fiction focused on unconscious fears rather than on violent realism. The 1956 movie *Invasion of the Body Snatchers* became a classic of cultural paranoia that would be made once again in the 1970s, suggesting how difficult it is to confine general apprehension in time.

Two television sci-fi series, *The Outer Limits* and *Twilight Zone*, mirrored deep anxieties and explored the uncomfortable psychological effects of mistrust. In 1961 Rod Serling, one of the best writers to emerge in the early years of television, produced a *Twilight Zone* story called "The Shelter" about a family that barricades itself and refuses to admit others when the sirens go off. The story describes how those locked out turn on each other to become a destructive mob. When the all-clear sounds everyone realizes that their once tranquil community has been destroyed as surely as if the bomb had fallen.[4]

In 1957 the National Committee for a Sane Nuclear Policy was founded with the support of the decade's most famous pediatrician, Dr. Spock. An advertisement for the group with the caption "Dr Spock is worried" showed Spock looking at **Political Reactions** a small girl, presumably fearing for her future. In 1959 polls revealed that 64% of Americans considered nuclear war the nation's most pressing problem. And although a test ban treaty was signed in 1963, the issue of nuclear proliferation remained an area of continuing concern. As late as 1984 Carolyn Forché would write in *Mother Jones* magazine, "We are the poets of the nuclear age ... there is no metaphor for the end of the world and it is horrible to search for one."[5]

In 1950 in the *Bulletin of Atomic Scientists*, a former head of the American Institute of Planners asserted that the American city was doomed anyway; congestion was to be dealt with by spreading out along escape routes. In 1951 the American Institute of Architects suggested that the new shopping centers being built everywhere could be useful as evacuation centers. At the same time the clergy were expanding their roles as spiritual leaders for a post-attack period, planning mass burials and how to justify survival to the living. Cremation was out, reported *Mortuary Science* magazine, since radioactive particles would be carried off in smoke. Some people took comfort in these bizarre details as if they provided some control over their lives. In 1950 the American Medical Association magazine, *Today's Health*, saw atomic attack as a challenge to "free men with strong hearts"—typical of the '50s assumption that "men" represented all human beings. *Hospital Management* astonishingly urged the stockpiling of whiskey and sodium bicarbonate. And psychiatrists suggested that if people were forewarned, subsequent chaos could be minimized. The assistant director of the National Institute of Mental Health wanted to organize the nation into small therapy groups with trained leaders to work through fears. One Yale psychologist urged the creation of pamphlets with reassuring information on survival, suggesting the formation of segregated areas for doomed radiation victims so that they would not demoralize survivors. Instead of using their expertise to try to prevent the next war as the atomic scientists had done earlier, most of these mid-'50s professionals continued to follow the government's lead in trying to convince people that establishment policies were rational. Until John Kennedy reminded Americans that after a nuclear attack "the living would envy the dead," many public figures continued to insist that discipline and preparation would make survival possible.[6]

Perhaps the unreal attitudes of some experts connected to the military-industrial complex were what Dwight Eisenhower feared was shaping the new American economy. People were persuaded that they could not turn away from military production in a world so full of dangers. Accepting the Cold War as a way of life made a policy of permanent military mobilization central to the American economy. The portion of the federal budget given to defense went from one-third in 1950 to one-half in 1960. By then the military establishment was solidly connected with corporate, scientific, and university communities employing millions of Americans.

Eisenhower, the soldier-president—to his credit—worried about giving more power to the military. In his farewell address he looked with nostalgia to a time when the armed forces played a subordinate role in American life—before there was a permanent armaments industry. He noted that 3.5 million men and women were currently engaged in the defense establishment. Wary of the dangers of militarism, he urged the "proper meshing of the huge industrial and military machinery of defense with our peaceful methods and goals, so that security and liberty may prosper together." Connected to these changes, Ike also recognized the technological revolution demanding huge task forces of scientists in laboratories. He praised "the free university, historically the fountainhead of free ideas and scientific discovery,"[7] and warned of the double danger that knowledge might become captive either of a technological elite or of the power of federal money to define the goals of research. Americans remain concerned with these issues. Eisenhower's warning alerted analysts to new dangers. But ending government funding that creates jobs on many social levels is not easy.

Cold War fears in the 1950s were frequently more imaginary than real. Many more Americans invited each other to neighborhood barbecues than threatened each other with guns from the roofs of fallout shelters. In spite of the official publicity, most people did not rush out to buy or build fallout shelters. Many simply accepted the more commonsensical reality that nothing would work against nuclear attack. They got on with their postwar suburban lives. Civil defense subsided as consumer pleasures grew.

The same technological and production skills that fired our defense efforts were turning 1950s America into a world of new things. Consumerism made it as easy to be distracted from the Russian menace as it was to ignore the one-third of the population who remained outside of the generally flourishing economy, the "other America" Michael Harrington clearly defined in 1962.

Suburban Living and New Technology in the Home

In the years between 1950 and 1970 the suburban population more than doubled, from 36 million to 74 million. People enjoyed living in the mortgage and building subsidized communities exemplified by Levittown. In the 1950s the "typical" American lived in suburbia. Everywhere groups of people established new roots with the help of money saved during the war from higher salaries and war bonds. If people shared no past experiences with new neighbors, they could still manage to focus on the future of the children most of them had in great numbers. Community efforts to build playgrounds, libraries, schools, swimming pools, and baseball diamonds brought many families together who did not know each other before the war.

The "flight" to the suburbs remained difficult for blacks.[8] Although over a million African Americans managed to move away from the inner cities after 1950, by 1970 the suburban population still remained 95% white. Even though it was true that the American Dream of family security embodied in home ownership was more possible than ever before, it was clearly not available to everyone. A gifted journalist, Thomas Hine, described the period between 1954 and 1964 in his book *Populuxe* (1986).[9] Hines pointed out that the number of better paying jobs running or maintaining new machinery was increasing faster than the number of low paying jobs was declining. The average industrial wage for white men had doubled since pre-Depression days, allowing many working class people to see themselves as middle class. No longer made up of small proprietors, much of this new middle class, which even included service workers, was employed by large corporations. Because of the smaller number of Depression-born adults, more wealth was shared by fewer people.

When Vice President Richard Nixon challenged Soviet Premier Nikita Khrushchev at a trade fair in Russia in 1959, he did not argue that Americans had little poverty nor did he champion the civic freedoms that define American democracy. Instead he made a big issue of American consumer production for easier living. Later called the "kitchen debate" because the two men hovered about a model American kitchen set up in a model home for fair visitors, the confrontation gave Nixon a chance to bombard the Russians with statistics on American consumption. He boasted that 30 million American families owned their own homes and that 44 million families owned 56 million cars and 50 million television sets—awesome evidence, he asserted, of the success of democratic capitalism.[10] The average working man, Nixon asserted, could easily buy the split-level house on display. He noted also that women bought an average of nine dresses and suits and fourteen pairs of shoes a year, trivial statistics that made Khrushchev furiously retort that Americans were just interested in surfaces, in "gadgets" and obsolescent machines. Khrushchev did not pick up on the fact that our huge defense industry continued to subsidize many consumer goods. Were Americans just self-indulgent pleasure seekers? Karal Ann Marling, in her challenging book *As Seen on TV: The Visual Culture of Everyday Life in the 1950s*, depicts the kitchen as a symbol of the domestic culture of the 1950s. The model on display in Moscow appeared to be designed around new family values—even though such values reached deep into a past where oven, hearth, and warm food traditionally suggested security. Marling suggests that the several kitchen models sent to Moscow were more than just gadgetry, providing "a working demonstration of a culture that defined freedom as the capacity to change and to choose."[11] By the end of 1959, women comprised over a third of the American work force. Whether they worked to pay for new appliances or because new appliances gave them more time for self-fulfillment remains a middle class issue. It has taken decades for Americans to acknowledge that many women have no choice about working outside the home. Their wages contribute to rent or mortgage payments and help pay for their children's basic needs.

The escape into different levels of consumerism was real in postwar America for the great number of people with good jobs. Five years after the war was over the amount spent on household furnishings rose by 240%. Four years after the war 20 million refrigerators and 5.5 million stoves were bought. The icemen who once delivered large blocks of ice to put in wooden chests became part of American myth. To many the well-furnished domestic nest supplied stronger moral protection from the bomb than the official shelters a few continued to buy. In her carefully documented book *Homeward Bound: American Families in the Cold War Era* (1988), Elaine Tyler May uses the word "containment"—the same word government officials used to define our relationship with the Soviet Union—to define the lives locked into the domestic scene during the period from 1946 to 1960, when real income rose by 20%.[12]

Most of the appliances created for the American home during these years—washing machines, blenders, toasters, electric razors, dishwashers, power mowers, even television sets—were simple in design to accord with a world in which people did their own household chores. Although wild colors came into the kitchen, and airplane models influenced some industrial architects, the basic domestic designs of this period reflected functional European modernism. In fact, certain classics of industrial design, like the sleek chairs fashioned by Charles and Ray Eames, became part of a rebirth of esthetic awareness emphasizing function and simplicity. Distinguished industrial architects and artists like Eero Saarinen and Raymond Loewy began to make their work available on a grand scale. Indeed, the most elegant of the period's new appliances remain in the collections of the Museum of Modern Art in New York City and in the Smithsonian collections in Washington, D.C.

The new emphasis on style in personal material surroundings also made choosing furnishings time-consuming and socially challenging. Taste started to be graded in popular magazines—fewer people wanted to be middlebrow when either highbrow or lowbrow items could suggest individuality and character. The ubiquitous picture window—sensibly created so that mothers could keep an eye on children from inside—also allowed neighbors to evaluate each other's home furnishings. If prewar furniture manufacturers could not always make the costly new styles available rapidly and cheaply, there was nevertheless no shortage of canvas butterfly chairs or curved boomerang coffee tables. As many as 5 million wrought iron butterfly chairs were manufactured at the time, copied from the original basic Knoll chair designed to be an example of excellence in inexpensive furniture.

Easy portability as well as functional design was another mark of a period when many Americans moved as often as every year. Hine remarks that a feature of the "populuxe" age was that everything had handles or was easy to lift. The demand for informality and flexibility supported the invention of small portable appliances. Nothing stayed in its traditional place anymore: washing machines were in the kitchen; television sets ended up in the dining room. And many carried their entertainment to the beach or office. Portable radios—ancestors of the boom box—began to intrude on parks and even on public transportation.

By the end of the decade pushbutton products defined a new life. Even if a cook did not know the difference between "puree" and "liquify," the blender appeared to take over all drudgery. Ads showed women talking on the phone as their wash whirled behind glass in a nearby machine, but they did not urge these women to learn new skills in their free time or offer them more stimulating lives. Too often "labor-saving" devices led simply to more labor in the home. No-iron fabrics and synthetic casual clothes made it easier for women to do all their own laundry. When market researchers discovered that women also wanted to feel useful, they urged producers to leave out essential ingredients in packaged mixes so that good wives could feel they were adding something of themselves to their family's lives when they baked a cake. Betty Friedan's 1963 classic *The Feminine Mystique* also helped women to recognize how extensively they were being manipulated to consume.

The Automobile and the Decline of Public Transportation

Men too were being promised every dimension of fulfillment with the new car model they would buy. Ads throughout the decade demonstrated the great exception to modest design, the tailfinned, chrome-embellished, gas-guzzling chariot of the 1950s—the family car. By 1955 General Motors had already played a nationwide role in getting rid of 100 pollutant-free electric transit systems, and GM also managed to replace electric locomotives with their own diesel powered engines. The excellent railroad system in place at the end of the war was stealthily and steadily dismantled, first by unprofitably polluting diesels, then by personal cars and trucks. For a time the concept of mass transportation disappeared, except for a few commuter lines linking suburbia to the downtown workplace. By 1961 the last interurban transit service in Los Angeles had been demolished, leaving the city entirely at the mercy of the automobile and the freeway.[13] At that time the Interstate Commerce Commission did not hesitate to censure General Motors for contributing to the downfall of many lines on the New Haven Railroad. At later dates, in rare cases, citizens would be able to restore some railroad lines, but in most places railroad beds were quickly sold. As long as there were parking places downtown many families also began to buy second cars.

Of course, profit margins for the manufacturers were higher on cars than on any vehicles of mass transportation. In 1955 General Motors became the first company to earn $1 billion in a single year as it produced its 50 millionth car. Americans relished their individual freedom on the road. Just as people did not want strangers in their fallout shelters, so most individuals preferred traveling alone. By the end of 1955 Americans had spent $65 billion on automobiles. Ideas like car pools and speed lanes did not develop until fuel became scarce and expensive in the 1970s.

Public transportation too often did not accommodate workers in new suburbs. And large families living at a distance from grandparents wanted reasonable and comfortable means to connect with relatives often miles away. Airplane or railroad tickets for a family of five were much more expensive than automobile costs in a society where gasoline prices were held to a minimum and buying cars on the installment system was encouraged. Big cars became a way of life as well as status symbols. As the decade wore on cars got longer and longer and more and more powerful. Car designers were challenged to produce new models every year so that the public would never be satisfied. Because almost no one thought about the environment or about the safety of high speed cars, Detroit cut back production on all six-cylinder models. The huge tailfinned Cadillac would later become a collector's item representative of the flamboyant excesses of the age—an American version of Queen Elizabeth's carriage.

Marty Jezer, in a grim survey that equates the 1950s with the Dark Ages, points out that '50s car culture destroyed America's long romance with the railroad—an important part of folk mythology connecting most Americans since the middle of the 19th century.[14] He might have looked more closely at Jack Kerouac's contemporary efforts to replace tracks with highways as a new source of adventure. But Jezer was right about the loss of the folk magic and the disappearance of the community experience railroads provided. The car began to represent a lonely danger. Jezer reminds us that in the popular cult movies of the 1950s, *The Wild One* and *Rebel Without a Cause*, cars are used not to liberate the spirit but to celebrate "alienation, isolation and death." It was somehow fitting that James Dean, a '50s symbol of the loner, should die young in a high speed car accident. The golden spike linking the East with the West that extended a sense of American unity through the railroads had long been forgotten.

By the end of the decade common sense returned to the car buyer. People refused to buy Ford's new Edsel, a pretentious gas guzzler. And many began to discover the Volkswagen Beetle. The German import, well made and cheap to maintain, became a challenge to Detroit. In 1950 a single dealer sold 330 VWs; by 1957 nationwide sales reached 200,000.[15] Many different new cars in many models were becoming as much a part of the American dream of entitlement as the Levittown single-family home expanded by later variations. With the National Defense Highway system firmly subsidized by the government, Americans were well on their way to becoming what Jane Holtz Kay would label in a 1997 book the "asphalt nation." Not only were people allowing the culture and history of inner cities to fall into neglect during the 1950s, but they were also creating a new highway culture of efficient standardization. Drop some Martians on a road in New Jersey or Wisconsin or California, and their choices for food, fuel, or lodging would be almost identical. The prewar guest houses with their antimacassars and shared bathrooms and the family restaurants with their community bowls of homemade foods—part of the traveling scene of the early 1940s—quickly disappeared. Standardization, usually cheaper, seemed better. Often it was.

Perhaps the mass production and efficiency Americans have always admired inspired many to think of the '50s as **Leisure** "fabulous." Coming after the poverty of the 1930s and the **Activities** austerity of the 1940s, the pursuit of happiness—as it found expression in the great range of material goods in the 1950s—made many forget the Cold War. Not just hula hoops, Davy Crockett hats, deodorants, and chlorophyll toothpaste, and Elvis Presley and Marilyn Monroe—the popular culture symbols of the time—but a world that seemed to cater to every possible taste emerged to satisfy a great variety of needs. This was also a period when many people were eager to travel to faraway places and to try new leisure activities like skiing, golf, and scuba diving. Airplanes and ocean liners suddenly became accessible to a middle class that before the war did not even take vacations.

Perhaps Eisenhower, the avuncular golfer in the White House, communicated a sense of new possibilities. Ike had after all ended the Korean War. And by 1954 Joseph McCarthy had become unfortunate history—a symbolic name representative of false accusations. No terrible assassinations marked the 1950s. The unrest that began to shape the civil rights movement was orderly and slow to ignite the public imagination.

The Eisenhower years must also be identified with the beginning of television, just as the 1940s must be identified in popular culture with the movies. In 1955, 32 million television sets were blaring in three out of four houses as well as in many bars and restaurants. *TV Guide* magazine appeared in 1952 to help people choose what programs to watch. TV dinners filled the new supermarket freezers by 1954, offering viewers the chance to eat in front of the set instead of at the dining room table. By 1956, Americans on average spent more time watching television than they did working for pay.[16] Advertising became a flourishing industry urging viewers to buy the items that sponsored their favorite shows. Later voters remembered Ronald Reagan's eloquent TV demonstrations of refrigerators. Many people in the '50s also had the chance to watch Nixon arguing with Khrushchev about materialism and rockets on TV.

The over 32 million people who owned their own homes and the 21 million who drove their own cars considered themselves "average Americans." Labor leader George Meany characterized the American working man as supportive of American society—not interested in recasting it in any socialistic way. What labor wanted, he said, was "an ever-rising standard of living . . . not only more money but more leisure and a richer cultural life.[17] The Russian success in putting up an orbiting satellite in 1957—the famous *Sputnik*—made Americans realize that better education ought to be included in the definition of the good life.

On a material level during the 1950s, America was demonstrating to the rest of the world that its form of government was the most productive. The whole country was like the model kitchen Nixon glorified to Khrushchev. We were trying to show off the goods available to everyone with middle class incomes. And bookstores began to stock self-improvement books alongside the shelves filled with do-it-yourself manuals. The American Dream took many shapes. In 1954 it was reported that 70% of all wallpaper bought was hung by amateurs, while 11 million self-styled carpenters sanded 180 square miles of plywood with 25 million power tools.[18] Everywhere people cultivated their own gardens and devoted leisure time to home improvements. They enjoyed doing such domestic activities. The divorce rate was the lowest for any decade in the century.

A *Reader's Digest* article also spoke of expanding cultural opportunities. Art museums, opera companies, and symphony orchestras multiplied during the 1950s. It was a decade that introduced Americans to many good foreign films and produced quality paper bound books, inexpensive reproductions of art, and unbreakable long-playing records. New technologies also allowed engineers to offer re-recorded jazz classics and lost operas. Although 8 million new cars were sold in 1955—a record at the time—and 1.6 million new housing starts were made that same year, the life of the mind also became important during the decade.[19] Perhaps the great number of people who had taken advantage of the G.I. Bill were responsible for expanding national interests beyond the world of sports. Between 1952 and 1961 the sale of books doubled as a result of what was called "the paperback revolution." Americans spent more money on tickets to classical music concerts than to baseball games and more on records and hi-fi equipment than on all spectator sports. Cities like Boston even created arts festivals where both professionals and amateurs could display their creations and poets could offer readings to a new listening public.

As people settled down to domesticity to compensate for the uprootedness of the war years and the fear of the Cold War, it became a paradox that materialism provided comfort. Americans saw themselves in close-knit nuclear families rather than as a lonely crowd. What is called "the culture of the Cold War" not only had an impact on the growing birthrate—in 1955 as great as India's—but also influenced the increased production of material goods. By the mid-1950s, with only 6% of the world's population, the United States was producing and consuming over one-third of all the world's goods and services. The gross national product, considered by many the most important index of economic success, leaped from $206 billion in 1940 to over $500 billion in 1960.

Economics and Employment

In place for defense reasons at the end of the Korean War, the military budget continued to provide economic stimulus for research and development in fields like electronics and aviation.[20] Easily available credit for installment buying encouraged Americans to purchase "consumer durables" on budget terms, while the booming public relations industry took note that people spent 35% more using plastic credit cards than they would using money.

In 1950 "plastic" entered the vocabulary of the American financial world with the creation of the Diners' Club card. American Express and credit cards from oil and phone companies and car rental services followed by the mid-'50s. Such installment purchases caused consumer indebtedness to soar during the decade, from $73 billion to $196 billion! Madison Avenue writers preached immediate personal gratification as a way of life, and manufacturers complied by building "planned obsolescence" into many new products. Along with new lives people were encouraged to refurbish their personal worlds. The Model T car that still drove and the turreted GE refrigerator still running when given away were treasures from the past. So many additional appliances appeared in new households that the use of electricity nearly tripled during the decade.

As the country's population increased by one-third between 1940 and 1960—in the Pacific states it rose by 110%—people needed more basic material goods. Half of the population in the Far West now lived in a state different from the one in which they were born. And one-fifth of the nation's new population had settled in California, which surpassed New York by 1963 as the most populous state.[21] From 1946 to 1958 venture capitalists invested huge amounts of money in mechanization and power. Air conditioning helped open new territories along with more available water. And the electronics industry also began to thrive. Industry experienced a great rise in output per man-hour as automation intensified postwar scientific management.

If many unskilled workers did indeed lose their jobs to machines, economists argued that technology would create many new ones. The first giant computer, built around the invention of the transistor during World War II, was marketed in 1950. IBM, the industry leader, could not turn computers out fast enough to satisfy demand. In 1954 they produced only 20; by 1957 they produced 1,250; only a decade later they managed to turn out 35,000. Factory sales increased from $25 million in 1953 to $1 billion by the end of the decade, bringing all sorts of new jobs into the marketplace.

The huge spending on research and development still used as much as 50% government funding to support the Cold War's defense needs. Long after World War II the electronics industry continued to sell costly weapon systems. In 1956 military items amounted to $3 billion—40 times the amount spent in 1947.[22]

With the new interstate highway system demanding construction workers, the government remained one of the decade's largest employers. Jobs in the public sector doubled between 1950 and 1970. And incomes rose enough to create an expanded middle class. The proportion of the population enjoying an income of $10,000 or more increased from 9% in 1947 to 19% by 1968. The proportion of those earning below $3,000 also fell, from 34% to 19%. As late as 1940 fewer than 2 million Americans had any education beyond high school, but the G.I. Bill enabled many ex-soldiers to become professionals. By 1960 college enrollment reached 3.6 million, creating a range of skilled graduates with higher salaries to spend.

Some believed America had experienced a bloodless revolution. But the statistics about personal wealth did not document great changes. In

1953 just 1.6% of the population, for example, held 90% of the corporate bonds. By 1968 only 153 Americans possessed nine-digit fortunes, while millions still lived in want. The gap between rich and poor actually increased during the 1950s, when 0.5% of the population owned 25% of all personal wealth. In 1957 a University of Wisconsin sociologist, Robert Lampman, produced research revealing that 32.2 million Americans (nearly one-quarter of the population) had incomes below the poverty level.[23] And many people still lacked minimal comforts like indoor toilets and hot water and heating systems. Because there was so much visible well-being it remained easy to ignore "the other America."

Along with all the new homeowners, but not living beside them, grew a varied culture of poverty that included old people, Puerto Ricans, Mexican Americans, and residents of Appalachia as well as many rural citizens who wanted to remain on farms. From 1948 to 1956 the American farmers' share of the wealth fell from 9% to scarcely 4%. Small farmers could not profit from the mechanization that was creating agribusiness to make the wealthy wealthier. Even during this period of baby boom, the farm population declined by 9 million from 1940 to 1960. By the end of the '60s only 5% of the American population remained on farms.

Yet, paradoxically, many unlikely people seemed to have more material goods. In a place as poor as Harlan County, Kentucky, a depressed coal mining community, 40% owned homes; 59% had cars, 42% telephones, 67% TV sets, and 88% washing machines. Michael Harrington noted that in the most powerful and rich society the world has ever known the poor remained "the strangest in the history of mankind." An American prophet, Harrington wrote a number of essays during the decade passionately reminding readers that the misery of the poor "has continued while the majority of the nation talked of itself as being 'affluent' and worried about neuroses in the suburbs."[24]

It was true that more Americans owned their homes in the 1950s than at any other time in the country's history. The 1949 National Housing Act had promised to build 810,000 low-cost homes so that every American family could have "a decent home and a suitable living environment." But by 1964 only 550 units had been built. The Federal Housing Authority made matters worse by refusing to allow integration in public housing projects. Michael Harrington insisted that it would take an effort of the intellect and will even to see the poor.

Many Americans later learned much from Harrington's book *The Other America*, the collection of his research on the poor. But almost everyone knew about John Kenneth Galbraith's 1958 bestseller on the American economy, *The Affluent Society*. Not just concerned with examining America's newly defined wealth, Galbraith also seriously considered the remaining poverty. He attempted to shatter the myth that increased production would destroy poverty. Better distribution of wealth did not eliminate the poor. Although by 1960 per capita income in the United States was 35% higher than in the war boom year 1945, the very poor were still with us.

And public spaces deteriorated as surely as transportation systems decayed. The cities became impoverished as money set aside for low income housing remained unused or was spent inappropriately on soon to be destroyed high rise buildings. Not until the social and environmental movements of the 1960s formed would many Americans begin to recognize that public spaces were as important to a democracy as personal consumer goods. The appeal of a simpler life had always been a powerful force in America's spiritual heritage, but the abundance of the 1950s made it hard to escape the materialism that defined the times.

A famous passage from *The Affluent Society* epitomizes the dilemma of this period. Americans still need to think seriously about the implications of the story John Kenneth Galbraith tells:

> The family which takes its mauve and cerise, air-conditioned, power-steered and power-braked automobile out for a tour passes through cities that are badly paved, made hideous by litter, blighted buildings, billboards and posts for wires that should long since have been put underground. They pass on into a countryside that has been rendered largely invisible by commercial art. . . . They picnic on exquisitely packaged food from a portable icebox by a polluted stream and go on to spend the night at a park which is a menace to public health and morals. Just before dozing off on an air mattress, beneath a nylon tent amid stench of decaying refuse, they may vaguely reflect on the curious unevenness of their blessings.[25]

By the end of the decade the hazards of successful free enterprise had become as real as the Cold War anxieties that Communism had provoked.

NOTES

1. Douglas T. Miller and Marion Nowak, *The Fifties: The Way We Really Were* (Garden City, N.Y.: Doubleday, 1975), 51, 52.

2. *Time*, February 5, 1951.

3. Miller and Nowak, *The Fifties*, 55.

4. Paul Boyer, *By the Bomb's Early Light: American Thought and Culture at the Dawn of the Atomic Age* (1985; new ed., Chapel Hill: University of North Carolina Press, 1994), 354.

5. Quoted in ibid., 363.

6. Ibid., 327–332.

7. See Dwight D. Eisenhower, "The Military-Industrial Complex," in William Chafe and Harvard Sitkoff, eds., *A History of Our Time: Readings on Postwar America*, 4th ed. (New York: Oxford University Press, 1995), 120–122.

8. Elaine Tyler May, *Homeward Bound: American Families in the Cold War Era* (New York: Basic Books, 1988), 166.

9. Thomas Hine, *Populuxe: The Look and Life of America in the '50s and '60s* (New York: Knopf, 1986), 16–17.

10. May, *Homeward Bound*, 163–165.

11. Karal Ann Marling, *As Seen on TV: The Visual Culture of Everyday Life in the 1950s* (Cambridge, MA: Harvard University Press, 1994), 283.

12. May, *Homeward Bound*, 165.

13. Marty Jezer, *The Dark Ages: Life in the United States, 1945–1960* (Boston: South End Press, 1982), 140–143.

14. Ibid., 145–146.

15. Miller and Nowak, *The Fifties*, 142–143.

16. Ibid., 7.

17. *Reader's Digest*, June 1955.

18. Miller and Nowak, *The Fifties*, 9.

19. William E. Leuchtenburg, *A Troubled Feast: American Society Since 1945*, updated ed. (Boston: Little, Brown, 1983), 64–65.

20. Ibid., 37–39.

21. Ibid., 42.

22. Ibid., 46–47.

23. Quoted in ibid., 50.

24. Michael Harrington, *The Other America: Poverty in the United States* (Baltimore: Penguin, 1963), 170.

25. Quoted in Stephen J. Whitfield, *The Culture of the Cold War* (Baltimore: Johns Hopkins University Press, 1991), 76.

9

Television Defines Postwar America

Before World War II people shaped their opinions from what they read in newspapers or heard on the streets. By the end of the 1950s visual images taught Americans who they were. Although an advertising slogan of the decade boasted that movies were better than ever, and the introduction of drive-in theaters tried to accommodate both car culture and family—many had playgrounds, diaper services, and special foods for kids—the truth was that television was taking over as the main medium of communication. Gimmicks like three-dimensional films and aroma-ramas that puffed scents through the theaters' ventilation systems failed to bring in necessary crowds. Cinerama appeared in 1952, using overlapping cameras for a gigantic screen effect to extend the possibilities of adventure films. Pictorial innovations such as the famous chase across the face of Mount Rushmore in Alfred Hitchcock's *North by Northwest* (1959) suggested that the excitement of the big screen was far from over— but by then many movies were being created just for the living room viewer. Weekly movie attendance dropped from 90 million to 47 million in the ten years after 1946. By 1952, 19 million Americans had television sets and a thousand new TV appliance stores were opening each month.[1] When Lucille Ball bought the unused RKO film lot in 1955 to film *I Love Lucy*, the most popular sitcom of the decade, she became a pioneer producer in the new industry of making movies specifically for TV.

Critical feminists may attack *I Love Lucy* as another example of a ditzy housewife manipulating a loyal husband because Lucy's character's attempts at earning her own living remain

Popular Sitcoms

dreams. In fact, however, the show reflected different levels of media liberation. For one thing, Desi Arnaz played himself on the show—Lucy's Cuban bandleader husband, Ricky Ricardo. Far from the suburban organization man, Desi offered a vast audience the chance to appreciate Latino culture. He used his accent and charm to introduce viewers who knew nothing about Cuba to a different kind of civilization, while audiences enjoyed the tensions of the mixed culture marriage. Everyone knew that the slapstick character Lucy Ricardo played by Ball on screen was far from the brilliant business woman producing the most popular show on television. Lucille Ball's business skills established a tradition that made it easier for later talented women such as Oprah Winfrey to succeed in different roles.

Always torn between trying to please her husband and dreaming of being a star, Lucy Ricardo responded to everywoman's fantasies while coping with the social mandate of the stay-at-home '50s. Ball insisted on playing the role as a housewife, not as a star. Desi and Lucy represented caricatures that helped many—in this most married of decades—laugh at the disasters and peculiarities of marital stress. There was never any suggestion that divorce and extramarital love affairs were realities. Both characters emerged as sympathetic and vulnerable, far from sure of their social status. Their on-screen dealings with their neighbors' points of view offered some exposure to the world of compromise many Americans experienced in new housing arrangements everywhere.

The Monday evening show was such a success that Marshall Fields, the Chicago department store, changed its weekly Monday night clearance sale to Thursday. As early as 1952, 10.6 million households were tuning in to *I Love Lucy*, the largest audience thus far in history. By 1954 as many as 50 million Americans watched. The show allowed CBS-TV to make a net profit for the first time in 1953.[2] No problems emerged with Desi's being Latino—except behind the scenes when one producer argued that Americans would not accept Desi as a suitable TV husband for Lucy.

In 1947 Lucille Ball had been among the Hollywood stars who protested the activities of the House Un-American Activities Committee. On a radio show called *Hollywood Fights Back* she had read excerpts from the Bill of Rights. When the tabloid journalist Walter Winchell accused her of being a Communist in 1953, she acknowledged that she had joined the party to please her grandfather. But her television ratings were so high that Philip Morris cigarettes, Lucy's sponsor, refused to withdraw, demonstrating that in a capitalist society the bottom line frequently shapes ideals. Desi had left Cuba when Fidel Castro, the Communist leader, was just six years old. He insisted that both he and Lucy were 100% American. The only thing red about Lucy, Desi claimed, was her hair—and even that was dyed.

Sexist as Lucy's TV dilemmas appeared because she acted stupid, the situations described often challenged audiences to think more about marriage, especially when Lucy's pregnancy took center screen. The on-TV baby was another example of Lucille Ball's power to challenge network stereotypes. Before Lucy's baby all pregnancies had been hidden. CBS wanted her to stand behind chairs. Even the word "pregnant" was not to be used; she agreed to call herself an "expectant mother." By the time Desi, too busy on-screen to notice the change in his wife, acknowledged the great event, CBS had lined up a rabbi, a priest, and a minister to make sure the script was in good taste. But at the hospital it was Lucy who pushed Ricky in the wheelchair. When the baby emerged in January 1953, 68% of the television sets in the country were tuned in as 44 million people watched—twice as many as watched the inauguration of Dwight Eisenhower the next day.[3] As time went on Lucy and Desi followed their fellow Americans into suburbia, but their domestic adventures ended at the close of the decade when their real marriage, sympathetic as it seemed, collapsed. Lucille Ball kept financial control of ongoing programs she made by herself. She remains a perfect paradoxical feminist of the 1950s in terms of the vast power she exercised.

Almost all the earliest TV sitcoms centered on marriage or on the traditional family. Holdovers from the age of radio like *I Remember Mama*, a story of a Swedish American family, offered familiar happy assimilation stories. *The Goldbergs*, a radio success from 1929 to 1950, entered the TV scene in its old-fashioned form in 1955. Here again Americans had to confront the paradox of a highly professional woman, Gertrude Berg, celebrating the perfect stay-at-home mother, Molly Goldberg. Berg had written, directed, and produced more than 5,000 radio scripts when she turned her talents to television and continued to honor the good humor, wisdom, and generosity of Molly Goldberg—an antidote to the negative stereotypes of the Jewish mother many male writers from playwright Clifford Odets to novelist Philip Roth had delineated.[4] Molly Goldberg, like Lucy Ricardo, usually got her own way, but her power too was indirect. Audiences could never imagine either of these women taking part in any political cause. Molly used her new immigrant's common sense to help others achieve family warmth and idealized old-fashioned values. Critic Charles Angoff described her in 1951 as "Molly the Mixer and the Fixer."[5] In Molly Goldberg's media world the neurotic tensions and stress of Jewish life in the big cities of America melted into an assimilationist belief in immigrant possibilities. Far from stupid, helpless only insofar as her malapropisms amused, Molly Goldberg represented not just a good Jewish mother but a good example of an American mother: "Jake [her husband] wants the children to have everything money can buy," she said in defining her values. "I want them to have everything money can't buy."[6] In the years before World War II the family conflicts and the intrusive supporting community had been real to many urban Americans. But when the Goldbergs left the old neighborhood—following the rest of the middle class into the suburbs and sending their children to college—the audience dwindled. Younger people in the '50s did not relish immigrant folk wisdom. They needed the know-how that led to upward mobility, not the street smarts of city life.

Gertrude Berg suffered from the anti-Communist blacklist as Lucille Ball had not. Philip Loeb, who had played Molly's husband Jake on the radio and also for a short time on TV, was a victim of the infamous blacklist. Pressured by her sponsors to fire Loeb, Berg lived to see him commit suicide three years later. Gertrude Berg herself had belonged to a leftist group of artists that included the great singer, actor, and Communist sympathizer Paul Robeson. Because of this past connection NBC would not allow her even to be a guest on Milton Berle's television version of the *Texaco Star Theater*, another enormously popular show.

The suburban adaptation of the Goldbergs did not last the decade. Second generation immigrants were more interested in assimilation than in ethnic communities. And like most American consumers at the time, they, like Jake Goldberg, were deep into things that money could buy. *The Life of Riley*, another blue collar sitcom, also did not last long. Sponsors seemed reluctant to support shows about people whose purchasing power was small. Yet one working class saga, *The Honeymooners*, was enormously successful for the 39 weeks it aired. Based on story skits from Jackie Gleason's variety show, *The Honeymooners* dramatized the tribulations of a bus driver, Ralph Kramden, and his devoted crony Ed Norton, who worked in the sewers. No dream of upward mobility exists in their tenement. If there is any possibility of social change it must come from luck—like having a winning lottery number. The Kramdens would not have been able to afford the kitchen Richard Nixon showed Khrushchev as typical of the American working man's home. So it may be natural that Ralph Kramden, like his 1970s counterpart Archie Bunker, indulged in frequent bursts of anger. He did not resort to verbal attacks on minorities though, but made his sassy wife Alice the target of many abusive threats. Sharp-tongued in rebuttal, Alice averted physical abuse—yet the Kramdens' marriage lacked the good humor of the Goldbergs'. When Ralph boasted of a "big deal" he'd got into, Alice responded that the only big thing he ever got into was his pants. Such banter kept the marriage going. Many viewers wanted to believe that Ralph's threats to send Alice to the moon were a style of loving.

The working class sitcoms of the early '50s, with their realistic sets and financial problems, would soon be entirely replaced by stories and sets focusing on the affluent suburban family. Such new shows as *Father Knows Best, The Adventures of Ozzie and Harriet,* and *Leave It to Beaver* became part of a parade of unrealistic media sitcoms focused on family "togetherness," idyllic settings, and minor domestic problems. During the '50s there were no shows about African American families or uncloseted gays or any significant old people. A rare program about a single woman, *Our Miss Brooks*, a schoolteacher, made more of her search for a man than of the satisfactions found in teaching. More than one motherless family also appeared—an easy way to avoid dealing with housewives who wanted to be more than just mothers. To be sure, there were Native Americans in the series of shows about Davy Crockett and cowboy hero Hopalong Cassidy—among many Westerns satisfying demands for clear visions of good versus evil essential to the Cold War. The Lone Ranger's sidekick Tonto continued to support him for a modest number of adventures when the long-running radio serial also converted to TV. But they all had to head for the wilderness when the fantasies of suburbia got higher ratings than good guy–bad guy shoot-outs.

The early years of commercial television have nevertheless been called its Golden Age. Why is this? One reason was that **Serious** in spite of the blacklist the American public was offered a good **Drama** number of original dramas. Paddy Chayevsky's *Marty*—later made into a movie—allowed a vast 1953 audience to appreciate the dignity and poignance of working class life not offered in *The Honeymooners*. Reginald Rose's eloquent jury drama *Twelve Angry Men* also went from television in 1954 to the big screen in 1957 and would be reproduced again on television in 1997. The *Studio One* production in 1954 won three major Emmy Awards for television excellence. Rose had been another blacklisted writer. Just as Arthur Miller made people consider what Cold War fear was doing to America when he wrote the play about Salem witchcraft, *The Crucible*, in 1953, so Reginald Rose used *Twelve Angry Men* to make audiences consider how dangerous accusations without concrete evidence could be. *Twelve Angry Men* also openly aired the reality of race prejudice in the jury system, suggesting an important aspect of the growing struggle to broaden civil rights.

The chance to act on live TV in new plays before a real audience attracted remarkable young talents like Paul Newman, Joanne Woodward, and Grace Kelly. Commercials were few in the early years, and sponsors had not yet begun to dictate what should be in the productions. At the time sponsors often chose to be identified with one kind of spectacle. The Kraft Television Theater, Texaco Theater, Colgate Hour, Alcoa Hour, and General Electric Hour were names identified with certain kinds of productions. The Lux Video Theater produced two plays by the gifted writer William Faulkner in 1953 and 1954. Over 80% of the productions at the time were live. Dramas frequently catered to quality rather than to mass tastes. Later serious science fiction dramas reflected the anxieties of the Cold War as well—but series like *The Outer Limits* and *The Twilight Zone* provided forums for powerful talents like writer Rod Serling and provoked thoughtful audience reactions.

Variety Shows   In the earliest years of the 1950s, in spite of the self-righteous political mood of the country, there was real humor on TV, not the canned laughter and fake applause that later television shows exploited. Uncle Miltie's slapstick clown, played by Milton Berle with all the vaudeville trappings of the past, made every generation laugh. He was credited with making more people buy television sets than any other TV star. But his pie-in-the-face style grew monotonous; he was entirely off the screen by 1955. New wits took over. Phil Silvers' *Sergeant Bilko* reminded viewers of the wry ironies of army life. Groucho Marx conducted a quiz show, *You Bet Your Life*, making fun of his contestants with outrageous remarks. Comedian Ernie Kovacs used the visual magic of the medium itself for amusement in the way a magician can levitate or suddenly disappear. From 1954 to 1957 Sid Caesar's *Your Show of Shows* kept America laughing with jokes by such gifted writers as Mel Brooks, Carl Reiner, Larry Gelbart, Neil Simon, and Mel Tolkin. Their scenes from domestic life using a brilliant young comedienne, Imogene Coca, remain hilarious. Laughing at themselves, this group of writers enabled America to appreciate much social criticism in their skits of everyday life.

"There was no censorship," Tolkin said. "Everybody had the right to be an idiot."[7] *Your Show of Shows* represented a range of new talent not trained for radio or vaudeville. The skits emphasized the visual possibilities of television. And the show introduced new cultural forces to a broad American public: cool jazz, psychoanalysis, foreign films, and the new social habits of suburbia. As the audience expanded, some reviewers thought the show "too smart," but its influence remained to filter into *The Carol Burnett Show* and *Saturday Night Live* at later dates. Some of the writers believed the shows they were writing would become television classics: "We didn't want to do things off the headlines because it would die and we wanted to be immortal."[8] Yet as the tastes of a broader audience determined what sponsors would pay for, the New York wits were replaced by Lawrence Welk's old-fashioned amusement park band.

Comedy team Jerry Lewis and Dean Martin early on introduced much more action into their shows, taking advantage—like Ernie Kovacs—of the range of photographic possibilities television cameras came to represent.

Elvis Presley and Ed Sullivan   It was entertainer Steve Allen who first focused discussion on Elvis Presley's pelvic gyrations by making him stand still as he serenaded a tethered hound dog. But Jackie Gleason deserves credit for pushing Presley's talents on the 1956 *Tommy and Jimmy Dorsey Stage Show* in spite of the Dorsey brothers' protests. Gleason rightly recognized Elvis as another possible hero of working class culture. He labeled him a guitar-playing Marlon Brando who had "sensuous, sweaty, T-shirt and Jeans animal magnetism."[9] Elvis managed to step forward—in between the quaint clowns and trained animal acts—to send rock 'n' roll music into affluent suburban America. Although Dick Clark was on *American Bandstand* every afternoon in Philadelphia with well-groomed youngsters and modest songs, Elvis' ability to attract huge audiences suddenly put him in great demand. Milton Berle even hired him to inject life into his dying show—at what was then the outrageously high salary of $50,000 a week.

Like the rebel James Dean portrayed in 1950s movies and the exposer of phonies Holden Caulfield represented in the 1951 classic *Catcher in the Rye*, Elvis Presley became a symbol of youthful independence. By the singer's third appearance in 1957 on America's most popular variety show, *The Toast of the Town*, host Ed Sullivan defended Elvis as "a real decent, fine boy."[10] The press began to stress his patriotism and how good he was to his mother. Estimates are that over 82% of the American viewing audience saw Elvis on the Ed Sullivan Show—54 million people watched as the cameras shot him only from the waist up.

Fifty years later Elvis Presley would be esteemed by music critics not for his sensationalism but for the agility of his voice and for the variety and range of his ballads. The accusation that he borrowed much from African American gospel music and from black blues had to be understood the way blending of cultural currents must always be explained in a country made up of complex energies. Elvis's rock 'n' roll and rockabilly represented in music the integration of black and white folk cultures that the law attempted to bring about on the social level. Greil Marcus in his classic *Mystery Train: Images of America in Rock 'n' Roll Music* attributes Elvis' great popularity to the self-respect he offered people who were only on the edge of the new affluence. Marcus believes Presley managed to stabilize country music even as he pulled away from it. The power of his music stems from tensions. Although Elvis was a rebel, he made it clear how impossible it was to break away from his roots.[11]

If Elvis remained "king" after the 50 intervening years since appearing with Ed Sullivan, it may be because the tensions he communicated are still part of an upwardly mobile society. The country music Elvis Presley offered America in his own extreme forms continued to celebrate traditions people were losing in the decade after the war. To many, Elvis suggested how much Americans remained trapped by fate. Often his message seemed to be simply that his music passed on lost values from many different roots. Greil Marcus' belief that Elvis embodied "the bigness, the intensity, and the unpredictability of America itself" may well be true. Although many black musicians complained that Elvis stole their material, his African American audience endured.[12]

It is easy to make fun of "amateur hours" like Ed Sullivan's. Fred Allen, a witty radio comedian who did not survive on television, said that Sullivan would stay on the air as long as other people had talent. But there was talent—a prodigious amount. In the '50s Sullivan offered the public artists as varied as the violin prodigy Itzhak Perlman and the great black musical performers Ella Fitzgerald, Duke Ellington, and Lena Horne. At a time when black singer Nat King Cole could not get a sponsor for a television series because of his race, Sullivan made a vast audience aware that talent had nothing to do with race or ethnicity. As the nation's leading TV impresario for 23 years, Ed Sullivan shaped American values and taste. Money spent for music lessons and musical instruments soared from $86 million in 1950 to $149 million in 1960. During these early "golden years" Sullivan's Sunday night show brought families and neighbors together in living rooms to watch and discuss new talents.[13]

How much television influenced national values remains a chicken-egg dilemma. The new medium allowed many Americans for the first time to appreciate the best of the national pastime as big league baseball appeared on the screen. TV also exhibited cultures and countries never thought about in isolationist pre–World War II America. The video screen revealed aspects of nature never imagined before and expanded viewers' visions of what the global village contained. Such images could dispel fear.

Talk Shows and Politics In the early years of television broadcasting a few serious talk shows stood out. Not every woman wanted to be *Queen for a Day*—or even to *Strike It Rich*. Marya Mannes, an astute TV critic at the time, praised *The Open Mind*, which treated such issues as antisemitism, homosexuality, and mental retardation. *Omnibus* in 1956 offered a series of dramas on American history, reminding people of a tradition of heroes who combined knowledge and courage to prevail against compromised politicians. For a time Mannes had her own TV spot, but her refusal to tailor her comments for mass acceptability led to her dismissal. "The death of art," she wrote in 1953, "is to please all and offend none." Never sympathetic with those intellectuals who simply chose not to watch television, Mannes wanted imaginative people to play a bigger role in taking it over. "This communication—so direct and so limitless—is open to the thinkers and dreamers and creators of this country if they want it."[14] But she worried that the wreckers would take over television if the thinkers backed away. As a TV reviewer for *Reporter* magazine during the McCarthy period, Mannes had much to rage about—but she also celebrated a few brave men like Eric Severeid and Edward R. Murrow, TV commentators who had achieved national stature during the war.

As more and more people owned television sets they turned from twice a day newspapers and current events magazines like the *Saturday*

Evening Post and *Life* to the more immediate journalism of the television screen. Yet at the time more controversial opinions were available in print. Throughout the McCarthy period a number of courageous journalists like James Wechsler, Drew Pearson, Elmer Davis, Martin Agronsky, and I. F. Stone stood on the ramparts attacking McCarthy for irresponsibility. But television sponsors were reluctant to deal with controversy. *Town Meeting of the Air*, an open-minded program that debated serious issues, was dropped in 1952.

Ed Murrow, enormously popular since his broadcasts from the bombing scenes of London during World War II, bravely continued to pursue controversial issues. *See It Now*, Murrow's on-the-spot news show, made a symbolic effort to link Americans from the Statue of Liberty to the Golden Gate Bridge. In 1956 Murrow had even dared to interview Chinese Communist premier Chou En-lai when other reporters were having their passports lifted for any sign of sympathy to China. But it was Murrow's program on Senator McCarthy, based on a compilation of film clips from McCarthy's own long red-baiting career, that made Murrow and his news partner Fred Friendly heroes.

"A Report on Senator Joseph R. McCarthy" aired on March 9, 1954 without any promotion and no CBS logo. Murrow and Friendly used their own money to advertise the show. This brave exposure, as Stephen Whitfield remarks in *The Culture of the Cold War*, became in retrospect "the most important single show in the history of television." Murrow, he believes, saved "from utter disgrace a medium that had evaded the central issue" of the fear McCarthy engendered.[15] A year later the long supportive Alcoa Corporation withdrew sponsorship for *See It Now*. By 1958, this show too would be off the air. In the interest of complex truth, Erik Barnouw, a media historian, suggested that such television broadcasts should not be reliant on sponsors but be seen as necessary historic contributions to the democratic process.[16] Murrow's final show, *Harvest of Shame*, contributed another controversial chapter to his American vision: the plight of the migrant worker. By the end of the century many public political events—both in the halls of Congress and in controversial global situations—would appear on the small screen, including debates about funding for public broadcasting.

It was a matter of luck that the Army-McCarthy hearings held in 1954 also exposed McCarthy's antics to a large number of people, finally forcing his fellow senators to censure his behavior. The hearings were broadcast on ABC and Dumont, not the major networks, so only 60% of the television audience actually saw McCarthy bullying army witnesses.[17] But such publicity was enough. From that moment, television took on the role of helping Americans weigh their political judgments. As early as 1950, Senator Estes Kefauver had brought cameras in to his Senate hearings on organized crime. Televised nationally, Kefauver in 1952 gained a tremendous following as a corruption fighter; he started to think about the presidency. At the moment he announced his candidacy the television industry also awarded him a special Emmy for "bringing the workings of our government into the homes of the American people." By the time of the 1960 election Kefauver's star had fallen, but the televised presidential campaign debates between Kennedy and Nixon made people realize how influential images could be in choosing a winner. Visual charisma would continue to be a measure of success for America's politicians.

The Quiz Show Scandals   The Golden Age of television finally turned to brass during the quiz show scandals. From 1956 to 1959 one of the most popular forms of television entertainment was the question and answer show that heaped consumer goods or cash on people who knew the right answers about a vast range of trivia. On one show Cadillacs were given away as consolation prizes to losers. In a consumer age that often measured status by accumulated worldly goods, viewers found vicarious satisfaction watching contestants carry off huge quantities of stuff. But on the quiz show *Twenty-One* handsome young Columbia University instructor Charles Van Doren made money and things appear secondary to intellect. A member of a famous American family of scholars and writers, Van Doren thought his charm would bring increasing "respect for knowledge and education." He had hoped to make the life of the mind attractive through his own personal image—just as Elvis made himself representative of the vitality of rock 'n' roll. During his fourteen-week reign as a master of small facts, Charles Van Doren won $129,000, a huge amount at the time, and he was subsequently offered a permanent contract at NBC. At one point his appearance drew more viewers than *I Love Lucy* did. *Time* magazine put Van Doren on the cover as "a phenomenal mind."[18] When it was finally revealed that he had been given the questions in advance, the entire country was stunned.

Elvis, for all his flamboyance, remains in the American imagination as an authentic talent, but Van Doren emerged as one of Holden Caulfield's phonies. Van Doren confessed to a Congressional committee examining quiz shows: "I was deeply involved in deception. I have deceived my friends, and I had millions of them."[19] In his eagerness to make "eggheads" popular, Van Doren had overlooked the deeper mandate to respect the truth. CBS dropped all its quiz shows. The American public became disillusioned, not just with television but with the violation of public faith.

Television as Moral Education   Being an American in the 1950s was a challenge to loyalty on many levels. The presence of Edward R. Murrow on TV from 1951 to 1958 redeemed the medium from general accusations of narrow mindedness. To his credit Murrow represented decency in an uneasy political world. He not only extended the vision of his audience, but he also managed to get one air force officer who had been dismissed for the beliefs of his father and sister reinstated. Guilt by association was acceptable to McCarthy. But Ed Murrow shared Marya Mannes' fear that television was not fulfilling its potential for good. He saw the medium being used "to distract, delude, amuse and insulate us" instead of opening and educating American minds.[20]

Another effort to establish television as a source of moral education focused on the introduction of a variety of religious leaders. Big time televangelism got its start in the 1950s. Billy Graham, Norman Vincent Peale, and Fulton J. Sheen all had their own programs. In contrast with 1940, when less than half the population belonged to institutionalized churches, in the late '50s the 73% of Americans who identified themselves as church members welcomed religious television. In 1954, the same year that "under God" was added to the Pledge of Allegiance, a religious boom took place. On television the Catholic Monsignor Sheen, "sponsored by God," was so popular that he won a 1952 Emmy Award as TV's most outstanding personality. With a live audience of over a thousand, Sheen's show *Life Is Worth Living* reached another 25 million over the air to surpass Uncle Miltie for two years.[21] At one point Sheen almost beat out *I Love Lucy* in the ratings game.

Televangelism—like most news broadcasts at the time—was designed to harmonize with broad institutional complacency. These preachers focused on individual salvation, not on social action. The personal conversion they celebrated could ignore the poor that Michael Harrington wrote about and Dorothy Day served. Nor did the TV evangelists involve themselves in discussions of civil rights or nuclear disarmament. At a time when theologians like Paul Tillich and Reinhold Niebuhr were struggling to articulate what the good life should be and how the skeptic could come to terms with fundamentalism, the televangelists of the fifties offered easier paths away from Godless Communism. They did not challenge contemporary institutions. A 1954 survey revealed that nine out of ten Americans believed in the divinity of Christ and two in three accepted the existence of the devil. Pollsters reported that 46% of their respondents believed that the clergy were the most useful citizens.[22] The church seemed to be the one institution people trusted. Voters shared Dwight Eisenhower's belief that the American people would not follow anyone who was not a member of a church.

Did these theologians have any impact on the content of the television being offered children during the '50s? **Children and** Young children's programs, except for cartoons, were **Television** mild and educational, adapted to growing minds. In the norms adults were trying to establish for their own lives, many struggled to provide sensible entertainment for the boom generation of children.

Milton Berle even called himself Uncle Miltie because so many children enjoyed his slapstick show that their parents asked for his help in putting them to bed.

In the beginning gentle programs for preschoolers like *Kukla, Fran, and Ollie, Ding Dong School,* and *Captain Kangaroo* conteracted the violence of Saturday morning cartoons. These programs often dealt sensitively with specific problems children experienced, emphasizing rational approaches to conflicts rather than fighting. And there were educational programs for older children about zoo animals and space travel. But the amount of air time given over to shows that would enhance the lives of America's children was meager. From the beginning there was more interest in the buying power of little people than in their minds. By the end of the '50s the extreme violence that characterized American television at the end of the century would be available to everyone who switched on a station for news or sitcoms at almost any hour. One waggish critic remarked that more people were killed on television in 1954 than in the entire Korean War. Whether excessive exposure to murder, rape, and bizarre horrors of all sorts could create generations of criminals became an on-going debate. Statistics proved beyond doubt that the jail population was increasing, and a few sociopaths credited television with ideas they used for particularly horrible crimes. Children could see almost anything when they turned on the set. The TV spectacle of so much blood and cruelty, many feared, might produce generations of youthful viewers who would grow up completely callous to human suffering. In one of her best reviews on how television seemed to be depriving the young of their childhood, Marya Mannes introduced a Danish scholar who challenged America: "If fifty million children see terrible things like this every day," he said, "do you not think they will feel less about shooting and murder and rape? They will be so used to violence that it does not seem like violence anymore."[23]

Mannes characterized the Westerns that flourished for a short time as plays that "concerned good men and bad men who rode horses over magnificent country and decided issues by shooting each other." In clarifying how little educational value there was in such programs, she noted that they "were all very much alike in that they bore no resemblance to what used to be the pioneer West of the United States except in the matter of clothes and horses." What these Westerns did most successfully, she perceived, was "to sell a great amount of goods."[24] As children became the most promising group of consumers for televised products, Hopalong Cassidy items boomed. The grandfatherly cowboy became a children's idol, inspiring a line of toys that grossed $100 million in 1950. Howdy Doody, a freckled clown, also inspired quantities of consumer toys at the time. And Davy Crockett seemed capable of putting coonskin caps on every small head in America before overproduction led to warehouse surpluses.[25] Such toys often provided a source of community for kids of different backgrounds. Just as adults found a source of identity in discussing their cars or their hi-fi music equipment with each other, children came together with their collections of televised loot designed for young people.

Davy Crockett, a one-hour prime time Western series sponsored by Walt Disney, garnered the highest ratings of the decade. Not only did the show make children eager for coonskin caps, but it also inspired some parents to turn to the simplicity of the old West for housing and furnishing styles. Log cabins and wagon wheels were easy to copy even in suburbia. By the end of the decade the ranch house would become the most popular style among the choices at Levittown. The West brought back echoes of a simpler life and easier living. Dungarees became the classic weekend wear for suburbanites.

The television show *Disneyland* appeared in the early '50s, testing on air all the American themes that would be incorporated during the next decade into the sparkling California amusement park. At the time few realized that Walt Disney's construction of this utopian vision would come to represent a worldwide dream of American possibility. In 1954 when *Disneyland* first appeared regularly on TV, it was as a source of publicity for the Disneyland theme park Disney was building to represent his dreams. Some critics called the show an hour-long commercial. Fantasyland, Frontierland, Adventureland, and Tomorrowland, with all the star-studded glitz that attended the grand opening of the park, quickly became as real to the American imagination as America itself— perhaps more real. Child viewers eager to participate in the televised adventures Disney conjured up might indeed learn something from the details of the displays, but many reviewers criticized the brash commercialism. One described the theme park as "a giant cash register, clicking and clanging as creatures of Disney magic came tumbling down." Television previews had prepared visitors to Disneyland for necessary compromises, but it was the tension between perfection and reality, Karal Ann Marling suggests, "between the real and the more or less real," that really delighted so many visitors.[26]

On New Year's Eve in 1957, attendance at Disneyland reached 10 million. The kind of entertainment the theme park offered fit perfectly with the togetherness of the car-centered suburban family. On one admission Walt Disney's TV dream worlds conducted everyone from an imperfect present into an idealized past or a thrilling future. And Main Street, USA, like an exhibit at a world's fair, suggested that utopia was already possible in middle class America. Some children may have been inspired to pursue a study of Disney's themes even if many more were seduced into buying Mickey Mouse Club paraphernalia and other trademarked toys and T-shirts. Eager children often found both pleasure and instruction in Disney's optimistic distortions. In a world of chaotic diversity, Marling points out, "Disney motifs constituted a common culture, a kind of civil religion of happy endings, worry-free consumption, technological optimism and nostalgia for the good old days."[27] Such dreams could define survival.

If parents monitored the hours small children sat before their television sets they need not have been concerned. And adults did not have to worry about the disc jockeys shaping teenage taste at the time; Dick Clark's decency charmed everyone. Jukeboxes in popular hangouts still offered songs with inoffensive lyrics in the decade that saw the beginning of *Playboy* magazine and the post office acceptance of *Lady Chatterley's Lover.*

Concern over Television's Impact
Before the term "couch potato" became standard in the American language, people were uneasy about what television might do to the mind. "If a citizen has to be bored to death," President Eisenhower confided to his diary in 1953, "it is cheaper and more comfortable to sit at home and look at television than it is to go outside and pay a dollar [movie price at the time] for a ticket."[28] Most Americans would have agreed that television was simply for entertainment. People commented that the art of conversation was disappearing. By the 1960s, 32 million TV sets were in use. The A. C. Nielsen Polling Company estimated TV use in 1963 at 5.85 hours per day.[29] And by this date also over 22% of the people would own more than one television set.

Although the Little Leagues for boys' baseball expanded from 800 to 6,000 during the 1950s and the number of Girl Scout and Brownie troops doubled, parents continued to worry about the quality of their children's lives. Did television direct everyone to consumption instead of to more creative lives? A caustic young German commented that Americans no longer had opinions, they had refrigerators.

As the city on a hill America once represented to the world became a screen in the living room, people had to consider not only what television was doing to the American mind but also what impact the new technology would have on the rest of the global village we shared.

NOTES

1. Paul A. Carter, *Another Part of the Fifties* (New York: Columbia University Press, 1983), chap. 8.
2. David Halberstam, *The Fifties* (New York: Fawcett Columbine, 1993), 195.
3. Ibid., 200.
4. See Joyce Antler, "A Bond of Sisterhood," in *Secret Agents: The Rosenberg Case, McCarthyism and Fifties America*, ed. Marjorie Garber and Rebecca L. Walkowitz (New York: Routledge, 1995), 199–203.

5. Ibid., 200.

6. Ibid., 201.

7. Quoted in *New York Times*, August 16, 1996.

8. Ibid.

9. Karal Ann Marling, *As Seen on TV: The Visual Culture of Everyday Life in the 1950s* (Cambridge, MA: Harvard University Press, 1994), 177.

10. Ibid., 180.

11. See Greil Marcus, *Mystery Train: Images of America in Rock 'n' Roll Music*, rev. ed. (New York: E. P. Dutton, 1982), 193–198.

12. Ibid., 208.

13. Gary Nash, *American Odyssey: The United States in the Twentieth Century* (Glencoe, IL: Macmillan/McGraw-Hill, 1991), 507.

14. Quoted in Eugenia Kaledin, *Mothers and More: American Women in the 1950s* (Boston: Twayne, 1984), 111.

15. See Stephen J. Whitfield, *The Culture of the Cold War* (Baltimore: Johns Hopkins University Press, 1991), 164–166.

16. Quoted in ibid., 165.

17. Ibid.

18. See Marling, *As Seen on TV*, 183–186.

19. Quoted in Whitfield, *Culture*, 175.

20. Quoted in ibid., 155.

21. See Douglas T. Miller and Marion Nowak, *The Fifties: The Way We Really Were* (Garden City, NY: Doubleday, 1975), chap. 3.

22. Whitfield, *Culture*, 83.

23. Quoted in Marya Mannes, "The Small Screen," in *More in Anger* (Philadelphia: J. B. Lippincott, 1958), 92.

24. Ibid., 102.

25. Miller and Nowak, *The Fifties*, 348.

26. See Marling, *As Seen on TV*, 90, 93.

27. Ibid., 119.

28. Quoted in James L. Baughman, *The Republic of Mass Culture: Journalism, Filmmaking and Broadcasting in America Since 1941* (Baltimore: Johns Hopkins University Press, 1992), 75.

29. Ibid., 91.

10

Postwar Cultural Changes

Just as the theologian Reinhold Niebuhr struggled to articulate the deeper spiritual needs of this decade of affluence and conformity, so a great many secular thinkers during the same period wrestled with de-fining who the American people were. Were their

Critical Attitudes: Shaping the Good Life

needs different from those of other nations? "Exceptionalism"—the term historians use to assert national distinctions—was a popular idea. How had American attitudes about their nation changed in that period of great expectations that emerged after the war?

Looking at Herbert Gans' interviews with the people of Levittown as typical of the postwar exodus, students might conclude that the "good life" seemed attainable. Indeed, a later article in *Commentary* magazine dared to label the 1950s "the happiest, most rational period the Western world has known since 1914."[1] Yet a good number of social critics and historians concerned themselves with the anxieties of the postwar world. Greater affluence could never be an adequate measure of national sat-isfaction if personal wealth denied community needs, as John Kenneth Galbraith suggested in his 1958 classic *The Affluent Society*. In an earlier book, *American Capitalism* (1952), Galbraith had expressed the view that the American talent for production could compensate for the tensions associated with unequal distribution of wealth. Theoretically, the expan-sion of the gross national product from $200 billion in 1940 to $300 billion in 1950 could have satisfied everyone's material needs. Yet, unlike the mood before the war, little incentive existed to turn to more drastic economic control. With the defeat of former vice-president Henry Wallace's Progressive Party in 1948, mainstream Americans seemed to be voting for the success of Harry Truman's association with a more moderate New Deal philosophy.

There was little reason to question the virtues of free enterprise. Yale historian David Potter called his 1954 cultural study of America *People of Plenty: Economic Abundance and the American Character*. Potter believed that the country's great wealth extended its liberal spirit. Yet some social critics did not wait for Michael Harrington's collected essays, *The Other America* (1963), to point out that cities everywhere had been diminished as money poured into suburban developments. Although a general condemnation of Communism made people feel patriotic about the range of American successes, thoughtful citizens felt the need to look more closely at the quality of life in less affluent communities.

Political theorists of the 1950s wanted to accept the idea that ideological struggles had ended (as '80s theorists liked to argue that history had ended) because Communism no longer had any appeal. The sociologist Daniel Bell subtitled a famous 1960s book, *The End of Ideology*, "On the Exhaustion of Political Ideas in the Fifties." Bell's followers believed that the creative social ideas of the early New Deal had disappeared in the anxiety over Communism. Yet as early as 1951—in the decade that represented the "end" of socialist ideology—serious new political magazines appeared. *Dissent* and *Liberation* offered forums for lively young critics of militarism and capitalism. The circulation of *Dissent* actually tripled in five or six years. And during the '50s I. F. Stone started his critical *Weekly*, fulfilling a public need to examine complacency in government.

At the height of consumer culture in 1954 Helen and Scott Nearing published a description of their austere 1930s lifestyle in *Living the Good Life*, subtitled "How to Live Sanely and Simply in a Troubled World." And Paul Goodman published similarly disciplined ideas in *Growing Up Absurd*. With his brother Percival he offered a positive vision in *Communitas: Ways of Livelihood and Means of Life*, showing the need for social planning to solve problems that caused individual dilemmas. Trying to extend a long tradition of utopian thinking to the search for the good life in the 1950s, Goodman concentrated on alienated young people— like the characters played by James Dean and Sal Mineo in *Rebel Without a Cause* (1955). How should individuals make their lives worthwhile? Even B. F. Skinner's behaviorist utopian classic *Walden II*, first published in 1948, found new young readers struggling to examine the possibilities of shaping the good life in controlled terms. Many sensed that the freedom advocated by the popular Dr. Spock might not raise citizens prepared for every social circumstance. Comparisons of childrearing theories at different periods in the 20th century provide rich material for debate.

Although critical—as most Americans then were—of the outcasts who called themselves Beats, Paul Goodman came to appreciate the Beats' loyalty to each other and their spirit of rebellion against materialism. He clarified their "Beatnik" frustrations and their political role even as he criticized Beat writer Jack Kerouac's novel *On the Road* (1957) for its indifference to institutions. The Beats wanted as much freedom to be themselves as possible. Yet although the "missing community" Paul Goodman sought was political—far from the Beats' world of drugs and ongoing travel—Goodman's books did not begin to reach the enormous number of Americans who were reading Nathan Glazer and David Riesman's 1950 sociological classic *The Lonely Crowd*, a book written for academics. The popularity of this book (which by 1971 was in its 23rd printing) suggested how vast was the number of people who began to recognize themselves, in Riesman's term, as "other-directed" types—not as the self-reliant individuals who inhabited prewar America. In his interpretation of America, group conformity rather than communities of creative individuals characterized postwar society. Exploring the shift away from 19th century assertive individualism to the sociable, well-adjusted human beings the comfortable, noncompetitive postwar society needed, Riesman provided a detailed examination of every area of American life. Childrearing, popular culture, the handling of money, and attitudes toward work could all be defined in Reisman's terms. Yet, paradoxically, at a time when many Americans were regarded as reluctant to be different, the new social climate also produced a rich array of individual thinkers—like Reisman himself. Ironically, the '50s, often labeled a decade of conformity and consensus, may well have been the 20th century's most creative period of social criticism.

Richard Hofstadter, one of the most distinguished historians of the era, noted, "For all their bragging and their hypersensitivity Americans are, if not the most self-critical, at least the most anxiously self-conscious people in the world." He went on to point out that they are "forever concerned about the inadequacy of something or other—their national morality, their national culture, their national purpose."[2]

Looking at the variety of '50s books critical of the times would be a worthwhile project for students who see the acquisition of wealth as the only American goal. Readers need to recognize that the American Dream has often been as concerned with personal fulfillment and social idealism as with the accumulation of money. The idea of the quality of life remained real to a number of practical political theorists. Liberal professor Arthur Schlesinger, Jr., in *The Vital Center: The Politics of Freedom* (1949), advocated the need for greater participation in new political groups like Americans for Democratic Action. In 1955 sage philosophical journalist

Walter Lippmann added *The Public Philosophy* to a long list of theoretical writings. He too urged enlightened political involvement to enhance the good life, while the European conscience of Hannah Arendt added a broader dimension to the American mind with *The Human Condition* in 1958. Conservative contemporaries could also find extreme reactions to conformity and community in the writings of Ayn Rand. In her novels and philosophical essays *Atlas Shrugged* (1957) and *For the New Intellectual* (1961), she argued for the power of the self-centered individual as the ultimate social good. Rand's many followers built a cult around hostility to altruism as they celebrated libertarian capitalism. Her novel *The Fountainhead* (1943), made into a movie in 1949, sold 2 million copies by 1952. Rand flaunted her own self-made refugee success by wearing a gold dollar-sign pin.

Magazines as different as *Life* and the *Partisan Review* encouraged people to think about national purpose—even as Eisenhower struggled to make a public statement about American goals. The president's parting warning that America was becoming a military-industrial complex surprised many; but government policies did not change. In some senses America seemed to need Cold War enemies to reinforce prosperity and fortify democratic communities.

The 1950s, as a decade of sociological discovery and cultural analysis, offered all class levels the chance to assess their personal lives. William H. Whyte, Jr.'s *The Organization Man* (1946) analyzing the structured business world was better known than the more hostile works of C. Wright Mills, *White Collar* (1951) and *The Power Elite* (1956). But Americans of all social levels appeared eager to explore the changes in life relating to their daily choices. As expenditures for advertising rose from less than $3 million in 1945 to almost $12 million in 1960, the consumer culture displayed undeniable power. With the 1950s invention of the plastic credit card, offering never-ending spending without ready cash, illusions of wealth grew. By 1996 Americans would charge over $1 trillion a year on plastic—and deal with stress and bankruptcy in dimensions never before imagined. Shopping became a new addiction, treatable by trained therapists.

Critical thinkers quickly grew aware of the influence of Madison Avenue advertising writers, not only in getting people to buy things but also in selling political campaigns. As television began to dominate communication, muckrakers shaped in prewar America emerged to attack the new consumerism essential to the flourishing economy. Vance Packard in *The Hidden Persuaders* (1953) and Russell Lynes in *The Tastemakers* (1949) examined the forces shaping popular tastes. In its fifth printing by 1955, Lynes' book helped people to escape their "lowbrow" private tastes and to appreciate what greater public consciousness could bring about in decorative arts, art, and architecture. In 1952 Mortimer Adler and Robert Hutchins completed editing the series, Great Books of the Western World in 54 volumes, defining the classics of the West everyone ought to buy—as Harvard's President Eliot had once done. Adler's classical tastes included few American writers, no moderns, no women, and no writers of color. Yet people creating new wealth at the time welcomed such help in shaping their judgments. Book clubs flourished as another way to educate different levels of taste.

In the visual world, similarly, culture critics Lewis Mumford and Jane Jacobs made people look around at American cities. With architectural points of view and social conscience they taught readers to value what was worth retaining from the past and what was essential to the changing quality of life in the present. Called "a seeker of a just society" by the *New York Times*, Mumford had been writing since the 1920s on almost every aspect of American life. Like the Nearings' testimonies to good lives lived over several decades, Lewis Mumford's books published in the '50s connected past observations with ongoing usable truths. And Mumford also published an array of new social commentary: *The Conduct of Life* (1951); *Art and Technics* (1952); *In the Name of Sanity* (1954), a criticism of the McCarthy period; and *From the Ground Up* and *The Transformations of Man* (1956). He was an example of a 1950s Renaissance man, a humanist valued not for narrow professional expertise but for the breadth of his mind and his social vision.

Jane Jacobs, like Michael Harrington, called attention to the decay in the inner city in a series of reports published in 1961 as *The Death and Life of the Great American Cities*. Although Mumford wanted more urban control, while Jacobs valued randomness, each called attention to the serious urban needs of the moment. Other journalists analyzed the problems of suburbia as well. John Keats' popular 1957 book *The Crack in the Picture Window* scrutinized suburban charms, while his 1958 volume *The Insolent Chariots* dared question the emerging world of cars—an obsession that would later lead Jane Holtz Kaye to label the America of the 1990s an "asphalt nation." Ever self-critical, Americans also bought many copies of Robert Lindner's *Must You Conform?* (1956).

Many women came out of World War II realizing that their gender roles were controlled by what society needed. If the **Women** domestic roles most played afterward appeared to reflect the mandates of the *Ladies' Home Journal* and the influence of Marynia Farnham and Ferdinand Lundberg's Freudian text, *Modern Woman: The Lost Sex* (1947), there were always a number of feisty women's voices promising more for women than suburban lives and many children.

The anthropologist Margaret Mead was in the public eye as long as Eleanor Roosevelt, reminding women of their cultural conditioning. Like Roosevelt she used women's magazines and newspapers to reach a broad audience. Although Mead accepted anatomy as destiny on one level, she was quick to point out ways to redefine the family. Mary Ritter Beard's classic of complex feminism, *Woman as Force in History: A Study in Traditions and Realities,* appeared in 1946 to alert others to the absence of important women in histories written by men. Beard urged scholars to struggle to understand the satisfactions of influence behind the world of power in order to understand why women put up with the injustice of gender roles. Few listened. In 1959 Eleanor Flexner published the definitive history of women's long, long, long political battles for suffrage, *Century of Struggle: The Women's Rights Movement in the United States.*

Although Betty Friedan's liberating attack on the feminine mystique would not crash upon the scene until 1963, a good number of concerned women had begun to articulate similar complaints. Dazzling critics like Mary McCarthy, Elizabeth Hardwick, Diana Trilling, and Marya Mannes wrote with passion throughout the '50s about what was happening to the minds of confined women. Other journalists, among them Freda Kirchwey, Dorothy Thompson, Lillian Smith, Aline Bernstein Saarinen, and Dorothy Day, demonstrated women's skills at interpretation of a range of social and esthetic problems. Foreign correspondents like Janet Flanner and Martha Gellhorn were prominent in demonstrating the power of the word in analytical commentary, and in 1951 Marguerite Higgins became the first woman to win the Pulitzer Prize in journalism for her reports on the Korean War. Students need to know as much as possible about the lives of such powerful women. Modern feminism began long before the noisy protests of the 1960s.

And if most therapists at the time indeed insisted that anatomy was destiny, there were also a few radical psychoanalysts like Karen Horney and Clara Thompson who recognized the role society played in shaping women's psyches. Unlike their more rigid colleagues, these analysts helped women regard themselves positively at a time when denial of access to many spheres and professions made women blame themselves for personal failures. Adjustment to domesticity was not among the goals they advocated.

The good life most '50s women struggled to clarify had to include both work and children. It had to be more than the either/or option—career or family—Betty Friedan recorded as typical before World War II. Energized by the statistical reality of long life with many possibilities ahead, '50s women came to feel that they could manage more than one existence. One of the appealing legacies of the New Deal described by historian Alan Brinkley was the "postwar faith in the capacity of America to rebuild and perhaps even redeem itself."[3] Women shared such faith—about themselves.

Creativity   Because of the G.I. Bill many educated citizens emerged in the 1950s to welcome and respond to the array of critical thinking. By 1960, as Todd Gitlin noted in his cultural study,

The Sixties: Years of Hope, Days of Rage, "the United States was the first society in the history of the world with more college students than farmers."[4] The great shift to white collar occupations enabled people with money and leisure to support a broad range of intellectual and artistic creativity.

In literature, music, dance, art, photography, and architecture, the 1950s could compete with the best decades of American achievement. New technologies growing out of the war produced long-playing records and better acoustics for concert halls. Engineers were able to recapture the sounds of early jazz and clarify the country voices of folk singers. Mass production of paperbound classics—in the European tradition—made it possible for Americans to own inexpensive books worth reading more than once. It would be a while before television made inroads into the number of serious readers. And Americans, as noted before, spent more money on classical concerts than on baseball games. By moving to new cities in the West in the late 1950s, baseball teams like the Brooklyn Dodgers and the New York Giants lost communities of followers as they made the national pastime truly national. The diminishing number of moviegoers in the '50s had opportunities to expand their cultural experiences. A number of remarkable foreign films such as *Wild Strawberries*, *Rashomon*, and *La Strada* made faraway talents accessible to many different human beings. On the big screen American "exceptionalism" diminished as people recognized what they had in common with the "foreigners" who had been viewed with such hostility during the war.

Because of World War II, prewar isolationism almost disappeared. Fulbright fellowships, funded by money owed the United States—as well as by American taxes—made new exchanges of students possible in many fields of study. Former G.I.s who had wed women from exotic places helped change earlier parochial attitudes. Small American towns began to house people with strange accents and different skin colors. And middle class Americans who had never left home now had money to travel abroad. Even American writers began to describe different experiences that could also become universal after the war.

Two classical war novels, James Jones' *From Here to Eternity* (1951) and Norman Mailer's *The Naked and the Dead* (1948), **Literature** remain testimonies to the fighting men of the time as well as skeptical statements about the nature and necessity of war. After *From Here to Eternity* became a movie in 1953, Frank Sinatra, who had been blacklisted for using a "Communist" songwriter, won the Academy Award that allowed him to make his comeback as a singer. Norman Mailer believed the writer's role was adversarial. As one of America's most gifted authors, he would go on to record a panorama of his country's social dilemmas before shifting to a more allegorical style. Of special interest in connection with the '50s view of war are the stories of Kay

Boyle, whose short fiction documents the rarely articulated lives of the occupation army and their army wives.

If Mortimer Adler thought his series of the Western world's great books would continue to determine the best tastes, he was mistaken. Educated readers began to heed a richer variety of viewpoints. The self-consciousness that emerged from the postwar search for identity no longer neglected the writing of women and people of color—even as talent remained the '50s criterion for judgment. After the war a great curtain lifted on the literary scene, revealing a tremendous operatic chorus of new and gifted performers.

The most common generalization about postwar fiction, connecting it with social criticism, is that it is a literature of alienation. Fifties writers depict individuals who no longer feel part of any community. J. D. Salinger's *Catcher in the Rye* and Jack Kerouac's *On the Road* describe wayward lives seeking release from the material goals of civilization. Whether or not American teenagers—or all teenagers—have often felt such "alienation" is worth discussion. Herman Melville's Redburn and Mark Twain's Huckleberry Finn, and even Louisa May Alcott's Jo March were not comfortable members of their own societies. In 1996, some 40 years after publication, *On the Road* sold 110,000 copies, demonstrating that it was clearly not a book for just one decade. In the '50s young women writers Carson McCullers, Flannery O'Connor, and Jean Stafford used a growing awareness of independent womanhood to express individual skepticism about social institutions.

Jean Stafford, Eudora Welty, Elizabeth Spencer, and Flannery O'Connor—all proud '50s writers—made much of place in shaping their characters. During this period many powerful Southern writers emerged, following the earlier examples of Allen Tate and William Faulkner, to demonstrate that regional consciousness could teach much about the broader human condition. The plays of Tennessee Williams and Lilian Hellman; the stories of Truman Capote, Gore Vidal, William Styron, Walker Percy, Shelby Foote, and Shirley Anne Grau; the poetry of Randall Jarrell and Robert Penn Warren helped keep the South a source of creativity. The only defeated section of the United States continued to offer the country impressive talent, adding to the national awareness of class as well as alienation. Searching for different levels of personal identity, the decade's literature offered a rich variety of complex individual worlds rather than established political contexts. The "dissidence from within," as the critic Richard Chase described it, may be "our most useful tradition." "In what other mood," he asked, "has the American mind ever been creative, fresh or promissory of the future?"[5] Like Norman Mailer, Chase believed that American writers often worked best in opposition to the mainstream culture.

Women writers distinguished by their work in other decades—Edna

Ferber, Gertrude Stein, Fannie Hurst, Pearl Buck, Katherine Anne Porter, Elizabeth Bishop, and Marianne Moore—produced some of their best writing during this period. Mari Sandoz's classic biography *Crazy Horse: The Strange Man of the Oglalas* was recognized as one of the best serious books on the West in 1954. Although few women would have labeled themselves feminists during the '50s, they nevertheless found writing a source of power. Shirley Jackson became a popular writer who managed to capture both the humor and the anxiety involved in domesticity. As her 1947 classic story "The Lottery" was suggestive of the danger of modern witch hunts, so her 1950s stories explored the deep anxieties of homebound women.

In his celebration of the next decade, *Gates of Eden: American Culture in the Sixties* (1977) Morris Dickstein attacked the writers of the '50s for being too concerned with the "elusive mysteries of personality"; too involved with "craft, psychology, and moral allegory;" yet readers must question whether or not these qualities do not continue to fortify the human spirit in ways that political attitudes may not.[6] The three-volume unabridged collection of Emily Dickinson's poetry appeared in 1955, suggesting how profound a writer could be without needing to mention the Civil War she lived through. In 1955 another elusive novel of American adventure on the road, Vladimir Nabokov's allegorical classic *Lolita*, was published in Paris. After rejection by five American publishers and much public protest, the story of the older man's obsession with a young girl would be in bookstores in the United States by 1958, on its way to the bestseller list. By the 1990s *Lolita* would be accepted as a classic. Students of the 1950s fantasizing about what books to take to a desert island or what to read during a long stay in outer space could find a huge variety of satisfying choices to deepen every level of consciousness.

Many of the women writers of the 1950s tackled the social and political issues of the day—even as they delved into personal domestic lives for material. Grace Paley, Tillie Olsen, Hortense Calisher, Harriette Arnow, and Mary McCarthy offered outright challenges to the current definitions of women's roles. The great angry poets of the next decade—Sylvia Plath, Anne Sexton, Adrienne Rich, and Denise Levertov—were all writing away in the '50s as they took care of their babies. Rich and Levertov would write their roles more specifically as political voices. Craft surely need not exclude awareness of the importance of social change.

Grace Paley and Harriette Arnow made social involvement part of the definition of being human. Gwendolyn Brooks, Ann Petry, Paule Marshall, and Lorraine Hansberry emphasized the distinguished tradition of black women, using their own culture to write about feminism and humanism. Hansberry could imagine a black heroine going to medical school at a time when the idea seemed preposterous. Brooks could write a poem about a journalist witnessing the horrors of Little Rock. In 1950 she won the Pulitzer Prize for poetry. Later Gwendolyn Brooks would be named poetry consultant to the Library of Congress, a job more recently redefined as Poet Laureate.

Strong writers from prewar days were still writing for a large audience. John Steinbeck, and John Dos Passos, Eugene O'Neill and Ernest Hemingway made their opinions heard. In 1952 Steinbeck wrote Adlai Stevenson, the defeated Democratic candidate, "If I wanted to destroy a nation I would give it too much."[7] In 1954, two years after he published *The Old Man and the Sea*, Hemingway won the Nobel Prize for a lifetime of carefully crafted writing about human courage.

Two of the decade's great men of letters were African Americans. Ralph Ellison and James Baldwin emerged during the 1950s as writers of special evocative skills—not as polemicists. The intensity of their articulation of experiences as black Americans expanded the consciousness of many white readers and inspired a growing tradition of 20th century black writing. Joining Lorraine Hansberry on stage, playwright Lou Peterson's *Take a Giant Step* opened in 1953 to warm reviews, remaining off Broadway for 264 performances. These black artists did not write solely to help African Americans recover their identity. They were well aware of the distinguished writers still on the scene in the '50s—Richard Wright, Langston Hughes, W.E.B. Du Bois, Zora Neale Hurston, and Jean Toomer. To be sure, many of their insights into the human condition cannot be separated from their color. But as black culture extended into the next decades, black writers spoke to more Americans of every color about the quality of American life. "You are white," Langston Hughes had written, "yet a part of me as I am part of you."[8]

On Broadway a bowdlerized version of Anne Frank's diary helped remind audiences of why they had fought World War II. The 1950s became a liberating period for a new generation of American Jewish writers. Saul Bellow, Bernard Malamud, Delmore Schwartz, Philip Roth, and even Isaac Bashevis Singer, who wrote in Yiddish and whose novels were translated into English, spoke to many kinds of Americans in much the same way Jewish American film makers had done at an earlier time. At this moment, when Jews and Catholics were beginning to be accepted on the faculties of elite colleges, gifted Jewish culture critics also emerged to explore their own roles in American civilization. Thinkers like Philip Rahv, Irving Howe, Lionel Trilling, Alfred Kazin, Norman Podhoretz, Diana Trilling, and Leslie Fiedler not only contributed original interpretations of American culture but also celebrated their personal—often ambivalent—success as they became more American than Jew. They too questioned the good life.

By the '50s earlier immigrant consciousness was melting into everyone's postwar identity dilemmas. Heroes of contemporary novels, with a sense of ambivalence about all their choices in life, belonged as much to John Updike and John Cheever as to Bellow, Roth, and Malamud. J. D. Salinger's character Seymour Glass is more Buddhist than Jewish. And Kerouac's Catholics also turn to the Zen religions of the East. Norman Mailer would not have been placed with other Jewish writers at the time, nor would Adrienne Rich. Finding out who you were remained one of the exciting mind-games of the '50s, a period when complexity was cherished. The 1947 Broadway musical *South Pacific*, enormously popular throughout the decade and adapted as a movie in 1958, made identity dilemmas seem easy to resolve as *Abie's Irish Rose*, a mixed culture drama, had done during the vaudeville ages. Assimilation remained an attainable ideal in many of James Michener's successful '50s novels. *Sayonara* (1957) and the *Bridges of Toko-Ri* (1954) also spread Michener's commitment to tolerance to the movies.

A few talented writers opted to drop out of society by becoming part of a drug culture that rejected connections with conventional communities. William Burroughs published *Naked Lunch* in Paris in 1959; Nelson Algren, *The Man with the Golden Arm* in 1947 and *A Walk on the Wild Side* in 1956.

Science fiction writers captured some of the most real social dilemmas of the time in books—as they were doing in original television dramas. Ray Bradbury published his classic on book burning, *Fahrenheit 451*, in 1953—the year before Joseph McCarthy was censured by the Senate. Andre Norton used intergalactic conflict to highlight human values, while Ursula Le Guin and Madeleine L'Engle began writing science fiction that appealed to both children and adults. In 1957 four of the best science fiction writers of the decade—Cyril Kornbluth, Robert A. Heinlein, Alfred Bester, and Robert Bloch—gained respect by lecturing at the University of Chicago.

Writing for young people has been another way for talented individuals to express ideas in a broader context. Helping children adapt to a new postwar world as they developed strong egos and an understanding of democratic choice were a number of distinguished writers who should be honored by the entire society—not just by the readers who award medals to writing for children.

Books for young people such as Jean Latham's on the doctor Elizabeth Blackwell and the biologist Rachel Carson not only described women who played roles outside the home but also stressed how they dealt with setbacks. In the 1950s Ann Petry and Dorothy Sterling both wrote about Harriet Tubman, the fugitive slave who helped many other slaves escape, making the point that black children had too long been deprived of knowledge of the bravery of their own forebears. And Elizabeth Yates wrote about Prudence Crandall as a pioneer in school integration at a time when many people, ignorant of the American past, believed such dilemmas began with the *Brown* decision in 1954.

Ann Nolan Clark's long experience in the Bureau of Indian Affairs enabled her to remind 1950s young people of the dignity of the Native Americans' nontechnological civilizations. Rachel Carson introduced children to the wonders of nature by educating their parents in elementary terms about the wilderness resources that many ignored at the time. "When I have something important to say," Madeleine L'Engle wrote, "I write it in a book for children."[9] The '50s baby boom may have made children especially visible, but it remains important for historians to be aware of the range of American myths—and realities—in books created for the young. Libraries have long played an underrated role in children's education, even as they have had to compete with schools for resources and with television for attention. During the 1950s special library rooms for children appeared in many places where mothers worked as library volunteers. And many children discovered E. B. White. *Stuart Little* had been a reading pleasure since 1947 and *Charlotte's Web* appeared in 1952 to the delight of Americans of all ages.

The poetry of the 1950s flowered in the midst of consumer delights. Not only did new poetry reflect the expanding consciousness of specific social groups, but a variety of experimentalists appeared evoking America on many other levels.

Older poets basked in their honors. Robert Frost continued to give readings that celebrated New England as a metaphor for the human soul. T. S. Eliot continued to manicure his British conscience. Marianne Moore, Louise Bogan, and Elizabeth Bishop published collections of distinguished work during the 1950s. And William Carlos Williams continued to produce volumes of *Paterson*. Wallace Stevens, vice president of a Hartford insurance company, managed to offer the decade several magical volumes, and the hospitalized fascist sympathizer Ezra Pound continued to write *Cantos* of distinction. e. e. Cummings also gathered together a summary of his life and work. And John Berryman began to celebrate sonnets.

Gifted young poets emerging at the time included Donald Hall, Richard Wilbur, John Ashbery, Randall Jarrell, Delmore Schwartz, Charles Olson, James Merrill, May Swenson, Denise Levertov, Sylvia Plath, and Adrienne Rich. Frank O'Hara helped shape a school of poets in New York City, and a Poets' Theatre flourished in Cambridge, Massachusetts. Yale University continued to offer gifted unpublished poets the opportunity to see their words in print. Perhaps the general prosperity made it possible for the great variety of new talents to take chances as poets. Visitors to America—chosen home of another great poet, W. H. Auden—could easily assume that this was a country that took poetry seriously. Too often historians who do not read poetry tend to neglect the cultural vitality of these times.

Indeed, Robert Lowell, the best known new American poet during the

'50s, quickly made his way into the academic canon, even as he extended his self-awareness into the confessional mode that would characterize much of the next decade's writing. With his solid New England ancestors and obvious talent, Robert Lowell sought a more complex identity in the '50s. As he exposed his manic depression and his family's quirks in his poetry, Lowell gave permission to a new generation of younger poets to set aside traditions and be themselves.

The most outrageous poet of the decade, Allen Ginsberg would remain identified with the Beat community and their hostility to law and order. As he shocked his listeners Ginsberg insisted on being the heir of Walt Whitman. A poem called "Supermarket in California" addresses Whitman as "lonely old courage teacher" and asks the great poet to tell us where we are going.[10] When Ginsberg read his famous long poem "Howl" in 1955 in a converted auto repair shop, the San Francisco City Lights Bookstore crowd greeted him with footstamping enthusiasm. By 1992 the City Lights quarto edition of Ginsberg's *Howl and Other Poems* would be in its 40th edition with 725,000 copies in print.

The Beats insisted that they stood for more than rebellion against the world of comfort and conformity. They too were trying to define the good life as they expanded America's consciousness. During the '50s and '60s Allen Ginsberg preached love to stunned audiences while taking off his clothes or playing finger cymbals for interminable amounts of time. Identifying with Buddhism even though one of his most famous poems, "Kaddish," was a Jewish prayer for his dead mother, Ginsberg joined Salinger in the long American tradition of looking East for philosophical wisdom. In the dedication to "Howl" he called Jack Kerouac "new Buddha of American prose" and asserted that Neal Cassady's biography enlightened Buddha. A distant neighbor in Paterson, New Jersey, William Carlos Williams, wrote a brief introduction to the text, recognizing that "this poet sees through and all around the horrors he partakes of."[11]

Writing of America, wondering if his country would ever be angelic, Ginsberg wanted his love to show. Yet his disappointments spoke to many of his followers even as his gentle spirit transcended the vocabulary that shocked. By the early 1980s Allen Ginsberg had become so respected as a representative of America's counterculture that the State Department sent him all over the world as an ambassador of freedom.

When Ginsberg died in 1997 his poetic vigor and personal kindness were honored in every community where poetry mattered. Harvard professor Helen Vendler noted that Ginsberg was a liberator. For many young people, Vendler suggested, Ginsberg offered "the first truthful words ever heard."[12] "How beautiful is candor," his American ancestor Walt Whitman had written—allowing Allen Ginsberg to continue a legacy of free expression touching every social and erotic experience.

"The real question"—asked by a dying friend of writer Grace Paley and included in the dedication to her collected stories—"How are we to live our lives?" was asked many times during this decade.[13] The '50s offered up no easy answers. Levittowners, black urban migrants, atomic scientists, victims of blacklists, and victims of quotas in professional schools—all struggled to define themselves in an affluent world that offered many the freedom Allen Ginsberg represented. Artists in other media also found that this moment offered time to explore new ideas and individual talents.

Visual Artists
In New York City during the 1950s a community of painters emerged—alongside the writers—with a body of work that was stunning and original. Again with the help of Fulbright grants and with the G.I. Bill, many young American artists were able to master European traditions and modern conventions. They learned to use the past in individual ways as they examined what artists in other parts of the world had been doing. New York at this time was still a haven for refugee artists as well as a home for a number of gifted painters who had been sustained by the New Deal's Works Projects Administration (WPA) programs for writers and artists. The artists who emerged in the 1950s calling themselves the New York School—or Abstract Expressionists—represented an astonishing array of vitality and originality. Always discussing each other's work and exhibiting wherever they could, the New York artists represented—as one of their group, Hans Hofmann, remarked—a true community of talents with nothing in common except their creative urge.[14]

Although the older artists, such as Willem de Kooning, Lee Krasner, Barnett Newman, Jackson Pollock, Robert Motherwell, and Mark Rothko, had been working in New York since before the war, it was not until the 1950s that their years of work culminated in financial success. By contrast, the group called the second generation of Abstract Expressionists, including Elaine de Kooning, Grace Hartigan, Larry Rivers, Helen Frankenthaler, Joan Mitchell, Clyfford Still, Ellsworth Kelly, Frank Stella, and Robert Rauschenberg, received almost immediate attention from both dealers and critics. Most of the Abstract Expressionists who had turned away from realistic representation were leery of being labeled. Indeed, Jackson Pollock may have spoken for all of them when he declared that modern artists were simply working and expressing an inner world. In their visual offerings they were expressing the energy and the motion of the unconscious in a new way. Like the writers—who were often close friends—the artists too were forging different identities as they reformulated the possibilities of modern art.

The remarkable artists of the New York School would not be distinguished by any one style or point of view but by their separate and daring originality. Larry Rivers would later assert that the artists of these times moved in all directions to make sure they were not repeating the past. No longer did any artist consider Paris the center of modern art.[15]

Although it took some time for Americans outside New York City to appreciate the forms, colors, and vitality of Abstract Expressionism, most people did not believe such experimental art was Communist-inspired or amoral, as Congressman George Dondero had insisted in the late 1940s. On the contrary, by the mid-1950s it was clear that such painting was a triumphant example of American individualism. That such extremely personal styles could find galleries and world markets was inspirational to experimental artists in subsequent decades, as well as to younger artists who found exuberance and spiritual community in New York.

Jackson Pollock, born in Cody, Wyoming, and trained by Thomas Hart Benton, suggested the depth of artistic excitement emerging in the art world. Robert Rauschenberg came from Port Arthur, Texas; Robert Motherwell from Aberdeen, Washington; Richard Diebenkorn from Portland, Oregon; Frank Stella from Malden, Massachusetts; and Joan Mitchell from Chicago to join those iconoclasts who were native New Yorkers, like Elaine de Kooning, Helen Frankenthaler, and Jane Freilicher. Louise Nevelson, who had grown up in Rockland, Maine—a "DAR town" that taught her hardship but recognized her talent—insisted that it was the spiritual climate of New York City that made Abstract Expressionism possible.

Moreover, the tradition of representational art continued to thrive during the '50s in different shapes and forms. Realists of many varieties— urban, regional, and magic—prospered. Two generations of Wyeths increased their following as illustrator Norman Rockwell continued to enchant Americans with *Saturday Evening Post* magazine covers, 322 in all, depicting everyday scenes. Rockwell also helped define the good life as most imagined it. In the '50s he did not hesitate to picture the poignance of school integration in a painting he called "The Problem We All Live With." And Jacob Lawrence, a distinguished African American artist, saw his stunning series of paintings on recent black migration from the South bought by the Museum of Modern Art in New York City and the Phillips Gallery in Washington. In New York realists like Isabel Bishop, Raphael Soyer, Reginald Marsh, and Alice Neel demonstrated an esthetic passion for rich detail, while social realists like Ben Shahn and Jack Levine and Hyman Bloom continued to turn satire into palpable beauty. When Congress wanted to deny Levine's *Welcome Home*—an indirect criticism of war—the right to be an entry in an international exhibition, Eisenhower protected the artist's freedom of expression. Older moderns like Stuart Davis, Arthur Dove, Marsden Hartly, John Marin, and Charles Sheeler refined their talents in other parts of America. They managed to survive with obvious skill.

As did the great original painters of the 20th century Georgia O'Keeffe and Edward Hopper, who refused identity with any school or movement. Like Robert Frost and Eugene O'Neill—writers who had created intense individual visions of America—O'Keeffe and Hopper managed to define the loneliness and beauty of American life on their own terms. Over several decades they defined cities and people and nature in ways that also enriched American self-awareness. During the '50s many people were affluent enough to buy inexpensive reproductions of their work.

In Washington, D.C., the National Gallery of Art continues to make quantities of reasonably priced reproductions for visitors from all over the world. That the national museums in Washington charge no admission also makes traditional art accessible to everyone who wants to pursue the history of art and collecting in America. Citizens able to travel in the '50s began to learn new aspects of their own and other cultures.

Other Arts   By the end of the decade art could be included in the freedom of choice in the good life of a culture of abundance. Architects like Buckminster Fuller and Edward Durrell Stone also became useful as creators of "American" public buildings.[16] Built overseas, these "pavilions of plenty" were designed to show Communists— and those tempted by Communism—the range of American creativity, along with examples of consumer goods. The most popular exhibits involved Abstract Expressionist paintings and jazz. Such shows also offered American designers a chance to display their talents as commercial artists. Charles Eames, Raymond Loewy, and Henry Dreyfuss became known worldwide as distinguished industrial designers.

Architecture was valued during this moment of middle class prosperity. Many small-scale housing developments used talented architects to create new visions of the good life. In Lexington, Massachusetts, four such communities built after the war had their own swimming pools and shared common land. Before the decade was over a number of gifted architects also created new buildings for universities and industrial parks. Eero Saarimen, Louis Kahn, Mies Van der Rohe, Philip Johnson, and Walter Gropius brought new architectural vitality to America. Frank Lloyd Wright, usually identified with earlier decades, built his amazing Guggenheim Museum in 1959.

And sculpture—reflecting the New Deal heritage of support for artists—was sometimes designed to be part of the civic experience of architecture and planning in the '50s. In Philadelphia in 1959 the City Council mandated that art be 1% of the budget for all new buildings. Alexander Calder, a third generation sculptor, created mobiles to make people realize that some modern art could be moved by air currents, and David Smith, who came from a family of Indiana blacksmiths, demonstrated the power of mammoth welded sculptures designed to intensify the possibilities of visual experience. During the '50s other sculptors of ingenuity and originality, among them Jacques Lipschitz, Louise Nevelson, Louise Bourgeois, and Isamu Noguchi, would join with Joseph Cornell to remind viewers of the power of simple materials and found objects. The art world became ever more accessible as a source of self-esteem for creative personalities who felt free to turn from the conventional and traditional to explore new ways of looking at reality and new ways of using materials.

The 1950s may also have been the richest decade in American history for African American music. All the great classical jazz musicians and singers, including Louis Armstrong, Duke Ellington, Billie Holiday, and Ella Fitzgerald, performed during this decade. As the LP brought back the early sounds of King Oliver, Ma Rainey, and Bessie Smith, the new Motown sound began to shape itself in Detroit. Marian Anderson in 1955 became the first black woman to sing at the Metropolitan Opera, opening the stage for a great parade of superb African American singers. And although Paul Robeson—because of his Communist sympathies—had his request for a passport denied along with opportunities to sing and act, many recordings of his rich, deep voice remained to be transferred to the new vinyl LP recordings.

Music and Dance

The vitality and originality of the American art world also found its way into the practice of dance during the 1950s. This decade became a period when Americans made good use of both new immigrant and native talents to turn New York into the dance capital of the world. In 1948 Lincoln Kirstein, with the help of the great Russian trained choreographer George Balanchine, began to shape the New York City Ballet into what would often be called the world's greatest dance company. In 50 years the City Ballet not only created a whole range of complex and imaginative new dances, but Kirstein and Balanchine also created the School of the American Ballet to train a corps of dancers necessary to maintain the future of the ballet in the United States.[17] At a moment when competition with the Soviet Union was intense on a political level, New York provided Balanchine with the resources and the freedom necessary to produce unequaled dance productions. In subsequent decades cultural exchanges would enable great Russian dancers like Rudolph Nureyev and Mikhail Baryshnikov to join the American dance theater, where they both remained.

During the '40s and '50s modern dance pioneer Martha Graham—following the originality of her liberated predecessor Isadora Duncan—appeared with her trained company not only in New York City but also in cities all over America. Graham brought "the power of the Indian and the freedom of the Negro" into her choreography in a way that classical ballet could never do.[18] Although the dances of this decade turned to mythology and classical tragedy for human themes rather than to contemporary life, the integration—both racial and intellectual—of Graham's dance company was ahead of its time. Her '50s work also stressed the force of powerful women in a way unusual for the moment. A later biographer found it easy to describe Martha Graham as a woman who liberated both women and the dance. During the late '50s the State Department sent her dance troupe to Europe and Asia as cultural ambassadors.

In the United States, a country not known for receptivity to the dance at any time, the '50s represented a golden age of choreography. Dancers from an earlier period like Ted Shawn and Ruth St. Denis and new talents like Merce Cunningham, Doris Humphrey, and Katherine Dunham added to the richness. Agnes De Mille not only provided Broadway with spectacular choreography for many new American musicals but also produced these works all over the country. When the movie version of *Oklahoma!* came out in 1955, reviewers regretted that the film diminished the vigor of DeMille's dances. Jerome Robbins, on the other hand, became a musical choreographer who used films to make his talents more visible. *On the Town* celebrated New York City in 1950; *West Side Story*, available on film in 1961, put Shakespeare into street gang terms with the help of Leonard Bernstein's music and Stephen Sondheim's lyrics. This production remains an American classic—a Broadway opera expressive of both racial tensions and the ongoing universality of young love.

When Alvin Ailey founded his African American Dance Company in 1948, he could not have anticipated how enthusiastic the world would become about his imaginative creations. Born in Texas, Ailey studied in California, worked in New York City, and produced ballets in London, Paris, and Denmark. For over forty years he was celebrated as one of America's best known cultural ambassadors. Estimates suggest that 18 million people in 67 countries enjoyed the pleasure of witnessing his troupe. Many who attended could not speak English but they could understand the beauty and power of movement. All over the world audiences welcomed *Revelations*, Ailey's exploration of the motivations and emotions behind American Negro religious music, for its clarity and depth. Like the other gifted black artists of the '50s, Alvin Ailey created work designed to bring human beings together, not to separate the black experience from the white American experience. His choreography demonstrated the universality of intense human emotions.[19]

Why is it that the rest of the world so often honors achievements Americans themselves cannot see? As students concentrate on the politics of any decade they need to try to stretch their vision of the way people define themselves. Because the '50s emerge as such a complex period, the challenge to explore the range of possibilities in American life during this decade should be exciting. The pursuit of the good life as many saw it—in sociology, literature, and the arts—may well have been what was truly "exceptional."

NOTES

1. Cited in Morris Dickstein *Gates of Eden: American Culture in the Sixties* (New York: Basic Books, 1997; reprint, New York: Penguin, 1989), 26.

2. Richard Hofstadter, *Anti-Intellectualism in American Life* (New York: Vintage Books, 1962), vii.

3. Alan Brinkley, "The New Political Paradigm: World War II and American Liberalism," in *The War in American Culture: Society and Consciousness during World War II*, ed. Lewis A. Erenberg and Susan E. Hirsch (Chicago: University of Chicago Press, 1996), 326–327.

4. Todd Gitlin, *The Sixties: Years of Hope, Days of Rage* (New York: Bantam Books, 1987), 21.

5. Quoted in "Our Country and Our Culture (Part 3)," *Partisan Review*, September-October 1952, 567, 569.

6. Dickstein, *Eden*, 37.

7. Quoted in Eric Goldman, *The Crucial Decade—and after: America, 1945–60* (New York: Vintage Books, 1956), 325.

8. Langston Hughes, "Theme for English B," in *Black Voices: An Anthology of Afro-American Literature*, ed. Abraham Chapman (New York: New American Library, 1968), 430.

9. Quoted in a biographical article by Francis J. Molson. *Twentieth Century Children's Writers*, 2nd ed. (New York: St. Martin's Press, 1983), 468.

10. Allen Ginsberg, "Supermarket," in *Howl and Other Poems* (San Francisco: City Lights Books, 1956), 30.

11. Ibid., 8.

12. In Helen Vendler, "Two Poets," *Harvard Magazine*, September-October 1997, 62, 63.

13. Grace Paley, *The Collected Stories* (New York: Noonday Press, 1994), v.

14. See Dore Ashton, *The New York School: A Cultural Reckoning* (New York: Penguin, 1979), 79–84.

15. See Irving Sandler, *The New York School: The Painters and Sculptors of the Fifties* (New York: Harper and Row, 1975); also Barbara Rose, *American Art since 1900: A Critical History* (New York: Praeger, 1967); and Eleanor Munro, *Originals: American Women Artists* (New York: Simon and Schuster, 1979).

16. See Robert H. Haddow, *Pavilions of Plenty: Exhibiting American Culture Abroad in the 1950s* (Washington, DC: Smithsonian Institution Press, 1997).

17. See Lynn Garafola with Eric Foner, eds., *Dance for a City: Fifty Years of the New York City Ballet* (New York: Columbia University Press, 1999).

18. Don McDonagh, *Martha Graham* (New York: Praeger, 1973), 12, 297.

19. See Susan Cook, with Joseph Mazo, *The Alvin Ailey American Dance Theater* (New York: Morrow, 1978).

11

The Eye of the Camera

To end a discussion of the 1950s with an analysis of one movie that captured the diversity of the times—as *Casablanca* repre- **Film** sented the American myths of the 1940s—would be convenient. Unfortunately, the 1950s turned out to be much more complicated than the war years. Even the world of movies suggested a vast range of complexity. Among the 100 most important American films—chosen by 1,500 people connected with the American Film Institute in 1998 to represent the range of American experience—20 were made during the 1950s. From *Rebel Without a Cause, Giant, Shane,* and *On the Waterfront* to *Singin' in the Rain, Some Like It Hot, Sunset Boulevard,* and *The African Queen,* the mainstream movie industry—in spite of the Hollywood blacklist—managed to produce a rich variety of films reflecting the changing attitudes in the postwar world. To be sure, a number of blacklisted artists used assumed names or "fronts" to be able to keep on working. Yet if many talented individuals had unquestionably been stifled, others remained able to produce films of exceptional quality. Students viewing these movies in later decades need to reflect on the ideas expressed in the films—often underlying the obvious plots—about personal freedom and emotional commitment, along with the sense of changing racial and gender roles.

Not included in the mainstream, but also valuable as commentary on America, were Herbert Biberman's 1954 film *Salt of the Earth,* a realistic exploration of labor-management struggles, and Douglas Sirk's 1956 movie *All That Heaven Allows,* a "feminist" study of the choices available to a middle aged, middle class widow. *The Defiant Ones* (1958) made viewers confront in chain-gang terms how deeply black and white Americans were connected. In 1952 *Limelight*, the work of another outsider, Charlie Chaplin, was available to the public, even though it was picketed by the American Legion not because the film contained questionable material but because the organization saw Chaplin as "an amoral Communist." Never having joined any political organization, Charlie Chaplin was defended by the *New York Times* as a great artist who had given much pleasure to millions in many countries. Although Chaplin had made most of his films in America, he remained a British subject who in the '50s turned in his American reentry visa and refused to come back. His 1957 anti–red scare film, *A King in New York*, would not be shown in the United States until 1976. In the 1970s Chaplin also changed his mind about America. He returned to accept lifetime tributes from Brandeis University and the Lincoln Center Film Society.[1]

What is clear about a good number of films of the period not on the American Film Institute list is how accurately movies of every sort continued to reflect the social currents that were making the 1950s a different world. *The Fountainhead, The Man in the Gray Flannel Suit, Twelve Angry Men, The Caine Mutiny, Mr. Blandings Builds His Dream House, The Country Girl, On the Beach,* and *Marty* threw as much light on the '50s quest for the good life as the Doris Day comedies that ended in marriage and the Alfred Hitchcock mysteries that allowed beautiful women a measure of wit in overcoming fear and evil. Using movies as primary sources, imaginative history teachers could easily organize a complete course on the 1950s from a variety of different social or ideological viewpoints.

Photojournalism and Art

Few culture critics would dispute the power emerging from the great art form of the twentieth century, photography. In the '50s the strong American tradition of photojournalism became sure of itself as an esthetic offering. By the end of the decade art museums all over the country would begin to display the creations of the camera—not just as a record of the moment, but as art. Photographs, long entrenched as a necessary part of the country's social awareness, took on a new dimension as visual essays. From Mathew Brady's precise and painful work documenting the Civil War, through the Farm Security Administration's vast collection of photos of agricultural workers during the New Deal, to *Life* magazine's assemblage of heroic on-the-spot pictures made during World War II, the photograph had become as reliable a source of American history as the printed word. Some people even started to believe pictures to be more reliable than words. By the end of the 1950s such photographs— to the distress of many conservative scholars reluctant to extend the communication of events beyond official documents—became essential commentaries on American life. Any history of the contemporary world would be greatly diminished without photographs.

During World War II, a time when no consumer television existed, *Life*'s superb photographs brought the war into American living rooms. The early issues of the magazine offered new opportunities for some of America's most gifted photographers: Margaret Bourke-White, Robert Capa, Carl Mydans, Elliot Erwitt, Gordon Parks, and W. Eugene Smith, among others. They often risked their lives for the high quality of involved photography that created a sense of community among Americans as it made the war part of daily life. Capa, like the brave journalist Ernie Pyle, was killed at his work. More than one critic has remarked that photography remains the most democratic art because it records the lives of every social group and can be interpreted directly by any viewer. Even as photography became more professionally specialized, journalism also suggested possibilities for the skills of amateurs. After the war, along with the chance to buy good 35mm cameras at reasonable prices, every American had a chance to look at how much talented photographers could say with small cameras.

The two-volume picture books put together from *Life*'s enormous photo-archives might also be used as textbooks on American life. For the postwar years *Life: The Second Decade, 1946–1955* could answer student questions about changing customs, showing how farmlands disappeared into suburbs, and cities decayed.[2] Offering serious thinkers the chance to comment on what the photosequences suggested, *Life*'s editors at the time extended the visual into the philosophical, imitating the intellectual journals trying to accommodate affluence with social responsibility. *Life*'s readers also needed to define what the "good" American life could be. During the '50s the magazine sponsored a roundtable of thinkers attempting to connect the university with the public in what seemed a national commitment to examine the new lives of the middle class. In the photographic tradition of Lewis Hine, a famous early exposer of the incongruities of urban life, gifted photojournalists like Eve Arnold, W. Eugene Smith, Gordon Parks, Alfred Eisenstaedt, Martha Holmes, and Yale Joel captured daily activities that represented both "things to be corrected and things to be appreciated."[3] If *Life* directed much attention toward suburbia, helping to define its advertisers' new consumerism, it did not neglect the documentation of atomic blasts, or stories of Alger Hiss and Senator McCarthy. Pictures of high school teachers driving black students home from recently desegregated schools spoke to *Life*'s readers along with the photographs of lingering social hostility in the South.

Eve Arnold documented the lives of a clan rooted in Long Island since the 1700s—vigorous in civic virtue and in snobbery. A gifted photographer during many decades, Arnold eventually settled in England, but during the 1950s she often published in *Life*, offering social history as she saw it. She recorded the enthusiasm surrounding the popular evangelist Oral Roberts, and she documented the early days of Malcolm X among the Black Muslims. No one would have questioned the unbiased nature of her camera's lens. Arnold spent several days at one of Senator McCarthy's hearings and also managed to record the sit-in training given participants in the Congress of Racial Equality as they learned techniques for integrating lunch counters with dignity. At a time when sex discrimination existed in almost every labor union, she managed to capture angry picketers in front of a saloon where a woman had been hired as bartender. And she took dressing room photographs of women who later became American icons, Marilyn Monroe and Joan Crawford. Like other distinguished photographers of the 1950s, Arnold worked hard to document the incredible variety of the American experience. But by the end of the decade she came to believe that photographers no longer needed to be investigative reporters. Television had begun to take away one of their important roles. Nevertheless, the still photographs she valued had become an "acknowledged art form—viewed by millions."[4]

Looking back on what she also called a "decade of disillusionment" in *Flashback! The 50s* (1978), a book on her early years as a photographer, Eve Arnold declared her own life during the '50s to have been "free and adventurous"—both in the use of the camera and in the scope photographers had to range the world in search of subject matter. Her camera was not censored. And being a woman had not interfered with her choice of work. A colleague later commented that the '50s "was about people"; afterwards "it would be about photography."[5] Arnold's inclusive vision of the decade concentrated neither on the smugness she recorded at the McCarthy hearings nor on the consumerism identified with contemporary advertising, but on the possibilities of an America that could balance hope with disillusionment. Many Americans shared her double point of view.

The work of another important photographer during this decade can be viewed in *America Worked: The 1950s Photographs of Dan Weiner* (1989), edited by William Ewing after Weiner's early death in a plane crash. Influenced by the Farm Security Administration's archives of photographic witness, as well as by his employers at *Fortune* magazine, Weiner managed to communicate hope in most of the faces he recorded. Like a number of contemporary writers—John Updike, John Cheever, and Shirley Jackson—Weiner made much of the details of everyday life and the images of daily domesticity as a key to measuring the postwar world. One critic suggested that he treated the domestic life of the '50s as though it was as much a subject for revelation as a royal court or a famous battle scene.

On one level Weiner's '50s pictures document the conformity behind work stereotypes: salesmen, executives, mothers, and secretaries. Yet at the same time his images also capture what has been called the hardest subject of all to visualize—belief. Like many of the individuals interviewed in Levittown, Weiner's people "seem to have believed that the work they were doing and the things they were buying were going to make their country great and their lives happy." What Dan Weiner recognized and made clear in his photographs was the idea that "pride in work and faith in purchased goods" were essential to understanding the culture of the '50s. His personal vision offered a more complex interpretation of consumerism and the "good life."[6]

The photographer sophisticated critics singled out as the source for the most memorable images of the decade was Robert Frank, who captured public realities as Weiner captured private moments. Not a believer like Weiner, Frank brought the skeptical viewpoint of a naturalized immigrant to his commitment to discover and record the kind of American civilization the rest of the world was eager to imitate. An associate of Edward Steichen, Frank had been apprenticed to several European masters of modern camera techniques. He wanted to connect photography with more sustaining expression—to use his art to impart meaning and transmit emotion, not simply to tell a story. On a Guggenheim fellowship in 1955 he traveled all over America like his later friends Jack Kerouac and Allen Ginsberg, looking behind the myth of postwar prosperity and conformity pictured in magazines like *Life*. Frank ferreted out the loneliness and alienation that Weiner and Arnold had noted but did not underline. Yet he also suggested that the other side of loneliness might be a strong individualism. Conformity did not characterize his community images.

Robert Frank's pictures of gas stations, diners, jukeboxes, and the road itself became clearer symbols of American civilization to many people than the majestic landscapes of Ansel Adams and Eliot Porter. Looking everywhere for the ideas in things, Frank rejected much that was purely commercial or pretentious in favor of images like the jukebox that perpetuated the vitality of popular music. In the simplicity of a black funeral in South Carolina, he captured aspects of American religion that also transcended conventional rituals.

Robert Frank never pretended to be objective. His pictures were meant to be a personal response to the social, political, and cultural values of his new country. It was appropriate that Jack Kerouac should write the introduction to Frank's book *The Americans* (1959), culled from 20,000 photographs. Kerouac praised "The EVERYTHINGNESS" and "American-ness" of Frank's pictures—as pure as a "tenor solo in jazz."[7] He also felt the loneliness Robert Frank managed to convey.

Photography asserted its importance as a valid source for interpretation of the life of the 1950s on many levels—as photojournalism, personal witness, commercial persuasion, and esthetic creation. From earlier decades, artists like Ansel Adams, Edward Weston, Paul Strand, Imogen Cunningham, Dorothea Lange, and Walker Evans continued to enlarge the meaning of their craft. Pioneers like Margaret Bourke-White and Berenice Abbott also pursued their journalistic achievements at a time when women's skills were more apt to be challenged than before the war. During this period, too, fashion photographers Irving Penn, William Klein, and Richard Avedon had occasion to experiment with new angles of vision. And as Minor White tried to capture images of the spirit, Weegee continued to document the earthy in "the naked city" of New York. Looking at a retrospective of the 1950s' pictures of William Klein, Vicki Goldberg, photography critic for the *New York Times*, remarked that labeling the '50s—the organization man, the silent generation, "togetherness," and virgin brides—was like collecting "a set of rules waiting to be broken."[8] In the great richness of '50s photography she saw that the academic legacies of the decisive moment and the perfect print had disappeared as well.

The Smith brothers, Marvin and Morgan, left Kentucky in the back of the bus in 1910 and survived the Depression in Harlem as park laborers. Following the tradition of the distinguished African American photographer James Van DerZee, they managed to open a local photo studio to create "portraits of quality" for black citizens. During World War II Marvin became the first African American to attend the Naval Air Station School of Photography and Motion Pictures in Pensacola. And in the prosperous period after the war he used the G.I. Bill to study art in Paris with Fernand Léger. Although the twins worked through more than one decade as photographers of African American life, during the '50s they also worked behind the scenes in television. As many talented black performers and athletes began to command worldwide status after the war, Marvin and Morgan Smith produced for American history a distinguished archive of black achievement. Along with pictures of Harlem street activities, portraits of Fats Waller, Jackie Robinson, Count Basie, Duke Ellington, and Cab Calloway appeared in the brothers' gallery—the Morgans kept their studio until 1967. Gordon Parks, America's most famous African American photojournalist, managed to snap a portrait of the handsome identical twins, and he wrote the introduction for their later exhibition at the Schomberg Center, "Harlem: The Vision of Morgan and Marvin Smith."

The pictorial work Parks produced for *Life* for over two decades displayed another, more complete range of African American experience. Gordon Parks covered the story of the first black fighter pilots in World War II, but was denied permission to go overseas with them by politicians unwilling to give blacks visibility. The youngest of fifteen children of a Kansas dirt farmer, Parks would have to be included on any list of America's most talented photographers. He worked for *Life* both before and after World War II. Americans have had the chance to view his collected photographs in the art galleries of over ten cities and also to read Park's autobiographical novel, *The Learning Tree* (1969). Yet during the '50s Gordon Parks was twice threatened with lynching while photographing the civil rights struggles in the South. And later he would even be stopped by police in Beverly Hills for driving his Rolls-Royce—too slowly!

More focused specialists emerged in the photography profession during the '50s: "Ylla," the animal photographer, killed in a fall from a jeep in 1955; Laura Gilpin, who worked in industry at the time; Barbara Morgan, who caught the action of Martha Graham dancing. Skillful portrait photographers like Inge Morath, Lotte Jacobi, and Ilse Dorfman extended their sensitivity into the worlds of children, writers, and artists. Self-conscious artists like Marie Cosindas, Edward Weston, Ansel Adams, Eliot Porter, and Tina Modotti were refining their talents to create unforgettable images for America's museums.

During the '50s Diane Arbus, famous for photographs of eccentrics, studied with Lisette Model to learn how to shift her skills away from fashion photography. Her concentration on "freaks" seemed to match the words of writer Flannery O'Connor in adding another kind of awareness to contrast with the clichés of '50s normalcy. The nonconformist Arbus often used her camera to record the lives of those people others would turn away from on the street. She argued that she hoped to enhance the dignity of her photographic subjects. Diane Arbus believed there were valuable qualities in human beings nobody would see unless her camera recorded them. Her work represented the democratic commitment to individualism that characterized so much in this decade.

Noting the range of activities of women photographers of different ages during the '50s, students might consider how liberating mastering this technology has been for women. Many women felt free behind a camera to extend their experience. Although some critics thought women photographers expressed a passive need to participate in male accomplishments by photographing the worlds of men, others speculated that taking pictures offered women a different kind of power. Photography, Susan Sontag theorized, was a means to appropriate the thing photographed. It gave women a "certain relation with the world that feels like knowledge and therefore like power."[9] Did the essential art of the 20th century—photography—also help women to change the definitions of what was expected of them? To redefine their own worlds? Photographers of the 1950s again represented many different levels of freedom.

As early as 1938, in an essay on Walker Evans, the photographic recorder of the Great Depression, Lincoln Kirstein noted that the power of the visual arts to show us our moral and economic situation now belonged to **"The Family of Man" Exhibit** the photographer.[10] By the '50s social realities had changed, but the photographer's moral role remained the same. As the decade liberated individual photographers to experiment and produce diaries of American life, it also provided the resources and attention necessary to create an imaginative display of photographs that made use not only of American talents but also of the talents of photographers—both professional and amateur—from all over the world.

In 1955 when the Museum of Modern Art in New York City mounted a vast exhibition of photographs called "The Family of Man," there would be an enormous audience for the show. Photographer Edward Steichen, who organized and created this spectacular display, may have done more to clarify the power and value of photography than any other American. The impact of this exhibit on its viewers was so powerful that the United States Information Agency chose immediately to copy and rebuild it at trade fairs and consulates all over the globe. Over 9 million people eventually looked at Steichen's collected photographs. If William Carlos Williams' belief that there were "no ideas but in things" suggested that the film *Casablanca* might be seen as representative of 1940s mythology, the photographic display called "The Family of Man" suggested a similar representation of the cultural concerns of the 1950s. No other artifact of this conformist age of suspicion better expresses the quality of the '50s struggle to define the good life in the presence of the underlying anxiety shaped by the bomb and the Cold War.

A solid documentary text about the creation of the display, Eric J. Sandeen's *Picturing an Exhibition: The Family of Man and 1950s America* (1995) provides essential background material for study. To the mind of the '50s—as the cover of the catalogue declared—"The Family of Man" stood for "the greatest photographic exhibition of all time—503 pictures from 68 countries." Edward Steichen's introduction noted that the display "was conceived as a mirror of the universal elements and emotions in the everydayness of life." He saw the show as an affirmation of the essential oneness of the world. From over 2 million photographs submitted by both well-known professionals and unknown amateur photographers, Steichen and his colleagues picked the work of 273 different photographers to provide witness to "human consciousness"—not necessarily social consciousness—to the life cycle as all kinds of people experienced it. "I am no longer concerned with photography as an art form," Steichen said. "I believe it is potentially the best medium for explaining man to himself and to his fellow man."[11]

Attacked by later critics as "sentimental," *The Family of Man*—as it remained in print in picture book form—also made seventies viewers gasp at the gender specificity of its title. The '50s' acceptance of "man" as a generic term that included women had kept many people from recognizing that women were often unconsciously excluded in the prose of human rights emerging after World War II. Fortunately the show it-self—the images that defined the family—made no such gender distinc-tion. And many women photographers contributed to the exhibition. The 503 picture selections put together by Joan and Wayne Miller demon-strated as much about the lives of women and children as they told about the lives of men. And the captions chosen by Dorothy Norman managed to include quotations from the works of women writers as well as pub-lished texts from different cultures. It could not have been accidental that all four photos describing the solemn excitement of voting were of women. Later feminists would build on the title to create a more exclu-sive volume of photographs produced by the Ridge Press at Grosset Dunlap as *The Family of Woman* (1979).

As a young man Edward Steichen had created several photographs deemed American classics, such as his portrait of J. P. Morgan and his impressionistic vision of the Flatiron Building in New York City. Yet, like so many others, he was influenced by the powerful documentary archives of the Farm Security Administration to want to move people with pictures to bring about social change.

As a distinguished photojournalist of war Steichen had already held three shows of his war photography at the Museum of Modern Art—two of World War II and one of Korea. Believing that photography was a dynamic process of giving form to ideas, he had concentrated on col-lecting those pictures that revealed "the monstrous actuality" of war. But by the '50s he shifted his viewpoint. Instead of focusing on destruction he wanted to emphasize what was worth preserving. He too was trying to clarify the good life that might make political decision makers assess their activities differently. By displaying "the enduring human emo-tions" under the shadow of the bomb, Steichen tried to underline the value of life in "the most ambitious photographic exhibition" ever held. After "The Family of Man" opened in February 1955, *Life* magazine gave the show a nineteen-picture spread.[12]

What is sadly missing in the book of photographs—still in print in the 1990s—that defined the exhibit to future generations is the gigantic color picture of the hydrogen bomb. Steichen had arranged this horror as a backdrop to all the black and white photos. Perhaps the book editors felt that the room-sized photograph could not be realistically contained in a small volume of photos. But without it readers of the text missed the depth of Edward Steichen's intent. It was his desire to make the viewers recognize the reality of the bomb as they looked at all the rituals of human life it would destroy. Steichen had gone to the trouble of enlarg-ing a *Life* photograph of an H-bomb's total incineration of a Pacific atoll: Operation Ivy. In the world of black and white photographs that represented the daily activities of the family of human beings, the bomb's color reflected the elemental emission of colored light recorded by witnesses who watched the island disappear. Included among the words of wisdom that captioned the photographs was a quote from the modern philosopher and mathematician Bertrand Russell, underlining Steichen's views. "A war with hydrogen bombs," Russell declared "is quite likely to put an end to the human race."[13]

Those who know the exhibit only from the broadly circulated paperback catalogue also miss out on the distinctive style of the exhibition. The variety of shapes and sizes of the photographs created a visual syncopation and organization that pulled the viewer into the scenes of all the different lives existing in front of the outline of the bomb. During the 1950s the show broke every attendance record at the Museum of Modern Art. Many viewers acknowledged that it was the first time they had ever been in a museum.

"The Family of Man" was certainly not designed as propaganda for the United States. But its tremendous popularity spoke to the internationalism of an American government trying to bring about full acceptance of the United Nations both at home and abroad. To the credit of the United States Information Agency, which made reproductions of the exhibit to send to different parts of the world as publicity for the United States, all copies of the show included the H-bomb picture. Four full-sized and several smaller versions of the exhibit were also sent to different parts of America. By 1962 "The Family of Man" had made 91 stops in 38 countries. In Moscow 2.7 million people invited to a trade fair to inspect Nixon's kitchens often remembered with more enthusiasm "The Family of Man" exhibit set up next door. In Japan alone 621,000 people saw one of three versions, including over 28,000 citizens in the city of Hiroshima. More than half the city of Belgrade, Yugoslavia, went to see the show, as did almost 32,000 inhabitants in the city of Chicago.[14]

The USIA also gave out free catalogues to leading citizens in other countries—100,000 were offered in Amsterdam alone. And 300 prints of a 26-minute introductory black and white film, translated into 22 languages, were screened overseas in 70 countries. By the mid-1950s, 6 million copies of the paperbound book were in circulation, and an additional 4 million copies were also sold at bookstores for $1 apiece.

It would be ten years before enthusiasts came to recognize that some of the images were damaging to a new nationalism that did not want to see half-clad Nigerians or begging Chinese children. The desire for an international community led so strongly by Eleanor Roosevelt in the '50s began to disintegrate. Steichen had included a picture of the United Nations Assembly in the exhibit with a caption from the 1952 charter:

We, the peoples of the United Nations
Determined to save succeeding generations from the scourge of war,

which twice in our lifetime has brought untold sorrow to mankind,
and
To reaffirm faith in fundamental human rights, in the dignity
and worth of the human person, in the equal rights of men
and women, and of nations large and small. . . . [15]

Having considered this statement, some 9 million viewers would then
go on to examine the four images of women voting in societies far different from the United States. And they could also contemplate the cultural variety in rituals of love and death and in the patterns of work and
war. Above all, viewers would have to confront a vast number of photographs of the world's children—the representatives of the future—
playing and hoping under the shadow of the bomb.

Sentimental? Naive? Reflective of the baby boom? Perhaps. Steichen
had attempted to put forth a capacious middle ground some would find
too bourgeois. But recent replications of the show have left even new
viewers in tears. Steichen removed the photo of death by lynching. And
although he kept a picture of Warsaw Jews being marched to their deaths
in World War II, he also used the passage from Anne Frank's diary
asserting her belief that people were really good at heart—a quote that
would infuriate a later generation of Jews as too conciliatory. Images of
evil are not pure in this show. Belief in the family by its very nature
concentrated on images of love and possibility. The Cold War and the
new nationalism of 1955 remain visually dormant. Steichen's pictures
insist on the positive global power of what human beings have created.

In 1962 when Edward Steichen mounted his last show at the Museum
of Modern Art, he responded to a different social need. By then the
consumer society had forgotten both the hardships of the Depression and
the spirited commitment to World War II. Steichen chose to revive the
photographic archive of the Farm Security Administration's 1930s accomplishments—a reminder of a period of national disaster that might
occur again. "The Bitter Years" offered the public examples of "the en-
durance and fortitude that made the emergence from the Great Depression" to Steichen "one of America's victorious hours."[16]

Edward Steichen wanted his life work to be an encyclopedia of all
phases and activities of the United States and its people. Belief was essential to his mythical self-definition as he made people recognize the
humanizing value of photography. Yet in spite of Steichen's concern for
communication in "The Family of Man," it may be a final irony that the
show succeeded more in terms of its photographic beauty than its social
link to humanity. Nevertheless, students exploring the good life beneath
the surfaces of the 1950s need to look seriously at "The Family of Man"
as an American artifact suggestive of the high ideals of a moment when

images of the family could represent symbolic goodness to the entire world.

NOTES

1. See Stephen J. Whitfield, *The Culture of the Cold War* (Baltimore: Johns Hopkins University Press, 1991), 187–197.

2. New York Graphic Society, *Life: The Second Decade, 1946–1955* (Boston: Little, Brown, 1955), passim.

3. Quoted in ibid., 13.

4. Eve Arnold, *Flashback! The 50s* (New York: Knopf, 1978), 148.

5. Ibid., 2, 149.

6. Ingrid Sischy, "Photography: Belief," *The New Yorker*, May 22, 1989, 82.

7. Jack Kerouac, introduction to Robert Frank, *The Americans* (Paris: National Gallery of Art, 1958).

8. Vicki Goldberg, "William Klein, Impolite Photographer," *New York Times*, October 18, 1992.

9. Susan Sontag, *On Photography* (New York: Dell, 1973), 4.

10. Lincoln Kirstein, *Walker Evans Catalog* (New York: Museum of Modern Art, 1938).

11. Quoted in Eric Sandeen, *Picturing an Exhibition: The Family of Man and 1950s America* (Albuquerque: University of New Mexico Press, 1995), 8.

12. Ibid., 1, 2.

13. Quoted in *The Family of Man: Created by Edward Steichen for the Museum of Modern Art* (New York: Maco Magazine Corp., 1955), 179.

14. Sandeen, *Picturing an Exhibition*, 67, 48.

15. Quoted in *The Family of Man*, 184.

16. Quoted in Sandeen, *Picturing an Exhibition*, 178–179.

12

Conclusion

To be sure, the decade of the 1950s remains identified with ideological fears that may become ugly in America. McCarthyism so defined the extremism of its times that the decade's achievements are too often diminished. Because women during this paradoxical decade were offered few alternative career roles outside of mothering, much pity has been heaped upon them. But World War II had helped women recognize their rights, and they continued to work outside the home in growing numbers. Although denied access to professions and high paying careers, the women of the '50s did more than raise children. Too little has been written on *how* women managed to lead fulfilling lives—both as mothers and as part-time workers and volunteers—at a time when good jobs for women were scarce. Much still needs to be written on the varieties of voluntarism during this period. Social, political, and educational activities emerged not only to enhance many women's definitions of the good life, but also to improve the quality of American life for everyone.

The racism that has defined American history from the French and Indian War through the Civil War to the murders during the 1960s civil rights movement also existed in the '50s in many forms of harassment, segregation, and job discrimination. But the 1954 *Brown* decision on school desegregation and the integration of the army brought hope for modest progress. The presence during the decade of an incredible range of black talent: tennis player Althea Gibson, baseball great Hank Aaron, singer Billie Holiday, musician Louis Armstrong, writers Ralph Ellison and Lorraine Hansberry, jurists Thurgood Marshall and Constance

Baker Motley inspired many to hope that the American Dream—not of money, but of the fulfillment of the self—might actually be possible. As the G.I. Bill extended education and the society prospered, concern for equality of opportunity fell into place as part of the definition of the good life everyone was looking for. But it would be the next decade that would focus its attention militantly on "rights" as the means to self-fulfillment.

Few politicians cared about the natural environment during the fifties—or, worse, they continued to permit the destruction of valuable natural resources. Yet out of a world of indifference rose one of America's most important nature writers, Rachel Carson. Her writing was of such scientific clarity and literary grace that the whole world wanted to read her books. *The Sea Around Us* not only won the National Book Award in 1951 but remained on the bestseller list for 86 weeks. It was translated into 32 languages. Although her masterpiece on the effects of pesticides, *Silent Spring* (1962), brought the wrath of chemical manufacturers down upon her, it would later be declared a classic in the tradition of *Uncle Tom's Cabin* or *The Rights of Man*.[1] The impact this book had on the 20th century's careless attitudes toward the environment was, at the time, enormous. Like Edward Steichen, Carson made an effort to communicate with all levels of humanity in every part of the world—to underline the sense of beauty and wonder essential to the definition of a good life. She used her talents and knowledge not simply for personal success in the world of men but also to make the earth a better place for everyone to live in.

In 1956 Rachel Carson published an article on the importance of the education of children, not in a journal of science but in a women's magazine. "Help Your Child to Wonder" emphasized the importance of training children's intuitive sense to recognize that we are all part of the natural world.[2] The good life of the '50s had to contain a complex vision of the broadest human possibilities.

Emerging from over two decades of material deprivation and international strife, the Americans of the 1950s struggled to define themselves in an entirely different world. In spite of the fear of Communism, theirs was one of the most creative decades of the century in terms of critical intelligence as well as in all the arts and literature. To see the Americans of the 1950s solely in terms of their anxieties and their consumerism, or to define them solely as conformists, diminishes the importance of their broad and complicated contributions to the search for what really matters in life.

NOTES

1. Harriet Beecher Stowe's *Uncle Tom's Cabin* (1852) influenced public opinion against slavery; Thomas Paine's *Rights of Man* (1787) made people recognize the need for social reforms to help the poor.

2. Rachel Carson, "Help Your Child to Wonder," *Woman's Home Companion*, July 1956; rewritten as a book entitled *The Sense of Wonder* (1965).

As Ambassador to the United Nations, Eleanor Roosevelt fought the Cold War by emphasizing the worldwide significance of human rights. Her concern for workers, women, and children made her universally beloved.

Typing jobs were always available. Some women managed to use such skills to advance careers in special fields, but most remained secretaries. Radcliffe Archives, Radcliffe Institute, Harvard University

Senator Joseph McCarthy made a practice of waving papers he insisted were lists of Communists infiltrating the government. In 1954 he was censured by the Congress for recklessness. Photo by Tom O'Halloran. Library of Congress, Prints & Photographs Division

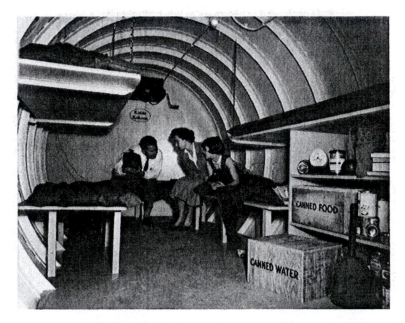

Fear of the Soviet Union's bomb drove a few Americans to delude themselves into believing that private shelters could save their families from nuclear attack. United Press International. Library of Congress, Prints & Photographs Division

Rosa Parks was arrested for refusing to give up her seat on a bus to a white man in Montgomery, Alabama in 1955. The bus boycott that ensued gave Martin Luther King a chance to display his remarkable leadership abilities. Library of Congress, Prints & Photographs Division

Levittown, New York. This entire project was finished in nine months. Open spaces were for schools and community recreation. National Archives

After the war the Levittown–favorite-style home among a few model choices was the Cape Cod cottage. Later the public preferred the ranch-style house. National Archives

The abundance of electricity after the war made all sorts of new appliances necessities for an easier life. National Archives

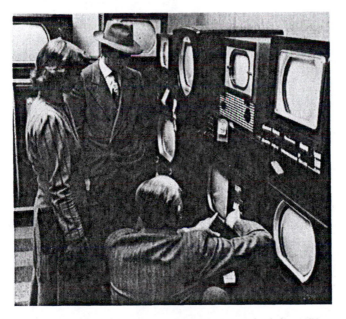

1950, Washington, D.C. TV demonstration. By the end of the 1950s people no longer went to the neighbors to watch popular programs. Some families even began to have two TV sets. National Archives

In 1958 "Super Giant" in Washington, D.C. experimented with carrying household merchandise as well as every kind of food. Available parking made it easy for customers to carry large purchases. National Archives

"Food Fair," Washington, D.C. Before the war butchers helped customers select meat. Now customers could make fast decisions with weights and prices clearly marked. National Archives

By the end of the decade the shopping mall included every variety of store and helped end small-town shopping. Here the central air conditioning made customers more comfortable while parking accommodated shoppers from different suburbs. Southdale, near Minneapolis, 1956. National Archives

New York City auto show at the Waldorf-Astoria Hotel, 1950. Marketers began to suggest that a better lifestyle, or a beautiful woman, came with the car. National Archives

Television began to be used as an educational tool for children studying at home. National Archives

In 1950 the good life in Tucson, Arizona included enough water for watering lawns that children could play on and for air-conditioning to make houses more comfortable. National Archives

In 1951 the good life in Detroit, Michigan included a family, a small house, and a reasonable car. National Archives

Lucille Ball, possibly the most popular artist in the United States during the 1950s, communicated many of the dilemmas of women in her television sitcom *I Love Lucy*, in spite of the housewife role she played. By permission of Photofest, Inc.

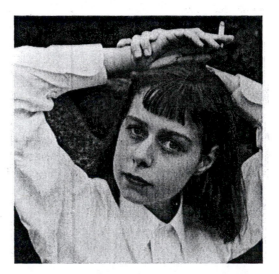

Carson McCullers's play *A Member of the Wedding* appeared on both stage and screen during the 1950s. Many gifted young writers flourished after the war: Ralph Ellison, Arthur Miller, Norman Mailer, Tennessee Williams, Flannery O'Connor, Robert Lowell, Allen Ginsberg, and Jack Kerouac also contributed to the feast of literary talent. Carson McCullers, 1940. Photograph by Louise Dahl-Wolfe. © 1993 Center for Creative Photography, Arizona Board of Regents, Collection Center for Creative Photography, The University of Arizona

Elvis Presley, "the king" of rock 'n' roll, not only won the hearts of thousands of teenagers but also helped to change popular music. With Buddy Holly, Chuck Berry, and Little Richard during the '50s, Elvis made a new music based on old sounds. Photo by Phil Stanziola. Library of Congress, Prints & Photographs Division

The Honeymooners represented working class people as laughable and lovable in spite of their toughness. By permission of Photofest, Inc.

Jackson Pollock One: November 31, 1950. Pollock's vitality and imagination made him a leader of the new abstract expressionist painters. New York in the 1950s became the art capital of the world. The Museum of Modern Art, New York. Sidney and Harriet Janis Collection Fund

In 1954 "The Family of Man" photograph display began at the Museum of Modern Art in New York and reached out to the world through traveling shows in the 1950s. Here the daughter of the ambassador from the Republic of China looks at an earlier picture of herself both on the wall and in the catalogue that spoke to millions of people. National Archives

Appendix A

THE BILL OF RIGHTS

ARTICLES IN ADDITION TO, AND AMENDMENT OF, THE CONSTITUTION OF THE UNITED STATES OF AMERICA, PROPOSED BY CONGRESS, AND RATIFIED BY THE SEVERAL STATES, PURSUANT TO THE FIFTH ARTICLE OF THE ORIGINAL CONSTITUTION.

Amendment I.

Congress shall make no law respecting an establishment of religion, or prohibiting the free exercise thereof; or abridging the freedom of speech, or of the press, or the right to the people peaceably to assemble, and to petition the Government for a redress of grievances.

Amendment II.

A well regulated Militia, being necessary to the security of a free State, the right of the people to keep and bear Arms, shall not be infringed.

Amendment III.

No Soldier shall, in time of peace be quartered in any house, without the consent of the Owner, nor in time of war, but in a manner to be prescribed by law.

Amendment IV.

The right of the people to be secure in their persons, houses, papers, and effects, against unreasonable searches and seizures, shall not be violated, and no Warrants shall issue, but upon probable cause, supported by Oath or affirmation, and particularly describing the place to be searched, and the persons or things to be seized.

Amendment V.

No person shall be held to answer for a capital, or otherwise infamous crime, unless on a presentment or indictment of a Grand Jury, except in cases arising in the land or naval forces, or in the Militia, when in actual service in time of War or public danger; nor shall any person be subject for the same offence to be twice put in jeopardy of life or limb, nor shall be compelled in any criminal case to be a witness against himself, nor be deprived of life, liberty, or property, without due process of law; nor shall private property be taken for public use without just compensation.

Amendment VI.

In all criminal prosecutions, the accused shall enjoy the right to a speedy and public trial, by an impartial jury of the State and district wherein the crime shall have been committed; which district shall have been previously ascertained by law, and to be informed of the nature and cause of the accusation; to be confronted with the witnesses against him; to have compulsory process for obtaining witnesses in his favor, and to have the assistance of counsel for his defence.

Amendment VII.

In Suits at common law, where the value in controversy shall exceed twenty dollars, the right of trial by jury shall be preserved, and no fact tried by a jury shall be otherwise re-examined in any Court of the United States, than according to the rules of the common law.

Amendment VIII.

Excessive bail shall not be required, nor excessive fines imposed, nor cruel and unusual punishments inflicted.

Amendment IX.

The enumeration in the Constitution of certain rights shall not be construed to deny or disparage others retained by the people.

Amendment X.

The powers not delegated to the United States by the Constitution, nor prohibited by it to the States, are reserved to the States respectively, or to the people.

Appendix B

UNIVERSAL DECLARATION OF HUMAN RIGHTS

Adopted and proclaimed by General Assembly as resolution
217 A (III) of 10 December 1948

On December 10, 1948 the General Assembly of the United Nations adopted and proclaimed the Universal Declaration of Human Rights, the full text of which appears in the following pages. Following this historic act the Assembly called upon all Member countries to publicize the text of the Declaration and "to cause it to be disseminated, displayed, read and expounded principally in schools and other educational institutions, without distinction based on the political status of countries or territories."

PREAMBLE

Whereas recognition of the inherent dignity and of the equal and inalienable rights of all members of the human family is the foundation of freedom, justice and peace in the world,

Whereas disregard and contempt for human rights have resulted in barbarous acts which have outraged the conscience of mankind, and the advent of a world in which human beings shall enjoy freedom of speech and belief and freedom from fear and want has been proclaimed as the highest aspiration of the common people,

Whereas it is essential, if man is not to be compelled to have recourse, as a last resort, to rebellion against tyranny and oppression, that human rights should be protected by the rule of law,

Whereas it is essential to promote the development of friendly relations between nations,

Whereas the peoples of the United Nations have in the Charter reaffirmed their faith in fundamental human rights, in the dignity and worth of the human person and in the equal rights of men and women and have determined to promote social progress and better standards of life in larger freedom,

Whereas Member States have pledged themselves to achieve, in co-operation with the United Nations, the promotion of universal respect for and observance of human rights and fundamental freedoms,

Whereas a common understanding of these rights and freedoms is of the greatest importance for the full realization of this pledge,

Now, Therefore **THE GENERAL ASSEMBLY** *proclaims* **THIS UNIVERSAL DECLARATION OF HUMAN RIGHTS** as a common standard of achievement for all peoples and all nations, to the end that every individual and every organ of society, keeping this Declaration constantly in mind, shall strive by teaching and education to promote respect for these rights and freedoms and by progressive measures, national and international, to secure their universal and effective recognition and observance, both among the peoples of Member States themselves and among the peoples of territories under their jurisdiction.

Article 1.

All human beings are born free and equal in dignity and rights. They are endowed with reason and conscience and should act towards one another in a spirit of brotherhood.

Article 2.

Everyone is entitled to all the rights and freedoms set forth in this Declaration, without distinction of any kind, such as race, colour, sex, language, religion, political or other opinion, national or social origin, property, birth or other status. Furthermore, no distinction shall be made on the basis of the political, jurisdictional or international status of the country or territory to which a person belongs, whether it be independent, trust, non-self-governing or under any other limitation of sovereignty.

Article 3.

Everyone has the right to life, liberty and security of person.

Article 4.

No one shall be held in slavery or servitude; slavery and the slave trade shall be prohibited in all their forms.

Article 5.

No one shall be subjected to torture or to cruel, inhuman or degrading treatment or punishment.

Article 6.

Everyone has the right to recognition everywhere as a person before the law.

Article 7.

All are equal before the law and are entitled without any discrimination to equal protection of the law. All are entitled to equal protection against any discrimination in violation of this Declaration and against any incitement to such discrimination.

Article 8.

Everyone has the right to an effective remedy by the competent national tribunals for acts violating the fundamental rights granted him by the constitution or by law.

Article 9.

No one shall be subjected to arbitrary arrest, detention or exile.

Article 10.

Everyone is entitled in full equality to a fair and public hearing by an independent and impartial tribunal, in the determination of his rights and obligations and of any criminal charge against him.

Article 11.

(1) Everyone charged with a penal offence has the right to be presumed innocent until proved guilty according to law in a public trial at which he has had all the guarantees necessary for his defence.

(2) No one shall be held guilty of any penal offence on account of any act or omission which did not constitute a penal offence, under national or international law, at the time when it was committed. Nor shall a heavier penalty be imposed than the one that was applicable at the time the penal offence was committed.

Article 12.

No one shall be subjected to arbitrary interference with his privacy, family, home or correspondence, nor to attacks upon his honour and reputation. Everyone has the right to the protection of the law against such interference or attacks.

Article 13.

(1) Everyone has the right to freedom of movement and residence within the borders of each state.

(2) Everyone has the right to leave any country, including his own, and to return to his country.

Article 14.

(1) Everyone has the right to seek and to enjoy in other countries asylum from persecution.

(2) This right may not be invoked in the case of prosecutions genuinely arising from non-political crimes or from acts contrary to the purposes and principles of the United Nations.

Article 15.

(1) Everyone has the right to a nationality.

(2) No one shall be arbitrarily deprived of his nationality nor denied the right to change his nationality.

Article 16.

(1) Men and women of full age, without any limitation due to race, nationality or religion, have the right to marry and to found a family. They are entitled to equal rights as to marriage, during marriage and at its dissolution.

(2) Marriage shall be entered into only with the free and full consent of the intending spouses.

(3) The family is the natural and fundamental group unit of society and is entitled to protection by society and the State.

Article 17.

(1) Everyone has the right to own property alone as well as in association with others.

(2) No one shall be arbitrarily deprived of his property.

Article 18.

Everyone has the right to freedom of thought, conscience and religion; this right includes freedom to change his religion or belief, and freedom, either alone or in community with others and in public or private, to manifest his religion or belief in teaching, practice, worship and observance.

Article 19.

Everyone has the right to freedom of opinion and expression; this right includes freedom to hold opinions without interference and to seek, receive and impart information and ideas through any media and regardless of frontiers.

Article 20.

(1) Everyone has the right to freedom of peaceful assembly and association.

(2) No one may be compelled to belong to an association.

Article 21.

(1) Everyone has the right to take part in the government of his country, directly or through freely chosen representatives.

(2) Everyone has the right of equal access to public service in his country.

(3) The will of the people shall be the basis of the authority of government; this will shall be expressed in periodic and genuine elections which shall be by universal and equal suffrage and shall be held by secret vote or by equivalent free voting procedures.

Article 22.

Everyone, as a member of society, has the right to social security and is entitled to realization, through national effort and international cooperation and in accordance with the organization and resources of each State, of the economic, social and cultural rights indispensable for his dignity and the free development of his personality.

Article 23.

(1) Everyone has the right to work, to free choice of employment, to just and favourable conditions of work and to protection against unemployment.

(2) Everyone, without any discrimination, has the right to equal pay for equal work.

(3) Everyone who works has the right to just and favourable remuneration ensuring for himself and his family an existence worthy of human dignity, and supplemented, if necessary, by other means of social protection.

(4) Everyone has the right to form and to join trade unions for the protection of his interests.

Article 24.

Everyone has the right to rest and leisure, including reasonable limitation of working hours and periodic holidays with pay.

Article 25.

(1) Everyone has the right to a standard of living adequate for the health and well-being of himself and of his family, including food, cloth-

ing, housing and medical care and necessary social services, and the right to security in the event of unemployment, sickness, disability, widowhood, old age or other lack of livelihood in circumstances beyond his control.

(2) Motherhood and childhood are entitled to special care and assistance. All children, whether born in or out of wedlock, shall enjoy the same social protection.

Article 26.

(1) Everyone has the right to education. Education shall be free, at least in the elementary and fundamental stages. Elementary education shall be compulsory. Technical and professional education shall be made generally available and higher education shall be equally accessible to all on the basis of merit.

(2) Education shall be directed to the full development of the human personality and to the strengthening of respect for human rights and fundamental freedoms. It shall promote understanding, tolerance and friendship among all nations, racial or religious groups, and shall further the activities of the United Nations for the maintenance of peace.

(3) Parents have a prior right to choose the kind of education that shall be given to their children.

Article 27.

(1) Everyone has the right freely to participate in the cultural life of the community, to enjoy the arts and to share in scientific advancement and its benefits.

(2) Everyone has the right to the protection of the moral and material interests resulting from any scientific, literary or artistic production of which he is the author.

Everyone is entitled to a social and international order in which the rights and freedoms set forth in this Declaration can be fully realized.

Article 28.

Everyone is entitled to a social and international order in which the rights and freedoms set forth in this Declaration can be fully realized.

Article 29.

(1) Everyone has duties to the community in which alone the free and full development of his personality is possible.

(2) In the exercise of his rights and freedoms, everyone shall be subject only to such limitations as are determined by law solely for the purpose of securing due recognition and respect for the rights and freedoms of

others and of meeting the just requirements of morality, public order and the general welfare in a democratic society.

(3) These rights and freedoms may in no case be exercised contrary to the purposes and principles of the United Nations.

Article 30.

Nothing in this Declaration may be interpreted as implying for any State, group or person any right to engage in any activity or to perform any act aimed at the destruction of any of the rights and freedoms set forth herein.

Note: This document can be accessed at the following Web site: www.un.org/Overview/rights.html.

Select Bibliography

The books—old and new—used to create this volume often contain valuable bibliographical essays of their own to help readers pursue opinions and analysis in depth. Particularly useful are the studies in Stephen J. Whitfield's *The Culture of the Cold War* (Baltimore, 1991) and the group of references in James T. Patterson's *Grand Expectations: The United States, 1945–1974* (New York, 1996). To make certain that the activities of American women are evaluated as broadly as possible, readers should consult Susan M. Hartmann's *The Home Front and Beyond: American Women in the 1940s* (Boston, 1982) and Eugenia Kaledin's *Mothers and More: American Women in the 1950s* (Boston, 1984) along with Elaine Tyler May's *Homeward Bound: American Families in the Cold War Era* (New York, 1988) and Stephanie Coontz's *A Way We Never Were: American Families and the Nostalgia Trap* (New York, 1992). Betty Friedan's *Feminine Mystique* (New York, 1963) is essential reading for the period from 1940 to 1970.

Questions about historical background can be answered in *The Readers' Companion to American History* edited by Eric Foner and John A. Garraty (Boston, 1991). Contemporary attitudes may be absorbed from the writings collected in *A History of Our Time*, edited by William H. Chafe and Harvard Sitkoff (New York, 1970), and from the two volumes of collected journalism, *Reporting World War II*, published in the Library of America (New York, 1995). David M. Kennedy's *Freedom from Fear: The American People in Depression and War, 1929–1945* offers a 1999 reassessment of what the New Deal and the war add to the present. No textbooks manage to communicate individual reactions to what happened during these times better than Studs Terkel's classics—*Hard Times: An Oral History of the Great Depression* (New York, 1970) and *"The Good War": An Oral History of World War II* (New York, 1985).

William E. Leuchtenburg's *A Troubled Feast: American Society Since 1945* (updated ed., Boston, 1983) and William Chafe's *The Unfinished Journey* (New York, 1986) should also be familiar to students seeking a deeper background for these decades. Douglas T. Miller and Marion Nowak's critical history, *The Fifties: The Way We Really Were* (New York, 1975), and David Halberstam's sensitive journalism, *The Fifties* (New York, 1993), both enrich readers seeking different approaches to the same ten years. Nicholas Lemann's 1999 book *The Big Test: The Secret History of the American Meritocracy* provides imaginative insights into the ways postwar educators attempted to create a new group of American leaders.

Useful for research are multivolume encyclopedias such as Mary Kupec Cayton, J. Gorn Elliot, and Peter Williams' three-volume *Encyclopedia of American Social History* (New York, 1993) and Stanley I. Kutler's four-volume *Encyclopedia of the United States in the Twentieth Century* (New York, 1996). Lovers of statistics should seek out the Bureau of the Census, *Historical Statistics of the United States, Colonial Times to 1970*, 2 vols. (Washington, DC, 1970), or the *Statistical Abstract of the United States*, published annually in Washington by the Department of Commerce.

Certain popular magazines defined American life during these two decades. *Life, Time, National Geographic,* the *Saturday Evening Post,* and *Ladies' Home Journal* all provide useful insights into how people lived and what they wanted. The advertisements in these magazines also reveal much about the "good life" being reinvented after World War II. Microfilms and on-line facilities now make these artifacts immediately accessible.

WORLD WAR II: BACKGROUND

Adams, Michael C.C. *The Best War Ever: America and World War II.* Baltimore: Johns Hopkins University Press, 1994.

Erenberg, Lewis A., and Susan E. Hirsch, eds. *The War in American Culture: Society and Consciousness During World War II.* Chicago: University of Chicago Press, 1996.

Fussell, Paul. *Wartime: Understanding and Behavior in the Second World War.* New York: Oxford University Press, 1989.

Goodwin, Doris Kearns. *No Ordinary Time: Franklin and Eleanor Roosevelt. The Home Front in World War II.* New York: Simon and Schuster, 1994.

Kennedy, David M. *Freedom from Fear: The American People in Depression and War, 1929–1945,* vol. 9. Oxford History of the United States. New York: Oxford, 1999.

Lemann, Nicholas. *The Promised Land: The Great Black Migration and How It Changed America.* New York: Vintage Books/Knopf, 1991.

Litoff, Judy Barrett, and David C. Smith, eds. *Since You Went Away: World War II Letters from American Women on the Home Front.* Lawrence: University of Kansas Press, 1991.

McCullough, David. *Truman.* New York: Simon and Schuster, 1992.

O'Neill, William L. *A Democracy at War: America's Fight at Home and Abroad in World War II.* Cambridge, MA: Harvard University Press, 1995.

Smith, Page. *Democracy on Trial: The Japanese American Evacuation and Relocation in World War II.* New York: Simon and Schuster, 1995.

Takaki, Ronald. *Strangers from a Different Shore: A History of Asian Americans.* Boston: Little, Brown, 1989.

Tuttle, William M., Jr. *"Daddy's Gone to War": The Second World War in the Lives of America's Children.* New York: Oxford University Press, 1993.

MOVIES

Christenson, Terry. *Reel Politics: American Political Movies from "Birth of a Nation" to "Platoon."* New York: Blackwell, 1987.

Doherty, Thomas. *Teenagers and Teenpics: The Juvenilization of American Movies in the '50s.* Boston: Unwin Nyman, 1988.

Dowdy, Andrew. *The Films of the Fifties: The American State of Mind.* New York: Morrow, 1973.

French, Brandon. *On the Verge of Revolt: Women in American Films of the Fifties.* New York: Frederick Ungar, 1978.

Gabler, Neal. *An Empire of Their Own: How the Jews Invented Hollywood.* New York: Doubleday-Anchor, 1988.

Gitlin, Todd. *The Sixties: Years of Hope, Days of Rage.* New York: Bantam Books, 1987.

Harmetz, Aljean. *Round Up the Usual Suspects: The Making of Casablanca—Bogart, Bergman and World War II.* New York: Hyperion, 1992.

Haskell, Molly. *From Reverence to Rape: The Treatment of Women in the Movies.* New York: Holt, Rinehart and Winston, 1974.

———. *Holding My Own in No Man's Land: Women and Men and Film and Feminists.* New York: Oxford University Press, 1997.

Kael, Pauline. *Deeper into Movies.* Boston: Atlantic Monthly Press, 1973.

Powdermaker, Hortense. *Hollywood: The Dream Factory.* New York: Universal Library, 1950.

Sklar, Robert. *Movie-Made America: A Social History of American Movies.* New York: Random House, 1975. Reprint, Bantam Books, 1987.

CHANGING SOCIAL ATTITUDES

Alsop, Joseph, and Stewart Alsop. *We Accuse! The Story of the Miscarriage of American Justice in the Case of J. Robert Oppenheimer.* New York: Simon and Schuster, 1954.

Anderson, Jack, and Ronald W. May. *McCarthy: The Man, the Senator, the Ism.* Boston: Beacon Press, 1952.

Caute, David. *The Great Fear: The Anti-Communist Purge under Truman and Eisenhower.* New York: Simon and Schuster, 1978.

Chambers, Whittaker. *Witness.* New York: Random House, 1952.

Fried, Richard. *Nightmare in Red: The McCarthy Era in Perspective.* New York: Oxford University Press, 1990.

Garber, Marjorie, and Rebecca L. Walkowitz, eds. *Secret Agents: The Rosenberg Case, McCarthyism and Fifties America.* New York: Routledge, 1995.

Haynes, John Earl, and Harvey Klehr. *Venona: Decoding Soviet Espionage in America.* New Haven, CT: Yale University Press, 1999.

Hellman, Lillian. *Scoundrel Time*. Boston: Little, Brown, 1976.

Hiss, Alger. *In the Court of Public Opinion*. New York, 1957.

Hiss, Tony. *The View from Alger's Window*. New York: Knopf, 1999.

Mumford, Lewis. *In the Name of Sanity*. New York: Harcourt, Brace, 1954.

Navasky, Victor. *Naming Names*. New York: Viking, 1980.

Powers, Richard Gid. *Not without Honor: The History of American Anti-Communism*. New York: Free Press, 1996.

Radosh, Ronald, and Joyce Milton. *The Rosenberg File: A Search for the Truth*. New York: Vintage Books, 1984; 2nd ed., New Haven, CT: Yale University Press, 1997.

Roche, John. *The Quest for the Dream: The Development of Civil Rights and Human Relations in Modern America*. New York: Macmillan, 1963.

Sayre, Nora. *Previous Convictions: A Journey Through the 1950s*. New Brunswick, NJ: Rutgers University Press, 1995.

Schrecker, Ellen. *Many Are the Crimes: McCarthyism in America*. Boston: Little, Brown, 1998.

———. *No Ivory Tower: McCarthyism and the Universities*. New York: Oxford University Press, 1986.

Trumbo, Dalton. *The Time of the Toad: A Study of Inquisition in America*. New York: Perennial/Harper and Row, 1949.

Weinstein, Allen. *Perjury: The Hiss-Chambers Case*. 1978. New York: Random House, updated 1997.

THEORIZING NEW SOCIAL PATTERNS

Bell, Daniel. *The End of Ideology: On the Exhaustion of Political Ideas in the Fifties*. Rev. ed. New York: The Free Press, 1965.

Carter, Paul A. *Another Part of the Fifties*. New York: Columbia University Press, 1983.

Degler, Carl N. *Affluence and Anxiety: 1948–Present*. Glencoe: University of Illinois Press, 1968.

Dickstein, Morris. *Gates of Eden: American Culture in the Sixties*. New York: Basic Books, 1977. Reprint. New York: Penguin, 1989.

Evans, Sara. *Personal Politics: The Roots of Women's Liberation in the Civil Rights Movement and the New Left*. New York: Vintage Books, 1980.

Fiedler, Leslie. *An End to Innocence*. Boston: Beacon Press, 1952.

Friedan, Betty. *It Changed My Life: Writings on the Women's Movement*. New York: Dell, 1977.

Galbraith, John Kenneth. *The Affluent Society*. Boston: Little, Brown, 1958.

Goodman, Paul. *Growing Up Absurd*. New York: Vintage Books, 1960.

Goodman, Paul, and Percival Goodman. *Communitas: Ways of Livelihood and Means of Life*. New York: Vintage Books, 1947.

Griffith, Thomas. *The Waist-High Culture*. New York: Universal Library, 1959.

Harrington, Michael. *The Other America: Poverty in the United States*. Baltimore: Penguin, 1963.

Hofstadter, Richard. *Anti-Intellectualism in American Life*. New York: Vintage Books, 1962.

Jezer, Marty. *The Dark Ages: Life in the United States, 1945–1960.* Boston: South End Press, 1982.

Larrabee, Eric. *The Self-Conscious Society.* Garden City, NY: Doubleday, 1960.

Lundberg, Ferdinand, and Marynia Farnham. *Modern Woman: The Lost Sex.* New York: Universal Library, 1947.

Lynes, Russell. *The Tastemakers.* New York: Harper and Bros., 1955.

Marcuse, Herbert. *Eros and Civilization.* With new preface. New York: Vintage Books, 1962.

Mills, C. Wright. *The Power Elite.* New York: Oxford University Press, 1956.

———. *White Collar: The American Middle Classes.* New York: Oxford University Press, 1951.

Mumford, Lewis. *The City in History: Its Origins, Its Transportations and Its Prospects.* New York: Harcourt, Brace and World, 1961.

———. *The Conduct of Life.* New York: Harcourt, Brace, 1951.

———. *From the Ground Up: Observations on Contemporary Housing, Highway Building and Civic Design.* New York: Harcourt, Brace, 1956.

Nearing, Helen, and Scott Nearing. *Living the Good Life: How to Live Sanely and Simply in a Troubled World.* New York: Schocken, 1955.

Niebuhr, Reinhold. *The Irony of American History.* New York, 1952.

———. *The Politics of Hope.* Boston: Houghton Mifflin, 1963.

Packard, Vance. *The Status Seekers: An Exploration of Class Behaviour in America.* Baltimore: Penguin, 1959.

Rubin, Joan Shelley. *The Making of Middlebrow Culture.* Chapel Hill: University of North Carolina Press, 1992.

Trilling, Lionel. *The Liberal Imagination.* New York: Macmillan, 1948.

TELEVISION

Anderson, Kent, *The History and Implications of the Quiz Show Scandals.* Westport: Greenwood Press, 1978.

Barnouw, Erik. *A History of Broadcasting. Vol. II: The Golden Web. Vol. III: The Image Empire.* New York: Oxford University Press, 1968, 1970.

———. *Tube of Plenty: The Evolution of American Television.* New York: Oxford University Press, 1990.

Baughman, James L. *The Republic of Mass Culture: Journalism Filmmaking and Broadcasting in America Since 1941.* Baltimore: Johns Hopkins University Press, 1992.

Jackson, John A. *American Bandstand: Dick Clark and the Making of a Rock 'n' Roll Empire.* New York: Oxford University Press, 1998.

MacDonald, J. Fred. *Television and the Red Menace: The Video Road to Vietnam.* New York: Praeger, 1985.

Mannes, Marya. *More in Anger.* Philadelphia: Lippincott, 1958.

Marcus, Greil. *Mystery Train: Images of America in Rock 'n' Roll Music.* Rev. ed. New York: E. P. Dutton, 1982.

Marling, Karal Ann. *As Seen on TV: The Visual Culture of Everyday Life in the 1950s.* Cambridge, MA: Harvard University Press, 1994.

POSTWAR CULTURAL CHANGE

Arnold, Eve. *Flashback! The 50s.* New York: Knopf, 1978.

Ashton, Dore. *The New York School: A Cultural Reckoning.* New York: Penguin, 1979.

Carson, Rachel. *The Sense of Wonder.* New York: Harper and Row, 1965.

Cook, Susan, with Joseph Mazo. *The Alvin Ailey American Dance Theater.* New York: Morrow, 1978.

Dickstein, Morris. *Gates of Eden: American Culture in the Sixties.* 1977. Reprint. New York: Penguin, 1989.

Frank, Robert. *The Americans.* Paris: National Gallery of Art, 1958.

Garafola, Lynn, with Eric Foner, eds. *Dance for a City: Fifty Years of the New York City Ballet.* New York: Columbia University Press, 1999.

Gates, Henry Louis, Jr. *Bearing Witness: Selections from African American Autobiography in the 20th Century.* New York: Pantheon, 1991.

Ginsberg, Allen. *Howl and Other Poems.* San Francisco: City Lights Books, 1956.

Guralnick, Peter. *The Last Train to Memphis: The Rise of Elvis Presley.* Boston: Little, Brown, 1994.

Haddow, Robert H. *Pavilions of Plenty: Exhibiting American Culture Abroad in the 1950s.* Washington, DC: Smithsonian Institution Press, 1997.

Mailer, Norman. *Advertisements for Myself.* New York: G. P. Putnam's Sons, 1959.

McDonagh, Don. *Martha Graham.* New York: Praeger, 1973.

Munro, Eleanor. *Originals: American Women Artists.* New York: Simon and Schuster, 1979.

New York Graphic Society. *Life: The Second Decade, 1946–1955.* Boston: Little, Brown, 1955.

Sandeen, Eric. *Picturing an Exhibition: The Family of Man and 1950s America.* Albuquerque: University of New Mexico Press, 1995.

Sandler, Irving. *The New York School: The Painters and Sculptors of the Fifties.* New York: Harper and Row, 1975.

Sontag, Susan. *On Photography.* New York: Dell, 1973.

Steichen, Edward, creator. *The Family of Man.* New York: Maco Magazine Corp. 1955.

Trachtenberg, Allen. *Reading American Photographs: Images as History, Mathew Brady to Walker Evans.* New York: FS&G, 1989.

Index

About the Author

EUGENIA KALEDIN is an independent scholar. She is the author of *Mothers and More: American Women in the 1950's* (1984) and *The Education of Mrs. Henry Adams* (1994). She has been a Fulbright Professor in China and in Czechoslovakia and is currently teaching at the Harvard Institute for Learning in Retirement.

DISCARD